THE
BODY OF
GOD

AN
ECOLOGICAL
THEOLOGY

Sallie McFague

FORTRESS PRESS

MINNEAPOLIS

THE BODY OF GOD
An Ecological Theology

Scripture quotations unless otherwise noted are from the Revised Standard Version of the Bible, copyright © 1946, 1952, and 1971 by the Division of Christian Education of the National Council of Churches. Used with permission.

Cover design: Ann Elliot Artz Hadland

Library of Congress Cataloging-in-Publication Data

McFague, Sallie.
    The body of God: an ecological theology / Sallie McFague.
      p. cm.
    Includes bibliographical references and index.
    ISBN 0-8006-2735-0 (alk. paper)
    1. Human ecology—Religious aspects—Christianity.
    2. Theology—20th century.   3. Theology—21st century.   I. Title.
BT695.5.M443   1993
231.7—dc20
                                                   93-6584
                                                      CIP

Manufactured in the U.S.A.   AF 1–2735

                                           12   13   14   15

Contents

Dedicated to Janet Cawley

Acknowledgments

I am deeply indebted to the following persons who read and commented on this manuscript: Carol Adams, Janet Cawley, Peter Hodgson, Gordon Kaufman, Catherine Keller, and Robert John Russell. From each of them I received extensive, incisive, and highly perceptive criticisms as well as suggestions for revision; few authors are so fortunate and I cannot thank them enough for the time and care that they gave my work. I am also very grateful to my superb editor, Michael West, and the other helpful people at Fortress Press, especially Lenore Franzen. I appreciate as well the careful proofreading of Barbara Hickey of Vanderbilt University. Finally, I want to thank the Vancouver School of Theology, its Principal, Arthur Van Seters, the members of the faculty and staff, and especially Seok-Leng Khor and Susan Lamey for their friendship and help during my sabbatical leave. The school provided me an ideal context for writing—and for hiking in the nearby rainforests.

Introduction

"The world is our meeting place with God . . . as the body of God, it is wondrously, awesomely, divinely mysterious." These are some closing words from my book *Models of God*, a book that dealt principally with immanental models—God as mother, lover, and friend of the world. My focus was a conscious one, meant to balance the heavy transcendence of the Christian doctrine of God. Yet I end the book aware that what is needed is not only immanental models of God, but a way of thinking of God's transcendence in an immanental way—that "the world is our meeting place with God."

The present essay, *The Body of God: An Ecological Theology*, is about that way of thinking. In one sense, it is a highly focused, limited project: it attempts to look at everything through one lens, the model of the universe or world as God's body. The ancient organic model, reinterpreted by both contemporary science and Christian incarnationalism, is a perspective from which to consider major theological issues: creation, sin and evil, christology, the transcendence and immanence of God, human existence, the natural world, eschatology, the church. Using the lens this model provides, we ask what we see and what we can say about various dimensions of the relationship of God and the world. The model of the universe as God's body does not see nor does it allow us to say everything. It focuses on *embodiment*, inviting us to do something that Christians have seldom done: think about God and bodies. What would it mean, for instance, to understand sin as the refusal to share the basic necessities of survival with other bodies? to see Jesus of Nazareth as paradigmatic of God's love for bodies? to interpret creation as all the myriad forms of matter bodied forth from God and empowered with the breath of life, the spirit of God? to consider ourselves as inspirited bodies profoundly interrelated with all other such bodies and yet having the special distinction of shared responsibility with God for the well-being of our planet? Such a focus causes us to see differently, to see dimensions of the relation of God and the world that we have not seen before.

But in another sense, the intention of this essay is not limited and focused, not just offering one among many other and equally adequate models of God and the world. I will argue that while Christian thought has neglected the organic model for the last several hundred years, this model is indispensable for our time. The organic model is certainly not the only context within which we need to understand ourselves, our world, and God, but it is a necessary one. The organic model is not only a fundamental way to reconceive Christian faith (for example, whatever else salvation might mean it ought to start with the well-being of bodies) but an offering that Christianity can make to the planetary agenda of our time, the agenda that calls for all religions, nations, professions, and people to reconstruct their lives and their work to help our earth survive and prosper.

In other words, the model of the body of God is only one model, but one that is neglected, essential, illuminating, and helpful both to Christian doctrinal reformulation and to planetary well-being. It represents one square in the quilt, one voice in the conversation, one angle of vision on the unbelievably difficult and complex issue of planetary health and the contribution Christianity might make to it. The essay is further contextualized by authorship and audience: I am a white, middle-class, American Christian woman writing to first-world, privileged, mainstream Christians (and other interested persons). The point of the essay is to help those of us from this background and with the power it carries to begin to think and act differently, *to think and act as if bodies matter*. They are not all that matters but they do, and if we believed they mattered and understood in detail what that belief entailed, how might that change our way of being in the world? I will argue passionately that the organic model might help us change. This is not a balanced essay, for balance often qualifies insight out of existence. We need to see and feel the illumination and power of this model in its breadth and depth by immersing ourselves in it, being willing to put on the lens it offers us through which to see everything.

Two further qualifications are necessary, one relating to race and gender issues and the other to scientific ones. This essay focuses on the basic physical needs of bodies (human and nonhuman) for food, shelter, water, space, and so on. Other related issues involve bodies, such as the profound oppression that some human beings experience due to their divergence from the "norm" of the white, male, heterosexual body. While we will be concerned with these forms of oppression in our analysis of the organic model, *The Body of God* cannot give the needed concrete, detailed attention to such complex issues as racial and sexual discrimination, physical violence, sexual abuse, or compulsory heterosexuality. Fortunately, scholars elsewhere are now carefully studying these various forms of bodily oppression. In its focus on basic physical needs, this book is meant to be a complement to analyses of these other, but related, kinds of bodily oppression.

This book is not about science, although it uses science as a resource for theology. The model of the world or universe as God's body is, I will argue, in keeping with the view of reality coming to us from contemporary science. It is a plausible theological response to that view of reality, a response that ought to make Christian interpretations of the relations between God and the world more credible than interpretations based on outmoded views of reality. This essay is not, however, about shaping theology to science, finding a tight fit between the two areas on particular issues. Rather, it is interested in a loose fit between the contemporary scientific picture and theological reconstruction. This is a *theological*, not a scientific, project. Just as theology has always understood its central beliefs in terms of the picture of reality current in different times, so reflective Christians today are also called to the task of understanding their faith in light of the current picture of reality. As a theologian, I am concerned with the broad parameters of the contemporary scientific picture of reality not only because the credibility of faith depends upon that connection, but also because the contemporary view tells us about our world in ways we desperately need to hear and heed. Science can be theology's partner by suggesting ways in which we can see ourselves living in *one* world and by warning us how we must change our behavior for the future well-being of this world.

The Body of God begins with an analysis of the ecological or planetary crisis that we face, suggesting that everyone has a part to play in the planetary agenda, including theologians. My contribution is the model of the body, a model that unites us to everything else on our planet in relationships of interdependence. In my own journey I have discovered the body to be central to Christianity, to feminism, and to ecology. The organic model suggests, I believe, a possible way to rethink humanity's place in the scheme of things: a postpatriarchal, Christian theology for the twenty-first century.

Chapter 2 moves into an analysis and criticism of the organic model in its classic form, which, because based on the human body, was hierarchical, anthropocentric (as well as androcentric), and universalizing. But another version of the model from the sciences (the common creation story) and from feminism suggests a different possibility: a way of thinking of bodily unity and differentiation that stresses the radical interrelationship and interdependence of all bodies as it underscores their radical differences.

In chapter 3 the character of the particular project on the organic model in this essay—a theology of nature—is specified. It is compared and contrasted with two other contemporary projects: creation spirituality and natural theology. The chapter also suggests criteria for reinterpreting Christian doctrine in terms of the organic model and gives reasons why one might be persuaded to adopt the model as a way of being in the world. (It is the most technical chapter and apart from the section entitled "Theology of Nature" could be skimmed or skipped by the general reader.)

The remainder of the book (chapters 4-7) looks at various dimensions of God and the world in terms of the organic model. We begin our reflections not with the theological circle within which we live (the body of God) but with the ecological—not with the divine "environment" but with our most humble one as creatures of the earth. While the model of the world (or universe) as God's body is central in this essay, it presupposes and learns from the common creation story and is also, as we shall see, deepened and qualified by yet another context—the liberating, healing, and inclusive love of Christ.

In chapter 4 we consider where human beings fit in the scheme of things from the perspective of the common creation story. Unlike many theological anthropologies that speak of human beings only in relationship to God, this one starts with our earthly context: our interrelationships and interdependence with all other creatures on our planet as well as our important differences from other life-forms. It gives an earth-up rather than a sky-down perspective and suggests, because the earth is our only home and the home of all other beings as well, that we must share the space. We must share it with other human beings, other animals, and the natural world. Not to do so is ecological sin.

From this modest, mundane, but highly significant starting point—one that decenters us as the goal of creation but recenters as us the caretakers of our planet—we move in the fifth chapter to a deeper context for understanding the relationships among all living things: the world (or universe) as God's body. We will suggest that the primary belief of the Christian community, its doctrine of the incarnation (the belief that God is with us here on earth), be radicalized beyond Jesus of Nazareth to include all matter. God is incarnated in the world. We will probe the model of the world as God's body to see what it means for an understanding of God and of ourselves. The model suggests that God is closer to us than we are to ourselves, for God is the breath or spirit that gives life to the billions of different bodies that make up God's body. But God is also the source, power, and goal of everything that is, for the creation depends utterly upon God. Thus, the doctrines of God's immanence and transcendence—God's nearness and distinction—as well as the doctrine of creation will undergo revision when they are seen from the perspective of the organic model.

In the sixth chapter the context for understanding our place in the scheme of things is now deepened and radicalized further through the story of Jesus. The liberating, healing, and inclusive ministry of Jesus that overturns hierarchical dualisms, heals sick bodies, and invites the outcast to the table should in our time be extended to a new poor—nature. In addition to including oppressed, ailing, and rejected human beings, the Christic paradigm should now be extended to oppressed nature. We human beings in our misuse and exploitation of the natural world have caused nature to be the new poor. Our christology will extend the shape of Jesus' ministry to the scope of the entire planet, taking seriously the ancient belief that the redeemer is the savior of the *entire* creation. The closing pages of the chapter will suggest how the doctrine of the trinity might look from the perspective of the world as God's body overlain by the liberating, healing, and inclusive love of the cosmic Christ.

We will, then, have completed our sketch of the overlapping circles—the common creation story, the world as God's body, and the Christic paradigm—that, for Christians in our time, gives a context for reevaluating who we are in the scheme of things. This context gives us a functional cosmology, a way of seeing ourselves living in the earth as our home, a home we share with many other beings as parts of the body of God and loved by God. In the last chapter we will gather together the insights from this new context as they relate to a new shape for humanity, a way of being in the world in keeping with who we are in the ecological, theological, and christological circles. Our new functional cosmology suggests that we have been recentered as God's partners to help life prosper on our planet—a high and daunting calling indeed.

You may read this book in two ways, depending on your time, background, and concerns. For full immersion, read the entire text including the endnotes, which expand points, converse with other positions, and provide relevant bibliographical material. For an approach that provides the basic substance but not all of the methodology, skim chapters 2 and 3 (focusing on "The Common Creation Story" and "Ecological Unity" in chap. 2 as well as "Theology of Nature" in chap. 3), and read the rest of the book, the endnotes where interested.

THE
BODY OF
GOD

Let others pray for the passenger pigeon
the dodo, the whooping crane, the eskimo:
everyone must specialize

I will confine myself to a meditation
upon giant tortoises
withering finally on a remote island.

I concentrate in subway stations,
in parks, I can't quite see them,
they move to the peripheries of my eyes

but on the last day they will be there,
already the event
like a wave travelling shapes vision:

on the road where I stand they will materialize,
plodding past me in a straggling line
awkward without water

their small heads pondering
from side to side, their useless armor
sadder than thanks and history,

in their closed gaze ocean and sunlight paralysed,
lumbering up the steps, under the archways
toward the square glass altars

where the brittle gods are kept,
the relics of what we have destroyed
our holy and obsolete symbols.

—Margaret Atwood

1 / THE CONTEXT

The Ecological Crisis

Walking home from school one day when I was in the second grade, I had the terrifying, yet oddly irresistible, thought that someday I would not be here any longer. I simply would not "be" at all. Christmas would come and I would not be here to open my presents, in the summer I would not go to our cabin on Cape Cod with the others, and, most unbelievable of all, on my birthday—*my* day—I would not be here to celebrate it. As with a sore that hurts when touched but one cannot leave alone, I brooded over this deeply frightening but strangely seductive thought for weeks. It was not primarily a thought of death, for it contained no illness, blood, or violence but, as I now see, a thought of extinction, a thought of no longer being in existence, a thought of annihilation. It is an unthinkable thought, a thought around which one cannot wrap one's mind, for unlike death, which assumes a life lived and lets the focus be on the richness and uniqueness of that life, annihilation or extinction looks beyond to the nothingness, the emptiness, that follows.

This thought, this unthinkable thought, is, however, now being forced upon us in ways far beyond my puny concerns with self. Earlier in the century we faced the possibility of nuclear extinction and now, ecological deterioration. Nuclear extinction would be the extinction of life, not my life or your life, but *all* life,

1

except perhaps for some grasses and insects. It would be a massive, appalling, and unnecessary annihilation and one for which *we* would be directly responsible. It is, of all thoughts of extinction, the most unthinkable and puts the contemplation of one's own end, by whatever means, in perspective. Once nuclear annihilation seeped into my consciousness, I viewed my own death (for I had now lived a life and could focus on it with gratitude) as insignificant. *The* issue was the extinction of life—the teeming, fertile, infinitely varied and endlessly interesting array of plants and animals. The more we meditate upon that possibility, especially in detail— from the extinction of early spring violets to the end of human children—the more nauseating, repulsive, and obscene it becomes. It is, indeed, the unthinkable thought, in part, of course, because *we* would have caused it.[1]

While the threat of nuclear extinction has not disappeared, a new one has emerged: ecological deterioration. To compare them as "quick kill" to "slow death" oversimplifies the situation. In fact, they are, significantly, quite different, and, curiously, ecological deterioration, the less "dramatic" of the two, may be more difficult for us both to face and to do something about. The nuclear threat is clear and stark: it involves someone pushing a button to begin the process of annihilation.[2] Ecological deterioration is subtle and gradual: it involves the daily, seemingly innocuous, activities of every person on the planet. Moreover, unlike the "egalitarian" destruction of a nuclear holocaust, ecological deterioration affects the human population along lines of class, race, and gender. Finally, the health and well-being of the planet is so complex that it may well lie beyond our best will and intelligence, whereas we at least know how to dismantle nuclear weapons.

A Lament for the Planet

As we begin to consider what theology done from an ecological context might be, let us take a closer look at each of these points, namely, the subtle, nondemocratic, and complex character of the ecological crisis. Ecological deterioration is sufficiently gradual that it can appear imperceptible. The changes happening on and to our planet as the result of the relatively innocent, as well as explicitly destructive, activities of over five billion human beings can become accepted with alarming speed and complacency. We hear such comments as "the winters seem warmer than they used to be," or "the fish in the lake are dying from something or other," or "I hear clear-cutting in the Northwest forests is pushing out the grizzly bears," but are not alarmed. These events are unpleasant and undesirable, but not distressing or foreboding. Ecological deterioration is more like alcohol or other drug addiction than war: it creeps up on us daily so that we become used to it rather than announcing destruction in the glaring headline it deserves—"War Declared on Planet." Like addiction, ecological deterioration is insidious. We become used to the smell of automobile exhaust fumes and open landfills, inured to the sight of dead rabbits and possums by the roadside, habituated to tall trees being felled to make room for more office buildings, accustomed to children playing on city sidewalks devoid of grass and trees. We become so used to diminishment, so used to environmental decay, that many even deny that it is occurring.

Many of us and many more of our children have never known wilderness, have never experienced nature relatively free of human tampering. We do not know "wilderness as a yardstick," which provides a measure of how we have changed the environment.[3] Fewer and fewer people worldwide live on farms, close to nature, and interact daily with its rhythms and creatures. Most of us, increasingly, live in cities where we are further removed from the "yardstick" of wilderness. Being in denial and distant from nature, we can and do refuse to acknowledge the insidious disease that is infecting the ecosystem that supports us all—from the microorganisms in the ocean to the human child. At most, we treat the problem like a bad cold that will eventually go away if we make a few minor life-style changes, such as recycling or car pooling. Profound life-style changes, especially for first-world people (the ones who use most of the energy and cause most of the ecological deterioration), are highly unpopular.

We are, then, dealing with a wily, crafty enemy: *ourselves*, as the perpetrators of the ecological crisis. Like addicts (and we are addicted to our nonecological, high-tech life-style), we find every available avenue to deny what others (extraterrestrial beings, if they are watching) would clearly see: that life on this planet is diminishing, both in variety and in quality, and we human beings, some more than others, are to blame. While we may be less obviously responsible for ecological destruction than we would be for a nuclear holocaust, we are, nonetheless, responsible.

But we are not all *equally* responsible, nor does the deterioration affect us all equally. In that sense, ecological blight is not fair; it is neither democratic nor egalitarian. This brings us to the second point: it affects people along class, race, and gender lines. Unlike a nuclear holocaust, which would wreak its greatest devastation on the inhabitants of first-world cities (since the power elite live in such places), ecological deterioration hits the poor, the weak, the vulnerable. In fact, those who feel the impact the most are the least responsible for it, and those most responsible are the least impacted. To put the matter in a nutshell, a third-world woman of color (as well as her first-world sister in the ghettoes of major cities) is the most impacted person on the planet. Her greatest ecological sin is probably ravaging denuded forests to gather firewood to cook her family's dinner. The most responsible person is a first-world, usually white, usually male, entrepreneur involved in a high-energy, high-profit business. His (her) greatest ecological discomfort is probably having to suffer through a record-setting hot weekend when the air conditioner broke down and no repair person would come to fix it until Monday. As more of the earth becomes desert, water scarcer, air more polluted, food less plentiful, the lines between the "haves" and the "have nots" will become even more sharply drawn. Justice for the oppressed will recede from view when resources become scarce. If the human population doubles in forty or fifty years, as appears likely, and the pressure on the planet for the basics of existence intensifies, those with power will do what is necessary to insure their own piece of the disappearing pie.

The population versus high life-style issue divides the developing from the developed nations, with each claiming *the* ecological issue is the *other's* excess. Both are critical problems, but since this essay is directed to middle-class Westerners, the focus will be on *our* excess, the highest energy-use life-style the world has ever known. If we refuse to moderate this life-style, we participate in systemic injustice, demanding an excessive piece of the pie. Unless and until we drastically modify our life-style, we are not in a position to preach population control to others.

To summarize the second point: even as ecological deterioration is less clear and obvious than the nuclear threat, so also it is less just. And it will become more unjust. Many people think that ecological devastation is a flora and fauna issue—a plant and animal rather than a people issue, referring principally to the loss of habitats for various species as well as to their extinction. But this is only partially true. The full truth is that we cannot live without the plants and animals and the ecosystem that supports us all. So the ecological issue is a people issue and, most especially, a justice issue, for the ecology, the environment, the home that we share is a finite one. If justice means, most basically, fairness, then ecology and justice are inextricably intertwined, for on a finite planet with limited resources to support its many different kinds of beings, both human and nonhuman, sharing fairly is an issue of the highest priority. We human beings are not the only ones who deserve a fair share, but we are among those who do and, in addition, we alone (to our knowledge) have the ability to make decisions about sharing along lines other than "might makes right," both for the needy of our own kind as well as other vulnerable species. This issue of justice and fair sharing will be a central one as we consider theology from an ecological context.

A third difference between the nuclear and ecological crises is the relative simplicity of the first and the almost inconceivable complexity of the second. While we should not underestimate the difficulty of nuclear disarmament or the problem posed by an increasing number of nations with nuclear capability, we at least know *what* we need to do to avoid a holocaust. But there is no formula for planetary well-being. Ecology, most simply, means planetary "house rules," knowledge of and obedience to the ways of living appropriately in our home, the earth. This sounds straightforward, but the more scientists discover about the incredible complexity of the interrelationships and interdependencies among the millions of species of plants and animals on the planet, as well as the myriad ways they interact with and depend upon soil, water, chemicals, atmosphere, gases, temperature, and so forth, the less certain they become about how we *should* act. We do not know enough, and we may never know enough, to prevent the ecological decay all around us.

And this is perhaps the key point: what if we cannot come up with a quick fix to the ecological crisis? If the flutter of a butterfly's wings in the Amazon Basin can affect the weather in Kansas City, then no amount of technical know-how can solve the problem. The interrelationships are too deep and complex for even our Western fix-it mentality.[4] This is not to say that knowledge is useless or is not a part of the solution. Of course it must be, but it is perhaps even more essential to realize our proper relationship to our planet. One of the most critical house rules we must learn is that we are not lords *over* the planet, but products *of* its processes; in fact, we are the product of a fifteen-billion-year history of the universe and a four-billion-year history of our earth. We are an intimate and integral part of what we want to know: planetary knowledge is self-knowledge. Hence, ecological knowledge is not about something "out there"; it is about ourselves and how we fit into the scheme of things. The most important ecological knowledge we can have, then, is not how we can change the environment to suit us (a tactic that may, in the long run, be not only impossible but disastrous for ourselves and other species), but rather how we can adjust our desires and needs to what appear to be the house rules.

In the end, "appear to be" may be as close as we can get to determining a life-style that actually promotes planetary well-being. Just as we may never know enough to change the environment to suit our desires, so we will probably never know enough even to fit in appropriately. In such a situation, restraint, doing less, pulling back, may be the better part of wisdom. This is not a popular suggestion; in fact, it would be considered "un-American" by some. To admit that we human beings have come up against our match—the planet itself—and cannot, must not, try to manage, control, and fix it, but instead ought to listen to it, learn from it, and restrain ourselves (our desires, projects, comforts, even our needs, as well as our population) is very difficult. Not to act, but to abstain; not to control, but to "let be"; not to solve the problem, but to simplify one's life; not to want more but to accept less: all this goes against the grain.

A sensibility of abstinence and restraint suggests that we assume an attitude of humility rather than of control, and realize that we are but one species in a world that, the better we know, the more complex, intricate, and mysterious we find to be. Such a sensibility will not deliver us from the ecological crisis but, with appropriate and thoughtful technology to help us learn more about our house rules (very different from a fix-it mentality), is a prudent posture. At least we should do *less harm.*

In a recent book on the economy and the environment, the authors conclude with these grim words:

> On a hotter planet, with lost deltas and shrunken coastlines, under a more dangerous sun, with less arable land, more people, fewer species of living things, a legacy of poisonous wastes, and much beauty irrevocably lost, there is still the possibility that our children's children will learn at last to live as a community among communities. Perhaps they will learn also to forgive this generation its blind commitment to ever greater consumption. Perhaps they will even appreciate its belated efforts to leave them a planet still capable of supporting life in community.[5]

Perhaps, but what a sense of loss, diminishment, and sadness these words convey! Rather than the parents' hope of a better future for their children, there is an unusual turnabout: a hope that the children will forgive their parents for ruining the present. One of the ways in which human beings throughout history have come to terms with their own personal diminishment and death is the knowledge that the world will go on for others—at least as good as it has been for them, and hopefully better for the children and the children's children. But that is no longer the case. Few of us dare imagine what life might be like one hundred years from now on our planet, and when the thought passes fleetingly through our minds, we are overcome with feelings of loss, emptiness, and sadness.

There will be something. It will not be like my childhood thoughts of annihilation, although some, perhaps many, species will be extinct. Ecological deterioration one hundred years from now will not call forth the existential exhilaration and horror of the unthinkable abyss. It will, I suspect, generate a different, far more mundane, kind of horror: the struggle for food and water, the stench of pollution in the sky and ocean, the battle for the decreasing parcels of arable land, the search for basic medical care and education. Succeeding generations will set their sights lower: they will not *expect* shade trees in the cities or forests in the country any more than they will *expect* a better future for their children. They will, among other things, learn to live with "much beauty irrevocably lost," but by then they may not even miss it. They will have grown used to a hotter, drier planet with many more people and many fewer trees, flowers, and other animals. Perhaps eventually they will even lose their sense of horror at the loss, the diminishment, that all of us have brought about in our own home, planet earth. Perhaps they will eventually learn not to feel the pain.

The Planetary Agenda

But even now we feel the pain, and for that we ought to be grateful. It may help us to change, and change we must at a very basic level. One of the ways to deal with ecological despair, the despair we feel when we think about the future we are willing to the next generation, is to refuse the role of victim, to become active, to participate in the vocation of the planetary agenda. In different ways each of us has a calling, is being summoned, to put our talents, passion, and insights into planetary well-being. Ecology is not an extracurricular activity; rather, it must be the focus of one's work, the central hours of one's day, however that is spent.

The planetary agenda involves everything and everyone. It involves everything because we now know that all things, all beings and processes on the planet, are interrelated, and that the well-being of each is connected to the well-being of the whole. The planetary agenda calls us to do something unprecedented—to think about "everything that is." Narrow, parochial agendas concerned with "me and my kind" not only go against our moral sense and religious traditions, but increasingly are seen to be against reality (which is, perhaps, why our moral sense and religious traditions reject them). We cannot save ourselves (and our kind) alone if salvation means the health and well-being of the planet and all its creatures, not merely the transformation of certain privileged individuals to another existence in another world. The planetary agenda, then, takes the wide and long view: it is concerned with the well-being of the diverse, rich plenitude of beings, human and nonhuman, that inhabit the planet, not just for the present and near future but, as Native American traditions insist, "for seven generations," or for as long as we can imagine. Maintaining the wide and long view is very difficult, for it goes against our way of thinking, which often leaves out most members of our real tribe — all other people on the earth as well as all other creatures.[6] Increasingly, we are recognizing the world as a tribal village, at least as it refers to all human inhabitants of the earth. But that recognition needs to be extended to all other living creatures and to the ecosystem that supports us all. As the pictures of planet earth from space vividly show us, we *are all* inhabitants of *one* space, *one* home, *one* finite, enclosed system. Our fate and our future are also *one*.

The planetary agenda that involves everything and demands that we think of everything that is, instead of just "me and mine," is neither romantic nor exaggerated. It is, on the contrary, necessary and realistic in the sense that it is what we must undertake, given the interconnections and interrelations that we now understand to be the nature of reality. *The* moral issue of our day — and the vocation to which we are called — is whether we and other species will live and how well we will live. The World Council of Churches summarizes this vocation, this planetary agenda, with its rallying cry of "peace, justice, and the integrity of creation." These issues, which at one time might have appeared separate or at odds with each other, must now be seen as profoundly interrelated if any of them is to be addressed.[7]

But each of us cannot live and work at this level of abstraction and generality. It is the horizon, the context, against which and within which we must view and interpret our own mundane, daily activities, but we cannot and should not live and work at the level of the planetary agenda. If the planetary agenda involves everything, it also involves everyone, but each of us *in and through the concrete activities of our daily lives.* The planetary agenda is a universal vocation, a calling (in the sense of an urgent summons to a life's work) to put our gifts, time, and energies into some small aspect of planetary well-being.

This vocation has two features: universality (everyone is called) and particularity (each is called to a concrete, specific task). The planetary agenda is obviously too large a task for any field of expertise or any one group of people. It may well be too great a task for all of us together, even if we put all our parochial, selfish concerns aside and gave it our best will, intelligence, and imagination. For the more we know about our planet and its workings and the more we think holistically about its well-being and how its human inhabitants can fit in appropriately, the more awesome the planetary agenda becomes. It may appear at first glance that some group of experts, perhaps the biologists or ecologists, hold the secret knowledge that will solve the dilemma, but, while we can and must learn our house rules from them, they cannot give us a magic formula. The issue before us is not only one of knowledge (though basic information about how our planet operates is critical, as we shall see), but also one of behavior. Everyone needs to see both the larger picture (the interrelations among all things and all beings) and how they fit in, that is, how each person's daily work contributes to planetary well-being.

There is no task too large or too small for the planetary agenda. From the child who learns to recycle to the economist who warns that our population growth is exceeding resources, all the daily activities of all people can and should become part of the planetary agenda. This agenda, then, is obviously not a pastime; it is not something reserved for one's leisure hours. It is concerned with how one conducts the main business of one's day, whatever that is—selling flowers, running General Motors, going to school, farming, cutting hair, working in a laundry, or driving a taxi. It is perhaps obvious how raising children, gardening, teaching, nursing, or caring for animals might contribute to the planetary agenda, but how does theology (let alone business, law, housekeeping, plumbing, or car manufacturing)? Some jobs and careers take more imagination than others to disclose their potential contribution, but these areas are often the very ones most in need of rethinking from a planetary perspective.[8] The issue is not *what* is done but *how* it is done. To be sure, there are some activities that from a planetary perspective are irredeemable, such as drug dealing, child labor, pornography, or the manufacture of nuclear or biological weapons. But most ways by which people earn their livelihood can be done from a narrower or broader (parochial or planetary) perspective. Each of these areas needs to say how it *might* fit into the broader perspective; from the planetary perspective, it *must* fit, or its legitimacy is in question. Especially those who control and manage the various arts and skills by which people earn their keep ought to be the ones who say in what ways they do fit or ought to change in order to do so.

The universal vocation of planetary well-being must coincide with our daily breadwinning activities. We cannot redress the ecological decay that has already taken place with marches, protests, and money-raising campaigns alone (though all of these activities are necessary). And we certainly cannot stop further ecological decline this way. We must, rather, *change the way* business, law, plumbing, childraising, government, education, medicine, car manufacturing, housekeeping, farming, logging—and theology—are carried on, from the parochial, narrow, short-term view to the planetary, wide, long-term perspective. The planet is not deteriorating because of what we do in our free time or on weekends; its problems come from the *center*, not the periphery of our lives, from how we understand the main functions of our society and how we conduct those functions. For the most part, neither the understanding nor the conduct of those functions has included the well-being of the planet as *a*, if not *the*, central concern.

Our personal and work lives are of course but one aspect of the planetary agenda. They are the focus of this essay since the change to an ecological worldview must take hold at the grass roots level. The new worldview must also, however, permeate all dimensions of our common life: our vote, our buying power, our ability to organize. Political and economic arenas are the most critical ones since the agenda in question is earthwide.[9] The concern of this essay, however, is to change sensibilities, change the *way* voters, consumers, and organizers engage in political and economic action, from an individualistic, short-term profit mind-set to one that takes the broad view and the long view — the well-being of the planet — as its foremost consideration.

Some have suggested that the model of conversation is a way to visualize the planetary agenda, the central vocation to which everyone is called and which includes everything.[10] This model underscores that no one field of expertise or effort, let alone any one person or group of people, has the preeminent or only voice. We do not need a monologue or even a dialogue, but a roundtable discussion in which all speakers are equal. This conversation must also include those on the underside of history, especially most women of the world, who have been voiceless in the past. One can even incorporate speakers who will represent the interests — be the voice of — the truly voiceless ones on the planet, namely, small children, all species of plants, and all animals except human beings.

The model has much to commend it: it acknowledges that what we need to know about ourselves and our planet cannot come from experts alone but must include the lived experience of peoples from both sexes, many races, various classes, different sexual orientations, diverse handicapping situations, and so forth. Since one, if not the, distinctive characteristic of human beings is our ability to communicate in language at a high level of precision and depth, the model of conversation is a natural and long-neglected (due to authoritarian hierarchicalism) paradigm for describing and mobilizing our many different contributions to planetary well-being. It calls up the image of everyone talking about the everything that makes up our planet and the various ways to insure the health of the planet from a multitude of different perspectives.

All models have limits, however, and the chief fault with the conversation model is its elitism. Not only are most life-forms on the planet without voice, including many human beings (all human infants, most poor people, and many of the elderly and ill), but voice in our culture, which means primarily access to the media, is controlled by those few with money and education. A more homey metaphor, one that has found favor among feminists, is that of a quilt, especially a crazy quilt, which has a pattern of sorts but one that emerges from the haphazard pieces that are sewn together. No particular expertise is necessary to make a contribution to such a quilt — even a child can do it (though this model also is limited to human beings). Many different hands work on a quilt. The quilting bee takes place in the round, with each person working on her or his own little square. No agreement or consensus is required, but each person must have some sense of the overall pattern emerging in the quilt in order to sew one's own piece in a suitable place. The quilt model emphasizes egalitarianism, the variety of different contributions, and the rather chaotic (complex, diverse) nature of the order that emerges. It suggests that the goal—having a serviceable, warm cover with pleasing variety—is sufficient for sewing one's square.

The quilt metaphor suggests a richer diversity of contributions than does the conversation model; it also sets no premium on verbal skills. The president of a company that makes packaging materials might sew her piece in the quilt by finding a way to reduce packaging by 50 percent; a child might sew his piece by drawing a poster for an Earth Day celebration. Models are not necessarily mutually exclusive. The conversation and quilt models have assets and limitations that help us grasp the planetary agenda, the agenda that includes everything and to which everyone is called, but called in radically particular, concrete ways. That is what makes it possible for each of us to count ourselves in. We are being called, as the saying goes, "to think globally but to act locally." We are not being asked to think about everything that is (what armchair philosophers and those who want to avoid doing anything cling to), but to add our bit to the conversation, to sew our piece into the quilt.

One Theologian's Response: The Model of the Body

Now I must become very concrete, very specific about my own piece for the quilt. I am a Christian theologian. That is how I spend the central hours of each day. I get paid for thinking about God, about how we do and ought to think about God and the world, and about ourselves in relation to God and the world. I do this within a particular tradition, the Western Christian tradition. I am also a feminist theologian, that is, one who has criticized the androcentric, hierarchical, dualistic models of God in the Christian tradition and suggested some alternatives.[11] More recently, as I recognize the interlocking character of oppression, most notably that of women and nature, I have become an "ecological theologian" as well. My theological and spiritual journey has led me, as it has led many others, to the realization that while all oppressions are different, indeed, radically different in the forms of agony they engender, oppressions are also interconnected, as the nature/woman oppression amply illustrates.[12]

When I consider what I—a Christian, feminist, ecological theologian—might offer to the planetary conversation, the small square that I might sew in the quilt, I return again and again to the puzzling importance of a common thread to my own journey. That common thread is the body and all its cognate forms and associations: embodiment, incarnation, flesh, matter, death, life, sex, temptation, nature, creation, energy, and so on (for definitions, see endnote).[13] In different and very complex ways, Christianity, feminism, and ecology have been sites of conflict on the issue of the importance and meaning of "body." A brief sketch will illustrate the point.

Christianity is the religion of the incarnation *par excellence*. Its earliest and most persistent doctrines focus on embodiment: from the incarnation (the Word made flesh) and christology (Christ was fully human) to the eucharist (this is my body, this is my blood), the resurrection of the body, and the church (the body of Christ who is its head), Christianity has been a religion of the body. Christianity during first-century Mediterranean culture, which was noted for its disparagement of the body and its otherworldly focus, defiantly proclaimed its message of enfleshment. And yet, the earliest Christian texts and doctrines contain the seeds that, throughout history, have germinated into full-blown distrust of the body as well as deprecation of nature and abhorrence and loathing of female bodies.[14] If Christianity is *the* incarnational religion, its treatment of embodiment, nature, and women is very strange indeed.

Feminism has a different but also contentious relationship to embodiment and nature. Western culture and religion have a long, painful history of demeaning the female by identifying her with the body and with nature, while elevating the male by identifying him with reason and spirit. As a result, feminists are of two minds about aligning themselves with embodiment of any sort. Some insist that to do so is to reinforce the stereotypes that have oppressed women for centuries, while others feel that the liberation and salvation of women rest upon such an identification.[15] Furthermore, many feminists claim, the social constructs of "woman" and "nature" that the dominant male patriarchal culture has assigned for its own benefit are principally ideologies.[16] It may be, then, that only as women define themselves in terms of embodiment and only as we all come to appreciate nature in its many different forms of embodiment (different from us and each form from all others) will we even have a clue of how to talk of women, body, and nature together.

When we turn to ecology, which deals with the interrelationship of organisms and their environment, one would think that bodies and embodiment would be a given.[17] However, even this is disputed.[18] Oversimplified, the debate moves between two models for understanding the natural order, an organic and a mechanical one, the world as body or machine.[19] The first model takes the perspective of the whole and sees all parts, from the largest to the smallest, as interrelated and interdependent; the second takes the perspective of the parts and sees them related only in terms of the larger parts being dependent on or influenced by the smallest. The first has been called holistic, with top-down and bottom-up causation, while the second is called atomistic or reductionistic, with only bottom-up causation.[20] Atomism, or the machine model, reduces all living things to their most basic chemical compounds, so that we and all other organisms are "nothing but" the chemicals in our bodies. The prevalence of the machine model for nature is very evident in the branch of ecology that relies on technological breakthroughs for managing the planet: like a machine, its inoperative or failing parts can be replaced with new, better ones that can service human needs and desires.[21] Hence, even in the study of nature, where one would expect organic thinking to be accepted without question, it is not.

The ambivalence and at times abhorrence that we see in Christianity, feminism, and ecology in regard to the body—in all its manifestations—indicates a deep sickness in our culture: self-hatred. To the extent we do not like bodies, we do not like ourselves. Whatever more or other we may be, we *are* bodies, made of the same stuff as all other life-forms on our planet, including our brains, which are on a chemical continuum with our physical being. We do not *have* bodies, as we like to suppose, distancing ourselves from them as one does from an inferior, a servant, who works for us (the "us" being the mind that inhabits the body but does not really belong there). We *are* bodies, "body and soul." One of the most important revelations from postmodern science is the continuum between matter and energy (or, more precisely, the unified matter/energy field), which overturns traditional hierarchical dualisms such as nonliving/living, flesh/spirit, nature/human being (for a definition of postmodern science, see endnote).[22] Whatever we say about that part of ourselves we call brain, mind, or spirit, it evolved from and is continuous with our bodies.[23] If we like the part of ourselves we call "mind" or "spirit," then we ought to honor that part which is its base or root—the body—for they belong together.

In other words, we ought to love and honor the body, our own bodies, and the bodies of all other life-forms on the planet. The body is not a discardable garment cloaking the real self or essence of a person (or a pine tree or a chimpanzee); rather, it is the shape or form of who we are. It is how each of us is recognized, responded to, loved, touched, and cared for—as well as oppressed, beaten, raped, mutilated, discarded, and killed. The body is not a minor matter; rather, it is the main attraction. It is what pulls us toward (and pushes us away from) each other; it is erotic in the most profound sense, for it is what attracts or repels.[24] It is bedrock, and, therefore, we ought to pay attention to it before all else.

Most of us live with the strange illusion that we are other than our bodies, that we and those we love can and will exist apart from them, that our spirits will live on, here or "in heaven," after death. Centuries of Christian speculation about life after death have encouraged a diffidence toward the body at best, distrust and hatred of it at worst. That attitude is at the heart of one of the central crises of our time: the inability to love the "body" of the earth. The ecological crisis will not begin to turn around until we change at a very basic level how we feel about bodies and about the material creation in all its incredible variety and richness of forms. It is not enough to change our life-styles; we must change what we value. We must come to value bodies, to love them, and, as we shall see, appreciate each of them in their differences from us and from each other. The body of the earth, teeming with variety, is but a tiny cell in the "body" of the universe, which includes all matter in all its forms over fifteen billion years of evolutionary history.[25]

We have moved from our body, from the body of each of us, to the body of the universe. In doing so, the notion of "body" has become far richer, deeper, and broader than we usually consider it to be. Often we think of human bodies and, in descending order, the bodies of animals beginning with mammals (does a virus or a plankton have a "body"?). We seldom think of trees or plants as bodies, but as physical structures. They are also bodies, matter, what all things are made of. *Body, then, is the model I suggest we investigate as thoroughly as possible for an ecological theology.* If what we need is a planetary rather than a parochial perspective, a broad rather than a narrow context, the model of body is one worth paying attention to. Unlike the models of conversation and quilt, which are limited to human beings, the model of body includes all life-forms, indeed, all matter on our planet (as well as in the entire universe). While body usually refers to living forms of matter, one can extend it analogously to whatever occupies space and is perceptible to the senses. Thus, we speak of the body of a mountain, heavenly bodies, or oceanic bodies. When cosmologists tell us that the atoms in our bodies were born in the supernova explosions of early stars, they are confirming this continuity of the material base of all that exists: body is a model that links us with everything in the most intimate way.

The use of the model of body as a way of interpreting everything that is, from an atom to the entire universe, stretches the notion in both directions: neither an atom nor the universe is a body, strictly speaking. The primary base or meaning of the model is our own bodies as well as the familiar bodies of other animals we see about us. Yet we do speak of any solid bit of matter, large or small, any material thing as a "body," and from what we are learning about evolutionary, ecological interrelatedness and interdependence, it is appropriate to do so: the atoms in *our* bodies were formed in the "bodies" of the early stars. "Body" does not, therefore, necessarily mean a living body, although that is its primary meaning; moreover, the lines between nonliving and living in evolution as well as their interconnectedness in ecosystems support the use of the model as a broad interpretive lens. Nonetheless, we must remember that it, like all models, is only one partial and inadequate way to interpret reality. With that qualification in mind, we would nonetheless insist that the model of the body is a rich, provocative, illuminating one. Body is the closest bit of matter to us (it *is* us); it is important to us beyond all telling; it gives us the greatest pleasure as well as the greatest pain we experience; it knits us together with all life-forms in networks of shared suffering and joy. In other words, it may be both the most intimate and the most universal way to understand reality.

One of the great assets of this model is that it links us first and foremost with the bodies closest to us: other human ones. While we are, indeed, distant cousins with the supernova, the notion of body calls up, first of all, the human body, our own and that of others. As an ecological model, it is extremely valuable in its extension, for it unites us to each and every body on the planet; but as a justice or liberation model, it is of equal value, for it forces us to think about human bodies that are hungry, thirsty, overworked, unhoused, sick, mutilated, imprisoned, raped, murdered. A focus on the body prohibits us from spiritualizing human pain, from centering on existential anxiety, from substituting otherworldly salvation for this-worldly oppression. *Whatever else* salvation can and ought to mean, it does involve, says the body model, first and foremost, the well-being of the body. A theology that works within the context of the body model claims that bodies matter, that they are indeed the main attraction.

But let us press this model one step further, to radicalize it to its roots. If we and everything else that exists in the universe are matter, are body, then can we also speak of "the body of God"? In fact, must we not do so? What would it mean to extend the model to God, the creator and redeemer of the universe?[26] Questions abound with this suggestion, and the rest of the essay will be concerned with looking at some of them, but, initially, the suggestion is merely to allow ourselves to think this unconventional thought. What if we did not distance ourselves from and despise our own bodies or the bodies of other human beings or the bodies of other life-forms, but took the positive evaluation of bodies from Christianity, feminism, and ecology seriously? What if, with Christianity, we accepted the claim that the Word is made flesh and dwells with us; with feminism, that the natural world is in some sense sacred; with ecology, that the planet is a living organism that is our home and source of nurture? What if we dared to think of our planet and indeed the entire universe as the body of God?

Since we now know that our bodies and spirits (or minds, souls) are on a continuum, is it so odd to think of God as embodied, since the Western tradition has always considered God in terms of personal agency (as having a will, mind, and spirit)? Remember that we are thinking analogically or metaphorically, that is, extrapolating from our own experience, what is familiar to us, in order to speak of what we cannot experience or know directly.[27] We are not describing God as having a body or being embodied; we are suggesting that what is bedrock for the universe—matter, that of which everything that is is made—might be, in fact perhaps ought to be, applied to God as well. We will deal later with some of the intricacies of this suggestion, of how it might be applied. At this point, we are only trying to free our Western, spiritualized, body-hating minds to consider the possibility.

Is it an impossible, abhorrent, or obscene thought? Should it be discarded out of hand? Or is it an interesting, inviting, provocative thought, and one that, as we have tried to show, has at least ambivalent credentials in Christianity, feminism, and ecology? Is the body model one whose day has finally dawned? Might we reflect on this model in all its richness and potential, embracing its positive aspects and not flinching from its negative ones? Could it not, because it is so central to us (what *are* we without our bodies?), be a way, a lens, a glass, by which we might see ourselves more clearly, see where we belong in the scheme of things—not as a spirit among bodies, but as a spirited body among other spirited bodies on our planet?

Perhaps the model could also be a lens or glass through which we might see that all of us "live and move and have our being" in God, in the body of creation, the universe. As the embodied spirit of all that is, God would be closer to us than we are to ourselves, for God would be the very breath of our breath. The model would be a way of speaking of the immanence of God. But it would also be a way to speak of divine transcendence, that Waterloo of Christian theology, which has pushed God out of the world and into another space.[28] In this body model, God would not be transcendent over the universe in the sense of external to or apart from, but would be the source, power, and goal—the spirit—that enlivens (and loves) the entire process and its material forms. The transcendence of God, then, is the preeminent or primary spirit of the universe. As we are inspirited bodies—living, loving, thinking bodies—so, imagining God in our image (for how else *can* we model God?), we speak of her as *the* inspirited body of the entire universe, the animating, living spirit that produces, guides, and saves all that is.

There is one obvious advantage to this model: it allows us to think of God as immanent in our world while retaining, indeed, magnifying God's transcendence. The model of the universe as God's body unites immanence and transcendence. At once a powerful image of divine immanence, for everyone and everything becomes potentially a sacrament of God, it is also, though perhaps not as obviously, an image of divine transcendence. The usual ways of speaking of divine transcendence in the Christian tradition have either been by means of political models (God is king, lord, patriarch) or through negative abstractions (God is eternal, *not* temporal; infinite, *not* finite; omnipresent, omnipotent, and omniscient, *not* limited spatially, or in power or knowledge). Political models describe "domesticated transcendence," for they are narrowly concerned with human beings and neglect not only all other life-forms but also the well-being of the planet as a whole and give no mention to the rest of the universe. Negative abstractions merely say what God is *not* (the *via negativa*) and are, as abstractions, far removed from the life and experience of believers.

But the model of the universe as God's body is, as I hope to show, a way to think about, reflect upon, divine transcendence—a way to deepen its significance to us. It is a form of meditation: the more we contemplate *any* aspect of our universe and especially our own planet, the more we know about it, delve into it, the more mysterious and wondrous it appears. Whether we look at the intricacies of the tiniest bits of matter through a microscope or contemplate the vast stellar reaches of the seemingly infinite space of the known universe, we are awed by the unbelievable detail of the smallest and the incredible massiveness of the largest aspects of the body of God. If Job had had access to microscopes or telescopes to convince his hearers of God's transcendence, he would have used them, for his strategy was similar to what I am suggesting: the cosmos is the picture we turn to when we try to imagine what divine transcendence is. The body of the universe is indeed attractive, for it lures us in its magnificence toward its source. But it is not only the microscopic and the macroscopic that reveal divine transcendence; it is also what we can see with our ordinary middle vision in the body of our own world: the return of the sun in the morning, the blooming of flowers in the spring, and, most especially, the eyes of another person loving us in our poverty and our need. Immanental transcendence or transcendent immanence is what the model of the universe as God's body implies, and it is, as I will try to show, what Christian incarnationalism implies as well.

If we find ourselves shrinking from the possibility of the model of the universe as God's body, let us recall that what become valuable by reflected glory are those aspects of our world that we elevate to represent God. Traditionally, it has been males and their roles (fathers, kings, governors, masters), the human mind (intelligence, purpose, intention), and the human heart (love, compassion, sacrifice) that have been esteemed as a result of their function as divine metaphors. As long as we refuse to imagine God as embodied, we imply (as we do when we refuse to allow the female to serve as a metaphor of God) that the body is inferior. We imply that bodies, because of how "our world" is constructed, do not merit divine validation. But in "another world," in another construction of reality, one that took the ecological context as the primary one, the body would be an appropriate model of God.

One theologian's contribution, then, to the planetary agenda is the suggestion that we look at the model of the body, and especially the universe as God's body. Let us summarize the main points made thus far: bodies are important (they are the main attraction) and we ought to honor and love them, our own and others; the body model gives us both an ecological and a justice context for theology, for it involves a planetary perspective while focusing on the most basic needs of human beings; the model of the universe as God's body suggests both an anthropology and a theology—a way of seeing our proper place as inspirited bodies within the larger body, within the scheme of things, and a way of seeing both the immanence and the transcendence of God—God as the inspirited body of the whole universe.

A Meditation on the Body

There are thousands of tasks involved in the planetary agenda, and there are undoubtedly hundreds of undertakings even for theologians to attempt. My contribution is, like all others, a limited and particular one: to meditate on the body as a model for doing theology in an ecological context. Like all models, this one will have assets and liabilities and will provide, at best, only one perspective. It will allow us to see some things and it will screen out others; it will take one aspect of our experience and use it as a lens through which to see other aspects; it will invite us to imagine boldly and radically while insisting that models do not provide descriptions.

At the outset we need to be aware of both the limits and the importance of such a meditation. Its limitations are perhaps obvious. Not only is this essay just one of the many tasks that theologians need to assume, but it deals with only one model. Many other models exist, some mutually exclusive of the body model, others complementary to it, and still others that correct its biases and partiality. If we keep these considerations constantly before us, then we will not be afraid to radicalize the model, probe it for what it can offer us, reflect upon its associations with imagination and boldness. Metaphors and models are *not* descriptions, and, to the degree we keep this in mind, we will be open to experience the potential insights they can offer us. Too often, especially when faced with novel metaphors for God, we shrink from them because we think they are attempting to define the divine nature and being. No human words can describe God, but it is difficult to remember that because our language, although always metaphorical when applied to God, sounds descriptive: God is father, God is loving, God is the creator. One of the advantages of a shocking or unconventional model such as the body of God is that we are less likely to take it literally than we are the above examples.

The limitations and partiality of the model of the body as a way of seeing ourselves, our world, and God might, then, be obvious, and we need have little fear in regard to literalization. The importance of the model may need more justification. The simplest way to test the importance of a model is to think about its most positive and negative characteristics. The body is rich in both, for, quite simply, like nothing else, it is a "matter of life and death." Everything else that we cherish depends upon it—appreciating the first leaves on a tree in spring, a child's smile, or a favorite piece of music: the body is the bottom line. The shock of the death of a loved one is precisely the blankness, the void, that replaces that person's rich complexity and special uniqueness, which are housed in the body. The body is the home of everything we value, both in ourselves and in others. The pain of this knowledge is so acute that we have tried as a species, since the beginning of human time, to separate the soul or spirit from the body and believe that the one can and does live on after the body dies. Perhaps, but we do not know. What we do know and what a meditation on the body will underscore is that *we are bodies*. This meditation will force us to look squarely at this reality as a way of thinking differently—that is, ecologically—about ourselves, about other human beings and other life-forms, and about God. While this meditation will have many dimensions, its central focus will always be this bottom line, the main attraction: *bodies matter*. It will insist, for instance, that salvation for our planet means, first of all, the health and well-being of the body of the world and the many bodies that constitute that larger organism.

While the positive characteristics of the body model can be epitomized by the phrase "a matter of life and death," the negative aspects are more subtle and diverse. Of course, the most negative aspect is simply that no matter what we do to delay the inevitable, it always comes: the body dies. But that does not begin to suggest the profound negativity with which we, and most other cultures, have regarded the body. Our meditation will reflect in some detail on this issue, as it will on the positive aspects of the model, but we might epitomize the negativity by suggesting that we both worship and abhor the body. These responses are now and have always been most obvious in response to women's bodies, since women have, it seems since the beginning of human time, been associated with the body.[29] The female body is the site of conflict where we see both worship and loathing of our bodies. The female body is an object in a way that the male body is not, and so reflecting on the way society treats the female body is instructive of how we feel about bodies. In our society, bodies, especially women's bodies, and often female child bodies, are to a degree that is increasing to the level of shock sexually abused, battered, prostituted, and raped. The very body that is worshipped—the Virgin Mary, Marilyn Monroe, Madonna body—is the one that in pornography and daily abuse is abhorred. Even when not physically abused, the body, especially the female body, is controlled by the "male gaze," becoming subject to self-abuse in order to satisfy this gaze, as evident in the prevalence of dieting as well as bulimic/anorexic behavior among women.[30]

A society that allows thousands of homeless people to roam the streets with no protection for their bodies; that spends, on the average, more for the last week of a dying elderly person's hospital care than for the medical needs of the first ten years of a child's life; that refuses in international congresses to join other nations in protecting biodiversity and limiting chemicals that contribute to global warming: this society hates the body, human bodies, and all other animal and plant bodies that make up the body of our planet.

Can there be any doubt that the body is a powerful model? Do we not see our lives, both positively and negatively, through the lens of the body? And is this lens, this model, not a distorted one? That is to say, "the body" is a social construction.[31] If we are going to use the body as a model for theological reflection, we must attend carefully to what we mean by body, who provides the meanings, and what the consequences of those meanings are. All models are, by definition, constructions. What we mean by body is a set of associations and stereotypes that are often assumed to be "natural" or "obvious" but are, of course, complex, highly nuanced networks of values and interests controlled implicitly (and at times explicitly) by those in power. It is no coincidence, for instance, that nature and the body (especially the female body) have received the same treatment in our society, for they have both been constructed from the same pattern. So, as we meditate on the model of the body, we will be involved not only in dealing with its accepted commonplaces and associations, but also suggesting other constructions, other ways of seeing and valuing the body.

We need, then, not only to affirm our embodiment, to accept the body as the main attraction, but to think *differently* about it as well. An ecological theology demands that we think about bodies and insists that we *change* our thinking. What resources are there to help us with this task? We will look at one of them, the so-called common creation story, in the next chapter.[32]

We know ourselves to be made from this earth. We know this earth is made from our bodies. For we see ourselves. And we are nature. We are nature seeing nature. We are nature with a concept of nature. Nature weeping. Nature speaking of nature to nature.

The red-winged blackbird flies in us, in our inner sight. We see the arc of her flight. We measure the ellipse. We predict its climax. We are amazed. We are moved. We fly. We watch her wings negotiate the wind, the substance of the air, its elements and the elements of those elements, and count those elements found in other beings, the sea urchin's sting, ink, this paper, our bones, the flesh of our tongues with which we make the sound "blackbird," the ear with which we hear, the eye which travels the arc of her flight. And yet the blackbird does not fly in us but in somewhere else free of our minds, and now even free of our sight, flying in the path of her own will.

—Susan Griffin

2 / COSMOLOGY

The Organic Model

The common creation story is both common and uncommon. It is common because it is the story of everything that is, of how the universe began fifteen billion years ago and how it evolved into some hundred billion galaxies of which our Milky Way is one. Hence, everything that exists—from the most distant galaxies to the tiniest fragment of life—has a common beginning and a common history: at some level and in a remote or intimate way, everything is related to everything else. We are distant relatives to the stars and kissing cousins with the oceans, plants, and other creatures on the earth. The common creation story is uncommon because it is the wildest, most outrageous, most awesome tale conceivable: from an initial explosion, an infinitely hot, infinitely dense matter/energy event billions of years ago, the entire universe has evolved into its present complexity, diversity, size, and age. The common/uncommon character points to one of this story's critical features: a kind of unity and diversity very different from that of the classical organic model. The particular kind of unity and diversity, one that is based on radical relationship and interdependence and yet produces the most stupefying array of diversified individuals, is well captured in this summary of the common creation story.

> Cosmology joins evolutionary biology, molecular biology, and ecology in showing the interdependence of all things. We are

part of an ongoing community of being; we are kin to all creatures, past and present. From astrophysics we know our indebt-
edness to a common legacy of physical elements. The chemical
elements in your hand and brain were forged in the furnaces of
the stars. The cosmos is all of one piece. It is multi-leveled; each
new higher level was built on lower levels from the past. Humanity is the most advanced form of life of which we know, but
it is fully a part of a wider process in space and time.[1]

This kind of organicism supports both radical individuality
and difference while at the same time insisting on radical interdependence of all the parts, and will be the heart of our new organic
model from the common creation story.

We will first contrast this model with the classic one, a model
that not only absorbs the many into the one, differences into a unitary
universalism, but is also anthropocentric and androcentric. A look at
the classic model will reveal its mixed record in Western, Christian
thought and its demise with the seventeenth-century scientific revolution. The surprising feature is how prevalent the model continued
to be within the Christian tradition, even though Christianity consis-
tently and vehemently separated the divine from any physical connection with the world except in the doctrine of Christ's incarnation.
The last few hundred years have been an aberration in human history, with its preference for the machine over the organic model.[2]
Whether we look at ancient cosmogonies, Goddess traditions, or
Native ones (just to take a sampling), we are struck by the widespread
acceptance, in one form or another, of the organic model as well as its
reemergence in contemporary movements such as deep ecology and
ecofeminism.[3] The body model is not only deep and old in human
culture but is also coming into its own once again. Models are not
adopted by majority vote, but they do gain in persuasive power if
they have helped millions of people for millennia make sense of their
lives and world. At least they merit serious analysis, which is what
we propose to give the organic model.

Our focus for reconceiving the organic model will be on the
common creation story coming to us from the sciences, which will
comprise the second section of the chapter. The reason for looking
to this story is simple: it is the view of reality current in our time.
Theologies always have paid and always should pay serious atten-

tion to the picture of reality operative in their culture.[4] If they do not, theology becomes anachronistic and irrelevant.[5] For the last several hundred years that picture was a positivistic, dualistic, atomistic one that forced both God and human beings out of the natural world and into an increasingly narrow, inner one. The world, machinelike and devoid of God except perhaps as the agent who starts it up, was understood within a history-nature split, with human beings on the history side and eventually, with the existentialists, limited to their inner anxieties and joys in their contact with God.[6] Moreover, and most significant for an ecological theology, this picture projected disembodiment: disembodied knowing (the Cartesian mind/body dualism) and disembodied doing (internal human peace or the forgiveness of sins became the principal action between God and the world).

But we now have another possibility: a story about our beginning and evolution that in significant ways is a story of embodiment. To see this story as organic, however, is an interpretation of it that not all share. Some cosmologists and biologists (as well as theologians influenced by them) describe the story in terms that we associate with life: interrelationship, interdependence, change, openness, novelty, beginnings and endings.[7] It can also be described in an atomistic or reductionist way, with a mechanical rather than an organic model.[8] The holistic or atomistic ways of viewing reality are constructions that have their contemporary scientific supporters, just as each has had its supporters for thousands of years. The reasons for supporting one construction over the other are important and complex but we do have a choice and, as I will try to show, there are persuasive reasons for embracing organic thinking.[9]

The final two sections of the chapter will focus on the nature of difference and unity in the common creation story. We will suggest that the kind of diversity the story supports is a wide and deep one, calling for both embodied knowing and embodied doing: that what we consider meaningful and true is profoundly influenced by the different ways we are embodied (our skin color, sex, class, and so forth), and that how we behave toward others ought to be profoundly influenced by the real differences that embodiment creates. Finally, we will analyze the kind of unity among all the diverse individuals in this story, what we will call an ecological unity. It is the kind of unity that

knits us all together in ways that are as profound and permanent as
are our individuality and our differences.

Our creation story is indeed a common/uncommon tale of
embodiment, one that will, we hope, help us to see both the one
flesh we share, as well as the infinite, wild, and wonderful diversity of shapes it has assumed.

The Classic Organic Model

The classic organic model is expressed in the phrase "the
church as the body of Christ" and pictured in Leonardo da Vinci's
drawing of a male figure with arms and legs outstretched to the
four corners of the cosmos. The classic model is based on the
human (male) body. This is the model on which our critique will
focus, for it is the one that has influenced Western Christendom,
but organic thinking is deep and diverse, and we first need to
sketch briefly its range and variety in preclassical as well as postmodern times.

One expects to find the organic model in ancient Goddess traditions and one does. The recent outpouring of materials documenting and analyzing the model establishes its almost universal
acceptance in ancient cultures.[10] It is no surprise, then, to find a
contemporary practitioner of wicca and Goddess traditions claiming that the earth is alive, part of the living cosmos, "a living body
in which we all participate, continually merging and emerging in
rhythmic cycles."[11] But one also finds a similar way of thinking in
a contemporary Native American when she writes that "the
planet, our mother, Grandmother Earth, is *physical* and therefore a
spiritual, mental, and emotional being."[12] Again, we hear the
theme emerge from the words of an ecofeminist: "*We are here*—
inextricably linked at the molecular level to every other manifesta-
tion of the great unfolding. We are descendants of the fireball. We
are pilgrims on this Earth, glimpsing the oneness of the sacred
whole, knowing Gaia, knowing grace."[13] The organic model is vividly expressed in an extreme fashion in a comment by a deep ecologist: " 'I am protecting the rainforest' develops into 'I am part of

the rainforest protecting myself. I am that part of the rainforest recently emerged into thinking.' "[14]

The range of contemporary cosmic, organic thinking is wide, diverse, and raises an interesting question: How has it survived? How has it managed to survive not only Christian asceticism and otherworldliness, but also scientific mechanism, Cartesian dualism, and the contemporary destruction of the planet? We find it not only in the Goddess and Native American traditions, ecofeminism, and deep ecology, but also, as we shall see, in the Christian tradition up through the Reformation (although with some ambivalence). It is also a central model in process theology. What postmodern science is telling us—that the universe is a whole and that all things, living and nonliving, are interrelated and interdependent—has been, for most of the world's history, common knowledge. That is, people living close to the land and to other animals as well as to the processes that support the health of the land and living creatures have known this from their daily experience. We, a postindustrial, urbanized people, alienated from our own bodies and from the body of the earth, have to learn it, and most often it's a strange knowledge. It is also strange because for the past several hundred years at least, Christianity, and especially Protestant Christianity, has been concerned almost exclusively with the salvation of individual human beings (primarily their "souls"), rather than with the liberation and well-being of the oppressed, including not only oppressed human beings, body and soul (or better, spirit), but also the oppressed earth and all its life-forms.

The organic model is reemerging as the original, primordial grass roots movement, not as another fad but as that which speaks to the deepest layers of our being. Many are finding it persuasive, that is, meaningful and true because it connects us to our most basic context, the source of our very life: the body of the earth to which we all belong. There is no more convincing form of persuasion than to be welcomed home and to feel at home, and for Christians who have been made to feel that we do not, in a fundamental sense, *belong* on the earth (for our home is in another world), the organic model invites us to be at home here on the earth. It is a difficult invitation to refuse.

But is it Christian? That is a complicated question that will demand much attention in this essay, but a historical sketch suggests that even within the Augustinian and Thomistic mainstream tradition most influenced by Greek dualistic antimaterialism the model survived, in one form or another, until the scientific revolution.[15] We can only suggest a few outstanding motifs in that history here. First, the organic model, relying on passages from Ephesians and Colossians dealing with the cosmic Christ, was transferred from a creation to a redemption context. Whereas Stoic cosmology saw the world as the visible body of the invisible deity, for the early Christians Christ became the head of the universe and the universe his body or, more typically, the church became the body with Christ as the head.[16] The important point here is that the model, while acknowledged and used, was narrowed to human beings and especially to those who acknowledged Christ as the deity. It lost its cosmic reach, the inclusion of the natural world and all human beings. Second, some early theologians did, however, speak of the world as a body filled with and ordered by the Logos in a manner similar to the Platonic World-Soul: the Logos as the intermediary between mind (God) and matter. Origen, for instance, wrote, "The cosmos is a 'huge animate being' held together by one Soul."[17] This way of thinking carries on the tradition of Wisdom as the intermediary between God and the world, a tradition that was comparatively relaxed in its attitude toward God (in the form of Wisdom or the Logos) and matter interacting or mixing.[18] But any intimacy between God and matter came to an abrupt end when, in the Nicene faith, the Logos became identified exclusively with the second person of the trinity, with the transcendent God.[19] The crucial factor in the increasing dualism appears to be Platonic and Aristotelian disparagement of matter: for Plato, reality and goodness were equated with incorporeality and even for Aristotle, matter is passive and at best has only potentiality.[20] Add to this the Neoplatonic chain of being in which matter is the lowest form of being and the stage is set for Augustinian and Thomistic dualistic antimaterialism.[21]

Given this highly ambivalent if not negative attitude toward matter, it is surprising that organic thinking survived at all into and past medieval culture. But it did, and with gusto. Carolyn Merchant, in her fine study of the model, writes: "For the sixteenth-century Europeans the root metaphor binding together the self, society, and the cosmos was that of an organism."[22] Organic thinking, she claims, permeated daily life, emphasizing the interdependence of the parts of the body, the subordination of the individual to the common good, and the permeation of the cosmos with vital life down to the lowliest stone. To be sure, the model was in significant ways deeply conservative because it relegated whole classes of people to "inferior" parts of the body. Nonetheless, its continued existence is notable in light of its obviously "pagan" credentials and the antimaterialism of Christian theology—Protestant as well as Catholic.

But the radical change that was to come—not from the church, but from the beginning of modern science, the substitution of the machine for the organic model as the major interpretive lens—was already evident in the ancient ambiguity with which nature was regarded. "She" was both the nurturing mother who feeds all creatures in the body of the earth and the scheming, chaotic whore who needs to be tamed.[23] The first obviously supports organic interdependence, while the second allows for and indeed encourages mechanistic control. Scientific discovery and technology, notably mining, needed a new root metaphor, and the machine model was perfect for the task as Francis Bacon, one of the "fathers" of modern science, illustrates when he speaks "of entering and penetrating into the holes and corners" to disclose the "secrets of nature."[24] One does not dig around in the orifices of the nurturing mother, but it is perfectly permissible to treat a lascivious whore that way.

It is doubtful whether Bacon or his brothers realized explicitly that with the rise of mechanism they were promoting a major new and fundamentally different way of construing the cosmos, society, and human existence—but they were. As Merchant puts it, "the removal of the animistic, organic assumptions about the cosmos constituted the death of nature,"[25] for "mechanism rendered nature effectively dead, inert, and manipulable from without."[26] Along with the mechanistic model arose a view of the self as a "rational master of the passions housed in a machinelike body," separated from nature and called to dominate it.[27]

If all this sounds familiar, that is because the machine model is the one that still controls much of our thinking in spite of the fact that contemporary science has replaced it with another possibility: a return to the organic model (although, as we shall see, with some important differences). The United States constitution, with its checks and balances, is built on the machine model, as are many other aspects of our culture: workers in our industrial plants are seen as interchangeable cogs programmed to perform certain functions; malfunctioning parts of our bodies (including the most vital ones) can be replaced with better parts from other bodies; and even the environment can be fixed with the right technology, according to some. We believe in, live in, the machine model as fishes live in the sea; it is not to most of us a construct, but the way things are. Americans believe that anything can be fixed, with the right know-how. It is a sensibility that above all else assumes the primacy of rational control: it is, in significant ways, the apotheosis of the human—over self, over nature, over God. One can and should control one's passions as well as the vagaries of nature and, except in dire emergencies, manage without divine assistance. It is significant that deism—the understanding of God as external to the world, intervening at most only to initiate creation and fill in the gaps in our present knowledge and power—accompanies the machine model.[28] And this is the God that is still all too current in many contemporary church circles: a personal, external superperson who intervenes in the lives of particular individuals at times of stress and despair to fix problems. God is the ultimate Fixer of a malfunctioning world machine.

Because we inhabit the machine model, because it is our "natural" way of seeing things, it is difficult to appreciate what we have lost. But we must try to appreciate this loss if we are to begin again to think organically. Most simply and most profoundly, we have lost the sense of belonging and the sense of life. We have lost the sense of belonging in our world and to the God who creates, nurtures, and redeems this world and all its creatures, and we have lost the sense that we are part of a living, changing, dynamic cosmos that has its being in and through God. We have lost this sense of belonging and of life, not as an intellectual matter, an idea, but as our daily sensibility that accompanies and qualifies all we do, the unquestioned milieu in which we conduct our lives. As twentieth-century people, we can never return to the naivete of organic belonging that permeated the lives of our foremothers and fathers.

But we can return *consciously*. And that is what this essay is about. It will not, however, be a return to the organic model we have been analyzing. The classic organic model had some significant assets that we have tried to highlight, but it also had some serious liabilities. As we set about reconstructing the organic model with the help of postmodern science, we need first to consider some of the problems with the traditional view, especially the Christian version.

Two issues are critical. First, in its primary form within Christianity, the church as the body of Christ, the model was spiritualized, excluding not only all of nature and most human beings but also the physical aspects of life, including sex and, therefore, women. Second, in its assumption that body meant *one* body, the human (and implicitly male) body, it was deeply conservative, at times verging on fascism. Let us look briefly at each of these issues.

There is a profound difference between the Stoic and early Christian notion, as seen in Origen and others, of the cosmos animated by the World-Soul or the Logos of God and the church as the body of Christ with Christ (and his representative) as the head of the body. The first is basically a sense of divine immanence in the entire natural order that includes all life-forms and all human beings. The second is a dualistic, hierarchical notion of exclusion, separating spirit from nature, human beings (and particularly Christians) from other creatures and the earth, and the head of a human being (rational, controlling part) from the body (physical, to-be-controlled part). In the Christian version of the organic model, the divine (here manifest in Christ) is not present in the whole of creation or even in the whole of the human being, but is located in and limited to the rational/spiritual part of the human being, the head. And since rationality was identified with masculinity, and the physical aspects of existence (including sex) with females, the dualism in the model further encouraged the disparagement and at times abhorrence of both women and sexuality.[29] We see in Christianity's version of the organic model an example of that tradition's typical disposition toward the physical realm: the use of it as a symbol of the spiritual life while discarding it as where we belong or where God can be found. The long and deep history of Christian asceticism, of despising the body, would be less curious if Christianity did not make extravagant embodiment claims in its doctrines of Christ, resurrection, eucharist, and ecclesiology.[30] The great fault with the Christian form of the organic model is its spiritualized, narrow focus: the image it calls up is of Christians (minus bodies) as members of the spiritualized, resurrected body of Christ. What it neglects is the rich, diverse, physical plenitude of creation—in other words, it neglects just about everything.

The second major difficulty with the classical organic model is that it assumed the body in question was a human, and implicitly male, body. The model was anthropocentric and androcentric, both features perhaps only to be expected in Western culture. What is more interesting and more problematic is what these features implied—the universalism or essentialism and idealism of the model; that is, the body forming the basis for the model was *one* body and it was the *ideal* human body. The Leonardo drawing personifies oneness and perfection: the body that stands at the axis of the universe is a perfectly proportioned young, physically fit, white, human male body.[31] This one ideal (human, male) body is the form and kind of body that stands behind and informs the traditional organic model. Thus, the organic model is a unitary notion that subordinates the members of the body as parts to the whole; it is concerned principally with human and especially male forms of community and organization;[32] and it supports essentialist thinking, for if there is only one body with one head, there can be only one point of view.

Let us look briefly at each of these points. One of the most severe criticisms against the organic model is its inability to take the freedom of individuals seriously: the harmonious functioning of the whole is, in a body, more important than the autonomy of its parts. In fact, one does not want body parts to act independently nor, if the organ in question is one body, can they. The concern with harmony has made some revolutionaries and liberation theologians rightly suspicious of the model, for it has deeply conservative and hierarchical tendencies. The head (of state or the church) tells the members of the body what they must do to insure the smooth functioning of the whole. Organic thinking was a central ingredient in fascism, especially Nazi ideology, but elements can also be seen in some forms of communism and, in fact, in any form of societal organization that works from the top down rather than the bottom up.[33]

A second implication of the unitary, ideal character of the classic model is its limitation to human (male) forms of association. While it is ostensibly a natural model, that is, derived from the physical, material level of existence, it functioned as a political one, limited to relationships among human beings and especially to public, civic, and hence mainly male forms of association. The model dealt principally with national, ecclesiastical, and local forms of governance, at least in its dominant Western form of the human (male) body. (An entirely different history, of course, as well as different uses and patterns of inclusion pertain in the organic model based on the female body as giving birth to nature and all its creatures.)[34] Hence, while the model was ostensibly organic, it functioned in a way very similar to the political model of God as king of his realm, a realm limited to human beings. In both instances, the entire natural order is neglected or at least marginalized, and personal or female forms of association disregarded (or, as in the case of the family, absorbed into the model with the father as its head).

Finally, the model supports a kind of universalism: *one* body underscores sameness, not difference, and, of course, the sameness in question is what derives from and benefits the head. In its classical form the model supports essentialist thinking: what is good for the head is good for the body and since there is only one head, there is only one form of the good. The same kind of model, an implicitly organic one, lies behind all universalistic, unitary statements, whether about "mankind," "humanity," "all men," or "all women" (or all children, all African-Americans, all poor people, all gays and lesbians, and so on). The assumption is that one head represents the body: the important point to notice is that the organic model relies once again on a human being, with its (superior) head and harmonious or at least controllable parts.

But what if the organic model did *not* assume a human (male or female) body for its base, but *bodies*, all the diverse, strange, multitude of bodies (matter in all its millions, perhaps billions of forms) that make up the universe? What if we changed our perspective from its narrow focus on the one, ideal, human (male) body as the base of the model to a cosmic focus, so that what came to mind when we thought of body was bodies—in other words, not sameness, but *difference*? What if, when we thought of our-

selves and all other creatures as organically interrelated and interdependent, we thought of the rich diversity and difference that
marks that kind of unity and not the sameness that comes to mind
with the image of the human body?

To do so, I suggest we look at the common creation story as a
resource for changing the organic model. That fifteen-billion-year
evolutionary story does not privilege any particular body, let alone
a lately arrived one on a minor planet in an ordinary galaxy (the
human body!). What it underscores, as we shall see, is the billions
of forms matter takes, the unbelievable diversity and difference of
the body of the universe. To anticipate only two implications of this
perspective: our focus would change from ourselves as the center
of things to appreciating the awesome, splendid, magnificent diversity of bodies; and, were we then to speak of the universe as
God's body, it would not be this or that body, and certainly not a
human body, but *all* the bodies that have ever been or ever will be,
from quarks and exploding stars to microorganisms and centi-
pedes, rocks, mountains, and water, but not forgetting tortoises,
pine trees, buttercups, giraffes, and, of course, human beings in all
their various shapes, conditions, and colors.

The Common Creation Story

The common creation story radicalizes both oneness and difference. From one infinitely hot, infinitely condensed bit of matter
(a millionth of a gram) some fifteen billion years ago, have evolved
one hundred billion galaxies, each with its billions of stars and
planets. On our tiny planet alone biologists have found in a single
square foot of topsoil an inch deep "an average of 1,356 living creatures . . . including 865 mites, 265 springtails, 22 millipedes, 19
adult beetles, and various numbers of 12 other forms . . . " (not to
mention the microscopic population that would include up to two
billion bacteria and millions of fungi, protozoa, and algae).[35] From
one millionth of a gram of matter, unimaginable unity, has evolved
unimaginable diversity, not only in the vast galactic realms of the
observable universe (what lies beyond this we do not know) but
also, in equally inconceivable ways, on our planet. The macro-

scopic and the microscopic join in astounding us with a totally new view of what difference and diversity mean. One of the great benefits of learning about the new creation story is that it helps us develop a new eye for difference, a new sense for perceiving difference, for it tells us about diversity in proportions and in detail unlike anything we have known before. Both the naturalist who documents thousands of different kinds of mushrooms and the astronomer who with increasingly powerful telescopes scans space discovering new galaxies agree on one thing: the complexity, diversity, and quantity of different types of matter. And yet, everything that is, from the fungi and protozoa on our planet to the black holes and exploding supernovas in distant galaxies, has a common origin: everything that is comes from one infinitesimal bit of matter. It staggers the imagination; it also will help us to think about unity and diversity in a new way.

We are looking at the common creation story as a resource for reconceiving the organic model in ways that avoid some of the liabilities of the traditional model so that we can interpret the relation between God and the world in ways commensurate with an ecological context. At the outset, however, we need to consider a possible liability of this creation story—the assumption that as the *common* story it is *one* story, a story that levels and homogenizes. Can it take into account as well as learn from the many different mythic creation stories, stories that without the benefit of science have helped people live in intimacy with and protectiveness for the earth? A simple and direct but by no means complete answer to this question is that many mythic stories of origins and development are profound expressions of different aspects of what the common creation story is also telling us. For instance, Native Americans do not find the notion of the radical interrelatedness and interdependence of all creation strange—they have always known it (unlike many Christians, who do find it surprising). This common creation story does not flatten out differences, at either the physical or cultural level; on the contrary, it strengthens them.

We might also ask a second question: Does the notion of the common creation story feed into the uncritical universalizing tendency—it alone has the truth—that characterizes modern and some postmodern science? Our answer is that the contemporary scientific view of reality is not monolithic (there is more than one interpretation) and that it is a *view* (a picture, not a set of permanent, absolute facts). As one philosopher of science, speaking of science and religion, puts it, "neither cosmology nor doctrine claim definitive descriptions of reality."[36] We will reserve the fuller treatment of this issue for later,[37] but it is essential at the outset to recognize that when we speak of the common creation story we remember that it is a story, a narrative of the beginning and evolution of the universe that, while accepted in broad outlines by the majority of contemporary practicing scientists, relies on many assumptions, includes many unknowns, and can be interpreted in a variety of ways (among them the atomistic or holistic ways mentioned earlier).[38] There are, for instance, questions about the big bang theory itself, and it behooves theologians to avoid linking doctrines too closely to any particular view of the beginning of the universe.[39] We should also remember that we approach this material from a theological perspective; hence, we should not attempt to enter complex, abstract intramural scientific debates that are beyond the capacities of laypersons. Our purpose is more modest: it is the practical one of attempting to understand what it means to take the cosmos as the context for doing theology. We are trying to take the context of the whole in which we exist, rather than merely a psychological or political context, as our theological standpoint in a way that emphasizes rather than sacrifices diversity. As we shall see, the common creation story may help us to reconceive the relation of God and the world in a number of other ways, but basic to them all is the radicalization of unity and difference.

What is this story? It is first of all a cosmology, that is, an account of the universe as a whole or of the whole of reality. Cosmology is not limited to scientific accounts; in fact, until recently most cosmologies have been religious, philosophical, or mythical.[40] For instance, during early medieval culture, when fact and value distinctions were unknown, cosmology was a joint enterprise of philosophy, religion, the arts, and the science of the day. One of the aims of this essay is to move us back in that direction, toward a unified view of reality, one in which theology is done in the context of and contributes to the picture of reality current in our time. Such a unified view would give us a functional cosmology, one in which we could understand where we belong, both as human beings and as Christians, in the scheme of things as currently interpreted rather than operating as many do in a schizophrenic fashion, now in a secular world and now in a religious one. We will reserve for later the theological implications of the common creation story, attempting here only to give its broad outlines in the most widely accepted form.[41]

Earlier in this century scientists became aware of a low-grade background radiation, which they eventually surmised was the leftover glow from the hot, early universe, the so-called big bang billions of years ago. This glow is the evidence for the beginning of the universe.[42] Since that time scientists have worked toward that moment, unfolding like a film run backwards the crucial periods of expansion, cooling, and condensation from which the initial explosion evolved into the present universe. They have not reached that moment, but have gotten very close, to before the first millisecond. At that time (although, since time and space were created by the big bang, the phrase is not really appropriate), the four fundamental forces of the universe (the strong and weak nuclear forces, electromagnetism, and gravity) would be united and, presumably, were we to reach it, we would have unravelled the mystery of the universe, attaining the Grand Unified Theory (GUT) or the Theory of Everything (TOE).[43] The utter simplicity and unity of the beginning is not the kind of unity in which the many are absorbed into the one, but a unity in which there is nothing but one. It is reductionism *par excellence* and provides the basis for some forms of reductionist thinking: if everything came from one infinitesimal bit of matter when the laws governing matter were also unified, then the explanation of everything including the minds and presumed spirits of human beings can eventually be understood by breaking wholes into their smallest parts. Reductionism, then, is an interpretive option. However, the utter simplicity of the beginning also suggests something else: everything that is has a common origin and is related. A more radical kind of unity cannot be imagined.

We know considerably more about the first three minutes after the big bang; in fact, these three minutes were among the busiest in the last fifteen billion years.[44] At the big bang itself, the universe was infinitely hot and infinitely condensed. But about one second after the initial explosion the temperature would have fallen to about ten thousand million degrees, which is about a thousand times hotter than the center of our sun. At this time the universe was composed mainly of photons, electrons, and neutrinos and their antiparticles, together with some protons and neutrons. About one hundred seconds after the big bang, the temperature was down to one thousand million degrees, and the protons and neutrons started to combine to produce helium and hydrogen. But within a few hours after the explosion, the production of helium and other elements stopped, and for the next million years or so, the universe just continued to expand without much else happening. Once the temperature dropped to a few thousand degrees, atoms began to form. Expansion and cooling continued, and eventually gravity condensed matter into the first generation of galaxies and stars. These stars eventually produced a second generation when they collapsed through a tremendous explosion (a supernova), spewing out the heavier elements of carbon and iron, elements essential for life. Our sun is a second- or third-generation star, formed about five billion years ago from debris of the supernovas.

For most of the lifetime of the universe, no fundamental changes occurred, and when they did occur, it was always due to temperature changes allowing simpler units to undergo revolutionary, drastic changes toward more complex, diverse ones. The irreversible direction of the universe is from simplicity to diversity. As we get closer to home in this story, to the history of our own planet, the same pattern applies. Our earth was formed, as were the other planets rotating around the sun, from a small amount of the cloud of gas contained in the debris of earlier supernovas. Initially the earth was very hot and had no atmosphere, but eventually it cooled and acquired one. It is believed that the earliest forms of life began in the oceans as a result of chance combinations of atoms into larger structures called macromolecules with the capacity to reproduce themselves and hence multiply. The next step is critical as it lies at the heart of evolution, in both its earliest and most developed forms: natural selection. As Stephen Hawking expresses it:

In some cases there would be errors in the reproduction. Mostly these errors would have been such that the new macromolecule could not reproduce itself and eventually would have been destroyed. However, a few of the errors would have produced new macromolecules that were even better at reproducing themselves. They would have therefore had an advantage and would have tended to replace the original macromolecules. In this way a process of evolution was started that led to the development of more and more complicated, self-reproducing organisms.[45]

This deceptively simple explanation of the process on our planet that led from unity, the initial macromolecules, to the incredible diversity we see about us (remember the rich life in an inch of topsoil!) contains some important and often misunderstood points. The process of evolution is through chance (random errors) operating at the local level; thus, any overall purposive direction, whether divine or of another sort, is highly problematic.[46] The process also relies on law or stability, that is, order. In fact, natural selection is the play of chance and order. It is, in other words, the heart of our interesting, complex, changing world. For without chance, there would be nothing new; without order, new things would simply vanish away.[47] The entire process, which is a highly complex one involving billions of local changes occurring in interaction with the varying environments of individual members of different species, is, nonetheless, in some sense *one* process. It began from the initiating macromolecules and yet has eventuated into a reality—all the life-forms on earth, from a virus to an elephant, from a plankton to a redwood—that is complex and diverse beyond all imagining. It is staggering both in the simplicity and seeming sterility of its beginning and the complexity, fertility, and diversity of its present reality. Moreover, in more or less intimate ways, all these life-forms are interrelated and interdependent: they form one whole with the life and death of the billions of life-forms interwoven with one another in profound as well as subtle ways that we are only beginning to understand.

To review the common creation story, here is a brief summary:

In the beginning was the big bang. As matter expanded from that initial singularity it cooled. After about three minutes the world was no longer hot enough to sustain universal nuclear interactions. At that moment its gross nuclear structure got fixed at its present proportion of three quarters hydrogen and one quarter helium. Expansion and further cooling continued. Eventually gravity condensed matter into the first generation of galaxies and stars. In the interiors of these first stars nuclear cookery started up again and produced heavy elements like carbon and iron, essential for life, which were scarcely present in the early stages of the universe's history. Some of these first generation stars and planets condensed in their turn; on at least one of them there were now conditions of chemical composition and temperature and radiation permitting, through the interplay of chance and necessity, the coming into being of replicating molecules and life. Thus evolution began on the planet Earth. Eventually it led to you and me. We are all made of the ashes of dead stars.[48]

"We are all made of the ashes of dead stars" causes us to reflect on the space and time frames of the universe, its incredible vastness and its aeons of time. Both are very difficult to imagine. We are not equipped for this task, for we have only middle vision, vision suitable for dealing with small things like a blade of grass and large ones like a mountain, but not the smallness of a nucleus of an atom that weighs 1,000,000,000,000,000,000,000,000 times less than a gram or the vastness of our own galaxy, the Milky Way, which is about 100,000 light years in diameter and contains between ten billion and one hundred billion stars (and this galaxy is but one among some billion others in the universe). Our eyes, ears, and language are suited to mundane things, earthly things, like cows, weather, and wheat that we can see, hear, and talk about in a middling way, not macrocosmically (their connections to the stars) nor microcosmically (the nucleus of their atoms).[49] Nor are we equipped to imagine the age of the universe; it is easy to say "fifteen billion years," but almost impossible to imagine. "Seven generations" is closer to the middle time sense we have than either the past of the universe (and its projected future of another fifteen billion years) or the less than a millisecond after the big bang when so much occurred. (Scientists have now worked back to within 10 to the minus 35 second, which is this much of a second: .00000000000000000000000000000000001.) The point of these exercises in space and time is not to generate sci-fi exclamations of incredulity, but a sober as well as awesome sense of our own history and place in the scheme of things. The story of the universe is *our* story, the common creation story of everything that is, and if we are to know how to think and talk about ourselves, our world, and God, it is essential that we learn something about it.

But the part of the story that is most important to us concerns the evolution of our own planet, which began some four billion years ago. In this story we have been following especially the way in which unity and diversity are understood as means of reconceiving the organic model. What began as one, nothing but one, when matter was infinitely hot and condensed, became over billions of years infinitely (for all intents and purposes) diverse. Both unity and difference are in the history of the universe radicalized beyond all imagination.

Two points emerge with particular significance: first, that the unity of nothing but one was the kind of unity at the *beginning* of the irreversible historical process and, second, that the kind of unity that functions among the unbelievably diverse bits of matter on our own planet now attests to a kind of unity quite unlike the unity of a head directing a body, for the connections are far more involuted and intricate. Once we move from the relative simplicity of the early universe and especially when we venture into the complexities of the evolution of the earth and its life-forms, these issues become highly contested.[50] We are not equipped and do not intend to enter that contest. What concerns us is the *direction* of the evolutionary process toward diversity (that it has occurred, not that there was any purposive intent that it should) and the *nature* of the connections among the different kinds of matter as characterized broadly by such words as "interrelationship" and "interdependence." This direction and nature are compatible with the most hard-nosed evolutionary theory, such as that of Stephen Jay Gould, who writes of "the 'pageant' of evolution as a staggeringly improbable series of events, sensible enough in retrospect and subject to rigorous explanation, but utterly unpredictable and quite unrepeatable."[51] The "wonderful life" that has evolved, in all its unbelievable diversity and complex interdependencies, is what is important, says Gould, not that its diversity and interconnectedness were willed by some principle or divine power other than the play of chance and law. While some may be interested in a conversation with contemporary science over the possibility of grounding a natural theology, that is, finding the hand of God in the evolutionary process, this is not the focus of the present essay. The concern here is with the possibility of a theology of nature, that is, using the picture of reality coming to us from postmodern science as a way to reimagine the relation between God and the world.[52] That picture is one in which a special kind of unity and diversity pertains, one which is quite different from the dualistic, hierarchical, conservative organicism based on the human body. What characterizes the common creation story above all else is the history of change from a simple beginning to its complex present diversity. On our planet this evolutionary process has eventuated in life, so that while one can characterize the entire universe in terms of a "historical, ecological, and multi-leveled view of reality,"[53] these words take on a special meaning when applied to the earth (and perhaps to other planets where life is present). For a particular kind of unity and diversity is the critical point, one that is based on radical relationship and interdependence and yet produces the most remarkable array of different individuals. This picture is a profoundly organic one, but it scarcely supports dualism or conservatism. Rather, its multiple levels suggest an "inverse hierarchicalism" (the higher mammals, including human beings, as dependent upon the lower forms, the plants); and it privileges matter rather than mind, inasmuch as matter is the source of everything, including mind.

To summarize: the distinctive aspect of the common creation story pertinent to the formation of an organic model of reality is the particular way both unity and differentiation are understood. It is a form of unity based on a common beginning and history, but one that has resulted in highly complex networks of interrelationships and interdependencies among all life-forms and supporting systems on this planet. It is a form of differentiation that boggles the imagination with its seeming excess of species (hundreds of kinds of mosses, thousands of varieties of mushrooms) as well as numbers of individuals within species. The fecundity, variety, and radical individuation of life-forms seems from an anthropocentric perspective exorbitant and unnecessary. The organic model that emerges from the common creation story is *not* the orderly, limited, clearly defined classic one based on the human (male) body, with its unity of the one ideal life-form, embodying difference only in its parts. Rather, it is wild, strange, and unconventional (from the perspective of the classic model), for in place of one, ideal body, it includes all the bodies that were, are, and shall be here on this planet and throughout the universe—from the slimy bodies of primitive worms to supernovas and black holes, from the elegant bodies of tigers and seals to coral reefs, viruses, and birch trees. And since this body includes everything that is, what characterizes it above all else is diversity, not sameness. But this diversity is interconnected in the most radical, profound way, for each and every thing emerged within a common history and, in some way, ancient or present, far or near, depends upon all the others. These interrelationships and interdependencies are often so remote that they seem to do little more than awe us ("we are all made from the ashes of stars"), but can be so close that our daily lives depend on them (our need for plants and water).

The substratum of this unity and difference is, of course, the matter/energy that comprises everything. The common creation story is the story of the physical universe, the story of embodiment, or, more precisely, the story of everything that exists on the matter/energy continuum. It claims that no special entity, principle, or substance needs to be or should be introduced to explain the evolution of the universe from its simple beginning to its present outcome—on our planet, to human beings with brains or minds (and some would claim, spirits).[54] For our purposes, the point to underscore is the focus of the common creation story on matter, physicality, embodiment.

Embodied Knowing, Embodied Doing

The common creation story allows for and indeed encourages a basic stance toward reality that privileges embodiment. It suggests that when human beings tackle the difficult issues of the meaning of things and the equally problematic issue of how to conduct themselves properly—in other words, the issues of truth and conduct, being and doing, what to think and what to do—they take with utmost seriousness the most fundamental thing about themselves and everything else: embodiment. These lofty issues that have often been dealt with in utter disregard and often disdain for the body (as, for instance, in Cartesian and other forms of idealism, not to mention Platonism, Neoplatonism, and contemporary deconstruction) would, from the perspective of the common creation story, start with the mundanity of embodiment and the peculiar forms of unity and differentiation characteristic of that story. This perspective would support, though of course not demand, a view of meaning and truth that takes seriously the diversity of embodied sites from which human beings make such claims: the sites that take into account race, class, gender, sexual orientation, handicapping situations, and so forth. Since there is no one universal, ideal embodiment but many, diverse forms of it, truth and meaning for human beings must begin from these embodied locations. The body matters, says the common creation story; in fact, it is the main attraction. Likewise, from the point of view of the common creation story, right action or praxis begins from embodiment as well. If we and all other life-forms are not incidentally but centrally and radically bodily, then the needs of bodies (all the different ones in the interconnecting network of life on the planet) provide the primary context for obligation.[55] Embodiment gives us a commonality with everything else on the planet (including even such remote bodies from ours as trees, rocks, and mountains) with which to reconceive our place in the scheme of things. If the ecological crisis is calling for an end to narrow anthropocentricism as our moral code (what is good for us and especially "me and my tribe"), then embodiment may move us not only toward a more biocentric and cosmocentric perspective but also toward a more inclusive sense of justice for the needs of *all* (embodied) human beings. In an embodiment ethic, hungry, homeless, or naked human beings have priority over the spiritual needs of the well-fed, well-housed, well-clothed sisters and brothers.

   We need to probe the issue of embodied knowing and doing more deeply, especially if it is to be recommended as a crucial element in Christian theological reconstruction, since Christianity, along with Western epistemology and ethics, has neglected it. Margaret Miles, in her study of Christian devotional practices, claims that the central project of Christianity "formulated doctrinally as the incarnation of God in human flesh, is carnal knowing, embodied knowing," which, as a form of experiential learning, should support the particular and concrete conditions in which all learning takes place. But, she insists, in Christianity the flesh was ignored in favor of a spiritual journey: "faith, knowledge of self and world, and spiritual progress came to be seen as abstract."[56] Yet Christianity merely illustrated in its own particular way the widespread Western preference for the abstract, the universal, and the disembodied.

But among some other important epistemological and ethical perspectives that take embodiment seriously[57] are two related forms that deserve special consideration, in part because their contributions have not been fully appreciated, but also because they offer insights particularly relevant to an organic model concerned with difference. They are attention epistemology and feminist epistemology. A brief look at each may help us to see the change that might take place in our understandings of knowing and doing were we to take embodiment as our starting point.

Attention epistemology is a rather abstract term for a very concrete and basic phenomenon: the kind of knowledge that comes from paying close attention to something other than oneself. It is best conveyed by a story from philosopher and novelist Iris Murdoch: "I am looking out of my window in an anxious and resentful state of mind, brooding perhaps on some damage done to my prestige. Then suddenly I observe a hovering kestrel. In a moment everything is altered. The brooding self with its hurt vanity has disappeared. There is nothing but kestrel. And when I return to thinking of the other matter it seems less important."[58] In spite of the disappearance of the hurt self, the experience is not, she claims, mainly therapeutic. "More naturally," she explains, "as well as more properly, we take a self-forgetful pleasure in the sheer, alien pointless independent existence of animals, birds, stones, and trees."[59]

Attention epistemology is listening, paying attention to another, the other, in itself, for itself. It is the opposite of means-ends thinking, thinking of anything, everything, as useful, necessary, pleasurable *to oneself*, that is, assuming that everything that is *not* the self has only utilitarian value. An attention epistemology assumes the *intrinsic* value of anything, everything, that is not the self. Each and every different entity in the universe has its own (from our point of view) "pointless independent existence" and the implicit assumption, therefore, is that we can *know* others, all others, not only human beings but "animals, birds, stones, and trees," only insofar as we pay attention to them. Since the existence of each entity and being is in and for itself (and not "for me"), then knowledge of *difference*, that is, of the teeming multitude and variety of things that comprise the universe, can occur only when we pay attention to radical particularity. In a passage that invites meditation, Murdoch combines art, morals, love, and reality: "Art and morals are, with certain provisos . . . one. Their essence is the same. The essence of both of them is love. Love is the perception of individuals. *Love is the extremely difficult realization that something other than oneself is real.* Love, and so art and morals, is the discovery of reality" (italics added).[60] In this enigmatic and fascinating statement, Murdoch seems to be suggesting that knowledge ("the discovery of reality") is directly connected with granting genuine autonomous, independent existence to others, refusing to take oneself and one's interests as the focus and point of reality. She also appears to be saying that the goal of knowing and doing (as well of art) is precisely this attention to (love of) other beings in their "sheer, alien pointless independent existence."

An attention epistemology is central to embodied knowing and doing, for it takes with utmost seriousness the differences that separate all beings: the individual, unique site from which each is in itself and for itself. Embodiment means paying attention to differences, and we can learn this lesson best perhaps when we gauge our response to a being very unlike ourselves, not only to another human being (who may be different in skin color or sex or economic status), but to a being who is *indifferent* to us and whose existence we cannot absorb into our own—such as a kestrel (or turtle or tree). If we were to give such a being our attention, we would most probably act differently than we presently do toward it—for from this kind of knowing—attention to the other in its own, other, different embodiment—follows a doing appropriate to what and who that being is.

Attention epistemology is not a recent arrival, gaining ground because it fits with ecological sensibility. Simone Weil expresses the deepest dimension of the Genesis myth when she writes: "God, if He exists, is good because He delights in the existence of something other than Himself."[61] The comment upon completion of creation, that everything that God had made was "very good," contains aesthetic delight in the existence of all the others (the day and night, ocean and sky, plants and animals, including great sea monsters, creeping things, and humankind). It surfaces in Aristotelian epistemologies such as that of Thomas Aquinas, who took seriously the empirical reality of different kinds of beings (in contrast to Platonic idealism) and more generally in the sacramental tradition that stresses the uniqueness of each creature's symbolization of divine grandeur.[62] One sees it also in Jonathan Edwards's "consent to being": "true virtue most essentially consists in *benevolence to being in general*," the attainment of a degree of objectivity in the sense of the acknowledgment that the realm of being is wide, diverse, and different from oneself.[63] There are aspects of attention epistemology in some contemporary theologies[64] and most especially, as we shall see, in feminist epistemologies, although for the most part these tend to limit the notion of difference to those among human beings. Ecofeminists, however, as well as some women scientists—most notably the Nobel laureate Barbara McClintock—have written eloquently and passionately about "loving perception of the nonhuman material world" and listening in order to gain "a feeling for the organism."[65] McClintock, a plant geneticist, insisted that "listening to the material," paying attention to the individual differences of corn plants, is essential to scientific discovery, for organisms have a life of their own (doing everything we can think of "better, more efficiently, more marvelously"). But in order to find this out, one must set dogmas aside and pay attention to the differences, even the differences among individual corn plants.[66] Feminist Marilyn Frye summarizes this kind of knowing well in her contrast between the arrogant eye and the loving eye: "The loving eye knows the independence of the other . . . It is the eye of one who knows that to know the seen, one must consult something other than one's own will and interests and fears and imagination. One must look at the thing. One must look and listen and check and question . . . The science of the loving eye would favor The Complexity Theory of Truth . . . and presuppose The Endless Interestingness of the Universe."[67]

Attention epistemology, the kind of knowing that focuses on *embodied differences,* is illustrated by feminist epistemology. Probably the most widespread criticism that feminists of many different persuasions have made against Western thought is that, while masquerading as universal human thought, it is really from the perspective of and for the benefit of men. This perspective is seldom acknowledged; in fact, innocence and ignorance join hands to strengthen the case of "objectivity." The sincere belief by the dominant voice (in the West, the voice of white, affluent, educated, straight males) that it speaks for everyone, makes it all the more convincing. The cloaked or masked character of essentialist thinking (thinking that merges all differences into one essence) must be, feminists claim, revealed for what it is: concrete, situated, particular, and limited. In other words, it is *embodied* thinking, as is all thought, including, of course, the criticisms by the feminists themselves.[68] Since time immemorial women have been identified with the body and, by extension, with nature, and while there are some feminists who focus on the female body as the primary context for thought and action, this focus can result in a new essentialism.[69] The feminists who have become increasingly conscious of the ways in which, within feminism itself, essentialism has cloaked the real embodied *differences* among women will be more important for our project, since we are developing ways of thinking and doing that underscore differences among bodies (as well as the special ways they are united). A case study will be instructive.

The contemporary women's movement began in the 1960s principally as a white, Western, middle-class phenomenon concerned with liberation from the particular forms of oppression these women experienced. But the movement was slow to realize the depths of its own universalist thinking, even as it increasingly criticized the social constructions of gender by the dominant male institutions of Western culture. Initially, feminists spoke from a position "as women," which assumes a monolithic voice. (Often still one hears the weary question, What is the women's point of view on this issue? as if there were *one*. The comparable question, What is the men's point of view? is never asked, for we assume that men have many, varied, different perspectives on issues—in other words, that they are the full human beings.) Increasingly, however, feminists have come to realize the radical differences that separate women, one of the most painful in this country being the history of relationships between white and African-American women during slavery when, among other things, white women were often mistresses over African-American women, who were in turn mothers by the husbands of their mistresses.[70] As recent feminists have become aware, *embodiment* is a complex notion, and it is no longer sufficient to speak of the "oppression of women." The way that a poor, Hispanic, lesbian woman experiences each of these forms of devalued embodiment in our culture is not simply additive; she is not poor *and* Hispanic *and* lesbian, but is herself all three at the same time and each qualifies and changes the others (if, for instance, she were poor but white and straight, her experience would be different).[71]

These feminists say that we need to overcome both "somatophobia" and "pletherophobia," disdain for the body and fear of different kinds of bodies.[72] These are issues about bodies that refer to devalued tasks done by those with particular kinds of bodies, as well as devalued differences associated with particular bodies. In our culture, for instance, men's work is associated with the mind and women's with the body; hence, we favor jobs requiring mental activity over those requiring bodily activity, especially those directly concerned with the body, such as cleaning up after it, feeding it, washing its clothes (the so-called dirty work). Moreover, body work is disdained because it is associated with women and certain races and classes; white, upper-class males seldom do it (except at the most elite level of clothes designer and chef). Our culture not only disdains the body but also fears the differences associated with certain kinds of bodies (such as those with wombs, frizzy hair, or dark skin). Our culture devalues these bodies as not simply different but inferior (in contrast to bodies without wombs or with straight hair and light skin). Another strategy of pletherophobia is to elide or pass over the differences in a well-intentioned search for equality; if bodies, in all their differences, are seen as the cause of discrimination, then the best strategy is to eliminate them, become sex-blind and color-blind.[73] But of course what emerges once again is "woman," the generic, nonhistorical, nonexisting essential woman, who is no particular woman.

While there are problems with radical particularity and difference without some forms of interconnectedness, recent feminist analysis and critique of essentialist thinking makes a substantial contribution to our organic model. It helps to remind us that the particular, concrete, situated *differences* among human beings, who at the same time exist together within the body of the planet, must be starting points for knowing and doing, for embodiment *is* radically particular.

We have been highlighting attention epistemology (and feminist epistemology as an example of it) as a kind of knowing and doing intrinsic to the organic model that emerges from the common creation story. Embodied knowing and doing rest not upon the one ideal body (the white, fit and able, male, human body) that would absorb all its parts and all differences into itself for its own well-being. Rather, embodied knowing and doing should rest, for all intents and purposes, upon the infinite number of bodies in all their differences that constitute the universe. That backdrop serves as the relativizing context for the more operable notion of the forms of embodiment on our planet: *all* bodies are included, but we can conceive of only a finite number and, in our daily lives, interact with many fewer still. But to be able to learn from and guide one's behavior through attention to others—to have an attention sensibility—one needs only a few others, perhaps only one other, for each one, in its own unique, different embodiment, is the *other*. If we were to see *one* other with full attention, that is, loving it, acknowledging that this something other than oneself is really real, then it might follow that we would have to acknowledge the reality of many, perhaps all, others. On such a basis we might build an ecological ethic—a way of being in the world that respects the intrinsic value of the many different beings that comprise our planet—and begin to see as well where we human beings, as particular kinds of beings with special gifts and limitations, fit into the scheme of things.

Ecological Unity

In the organic model derived from the common creation story we see forms of unity and diversity significantly different from those found in the classic model. Both unity and difference are radicalized. The oneness of everything at the beginning and hence a common history of kinship is of the most absolute sort imaginable; likewise, the multifarious character of the present universe in intricacy, complexity, and diversity at the macroscopic, microscopic, and middling levels approaches the realm of infinite difference. Thus far in this essay we have focused on the degree and nature of the differences since the classic organic model suppressed diversity and individuality. We have stressed the seemingly wild, profligate fecundity of the common creation story, the evolution and emergence on our planet alone of millions, perhaps billions, of different species of life-forms and within these species, often billions of individuals. Difference, individuality, and "unnecessary" largesse of numbers appear to characterize the diversity pole.

But what of the unity side? In the beginning everything was one, but what about now? How should we, using the common creation story as our resource, speak of the unity that connects this amazing array of a diverse, complex, intricate universe of individuals? The unity is ecological, and, as such, it is very different from the oneness of the beginning, as well as the subordination of the parts to the whole in the form of organic thinking based on the human body. It *is* an organic unity inasmuch as we now know that everything that is is related to everything else internally from the beginning. But this abstract statement does not in any way express the complexity, difficulty, and mysteriousness (at least to our present state of knowledge) concerning how any two or more things, life-forms, processes, or events interact and influence one another. We know that, speaking just of planet earth, physical reality is composed of systematically, internally interrelated parts, but how changes in particular parts affect other parts is so complex and often so highly nuanced that we may never be able to graph the relationships.[74] It behooves us, then, to at least grasp the big picture, to learn and be willing to abide by some of the most basic ecological interconnections that we *do* know.

By ecology we mean, most basically, the study of how the earth works; in other words, the house rules of our home. The word "ecology" is from the Greek *oikos*, house or home, so ecology is the study of organisms (which means us and all other life-forms) in their home (which means the interactions of all life-forms with one another and with their environment).[75] It is a complex study, but for our purposes, to try to understand ecological unity we will focus on a few critical notions.

The first task is to imagine the whole: two images come to mind here. One is the view from space (only possible in the last few decades) of the earth as a single, finite reality. The picture seen by billions of people of our green, white, and blue marble rotating slowly in the black emptiness of space is a moving sight: a lovely marvel of teeming life in a galaxy that to our knowledge contains no other fertile planets. For the first time, perhaps, we can appreciate the earth as vulnerable and fragile as well as precious in its specialness. It is also, as we now know, a closed system: while from the ground-up view, it may appear to have seemingly unending supplies of food and water for its inhabitants, from the sky-down view, it obviously must function within its limits: empty space is not an available resource. When populations of living creatures (of whatever kind, including human beings) exceed the resources of the planet, they will die.

So, the first image of ecological unity—the lone, fertile planet in space—tells us that we are all in this together. The health and well-being of the planet as a whole are not merely a desirable end; rather, they are a necessary bottom line.[76] And this leads into the second image, that of "home." We are not aliens or tourists on earth, as some religious traditions with otherworldly leanings would have us believe. We evolved on this planet, the product of its fifteen-billion-year history, and we belong here as solidly as do all its other life-forms, for we could not live nor could we have evolved elsewhere. We are, indeed, flesh of its flesh, bone of its bone. Thinking of the earth as our home in contrast to, say, thinking of it as a "hotel" is instructive.[77] If we belong here, if the earth is our home, then it follows that we will want to take care of it. The Western hotel sensibility views the earth as if it were set up for our convenience, with endless supplies of hot and cold running water, gourmet room-service meals, and luxurious fresh towels that, when we have used them up, can be tossed in the middle of the room as we drive on down the highway for more of the same. But we are coming to realize that the earth is not a hotel, and we had better start treating it as our home.

If the earth is our home, then we need to attend to some of its most basic house rules. Ecology is, as we have stated, a highly complex study; it should also be one of the most important areas of learning for all persons on the planet, for it concerns the fundamental workings of our home. At present, it is a little-known subject and scarcely taught in our schools. However, two of the most crucial house rules will illustrate both the necessity for learning at least the rudiments of ecology and the kind of unity among all life-forms and their environments that emerges from an ecological perspective.

The first rule is the Second Law of Thermodynamics, which is concerned with energy transformation. (It and the First Law form the most basic laws governing our home.) All processes, both animate and inanimate, occur through energy. Energy is involved whenever any work of any sort is performed; for example, when anything speeds up or cools down, is cooked or heated, moves, changes, or is altered in structure. The First Law says that while energy can be converted from one form to another, the *quantity* remains the same, but the Second Law, the critical one, says that the *quality* decreases. Thus, for instance, fossil fuels cannot be recycled back into coal but dissipate as gases into the biosphere. The quality decreases in any conversion of heat to do useful work, tending toward increasing randomness or disorder (what is called entropy).[78] The energy-use road is an irreversible one-way street: entropy increases and available energy decreases in a closed system. And this law operates even when it does not appear to, as, for instance, in a complex, orderly structure such as a city. The highly ordered structure of urban living demands an enormous amount of energy, and high energy use is the heartbeat of a modern city. Someone or something pays the price: "The device by which an organism maintains itself at a fairly high level of orderliness really consists in continually sucking orderliness from its environment."[79] There is no free lunch: for city dwellers to have heat and air conditioning, cars, computers, microwaves, planes, and so forth, other parts of the planet have to be sacrificed. The law means that the higher the life-style supported from various energy sources, the greater the damage done to the environment. Thus, a typical first-world baby will, over its lifetime, drain five times more energy from the environment than a third-world baby will. The implications for both population and life-style are immediately evident from this seemingly esoteric Second Law of Thermodynamics.

This law turns out to be at the heart of ecological unity, a kind of unity in which all the bodies of this organic whole, the earth, depend upon a supply of energy that, when used, becomes less usable or unusable. This is not the kind of unity in which parts are merged into a whole for the benefit of the one (head), but rather a form of unity that, in the final analysis, is bound to disintegrate *for all*, although at a different pace for different parts, depending on which parts do the "sucking" and which parts get "sucked." The prospects for injustice and oppression are evident—and they have materialized, as disproportionate energy use on our planet illustrates.

The bad news of the Second Law, however, is countered by the second house rule of our planet. It is derived from the very constitution of the earth: we are a planet and therefore we have a sun. The good news is that we do have an opening out of our closed system. We have (from our perspective) an infinite source of energy available from the sun, which has at least five billion more years of life. There *is* hope, but again we need to know how this energy source works. Just as with the Second Law, which tells us that energy transformation is irreversible and some parts of the environment must pay the price for energy use, so the energy from the sun has its strictures, most notably the availability of plants with their incredible feat of photosynthesis. The health of the planet depends *not* on the quantity and vitality of human beings (or on any of the other so-called higher mammals), but on the quantity and health of *plants*. The hierarchy of value and importance is reversed: we cannot live a day without the plants, but they would prosper indefinitely without us; in fact, given the rate of desertification and deforestation due to human actions, plant life would improve with our demise. Nonetheless, we do presently have a large supply of plant life, so the issue is how to live in a manner that is appropriate to its continuation and well-being. Again, there are many complex issues here, but looking at just one will highlight our central concern with the kind of unity an ecological perspective suggests.[80]

An ecosystem has two basic components, the abiotic ones (such as soil, water, chemicals, atmosphere, gases, sunlight, temperature, and so on) and the biotic components (the producers, the consumers, and the decomposers). The producers are the green plants, the self-feeders, which take the energy of the sun and convert it into carbohydrates, the basic stuff that all creatures feed on. The consumers feed from others in a chain from herbivores to carnivores. Human beings, at the top of the food chain, are the consumers *par excellence*: we produce no life-giving products, use the products available (the food, energy, and habitable lands derived from photosynthesis) with increasing profligacy, due to our burgeoning numbers and the high life-style of some of us, *and* we give nothing back. The decomposers, the organisms of decay such as bacteria and fungi, convert other organisms, dead ones, thereby releasing their constituent molecules so that the process of life can start over again. We do not even help this process, except to the extent that we eventually, if reluctantly, contribute our bodies to the decomposers.[81]

So, the hitch in the good news of the endless supply of energy from the sun and the process of photosynthesis is that the planet is still finite: there is only so much land and other ingredients, especially water, needed for the process to occur at a level necessary to supply the human population, which may reach ten billion in the next decades (not to mention the needs of other life-forms). Again, the implications are evident: population control and life-style changes. Indeed, unity in an ecological context is profoundly organic, profoundly concerned with bodies at every level and in every way. The interrelationships and interdependencies that we see in just a few simple house rules of our planet make that painfully clear. The unity that binds us together is a life-and-death one: who shall live and how well we (they) will live. And it is a we/they issue, for unless we accept the energy limitations of the planet, the basic reality of the planet will be, as it already is becoming, the control of the energy resources by the privileged and powerful as well as the virtual elimination of animal species that encroach on human desires or needs.

This little sketch cannot begin to suggest the complexity and gravity of the situation we face. At the very least, it is meant to highlight the need to think holistically, organically, about ourselves, other human beings, other life-forms, and the ecosystem that supports us all. In this essay we are concerned with a theological, not a biological or even an ecological task: we are asking how we should think about God and the world in light of the contemporary picture of reality, one that suggests novel and radical forms of both diversity and unity. We have so far, however, neglected one crucial difference that separates human beings from all other life-forms, and it may be the difference that makes all the difference: we are, to our knowledge, the only creatures on our planet who *know* the common creation story, the only creatures who not only participate in it but *know* that they do. We know a great deal about who we are in the scheme of things, of what our proper place ought to be, of how deeply and thoroughly we depend on all that is "beneath" us. We have, then, a choice: we can choose to be at home on our planet, learn to follow its house rules, value its fragility and beauty, share its limited resources with other human beings and other life-forms. We may decide not to do so, but we will not be able to say "If only we had known." We *do* know.

* * * * *

In this chapter we have been reflecting on kinds of unity and diversity, on that ancient puzzle of how the one and the many are related: How can things be so different, particular, and concrete and yet at the same time form a whole of some sort? We have suggested that the common creation story gives us a new way to imagine both the differences and the oneness. In closing, it might be helpful to look at a familiar example of ecological diversity and unity, perhaps most easily understood in a small space such as a tide pool. A pool, a mere foot or two across and a foot deep, can contain hundreds of plants and animals, many species as well as distinct individuals, all of which are united in complex networks of interdependence. The pool is, in miniature, a model of the kind of diversity and unity in all other parts of our planet and indeed in the entire planet itself. If one spends some time looking at the pool, one is struck by two things: how many different individual creatures and plants live there and how the whole forms a little world unto itself. It is a closed world except for the twice-daily visits of the ocean, feeding and cleaning the tiny enclosure.

One's experience with a tide pool is often a gradual deepening of delight in its particularity and diversity. The first impression is of a few bits of seaweed and something small moving on the bottom or sides of the sandy pool. But as one hunkers down and spends some time just looking at the pool, marvelous things begin to happen (it helps if you have picked up a brochure from the park office telling you the names and habits of the things you will see). The round or pointed or hairy things, brown or purple or striped, come into focus and you begin to see particular, distinct plants and animals. Green and pink anemones wave their tentacles in the air. Plastered against the rocks on the side of the pool are purple and orange starfish, curving their elegant feet tightly around one another. On each of them are tiny white bumps in intricate designs, every one appearing to be different. As the eye concentrates, you see coralline algae, tiny plants that look like the trees of the miniature world, providing food for many as well as cover for the hermit and purple shore crabs scuttling across the bottom. Out of the corner of your eye you see a shadow flash over the bottom of the pool—a sculpin, a tiny, highly disguised fish that, along with the scuttling crabs, gives movement to the pool. These few plants and animals are just a sampling of what lives in this self-contained world, for most of the life is microscopic. These creatures cause us to marvel at the diversity of the species, the intricacy and complexity of individuals, and the interdependence of the whole. Whatever survives here does so only through living with and off of the other life-forms. Nothing is an island unto itself, yet each *is* an individual. A tide pool's miniature world is a self-contained ecosystem except for its opening to the food-bearing ocean; it is a microcosm of our planet, also an enclosed space housing millions of diverse species and billions of individuals, open onto its source of food, our sun.

If we raise our eyes above the tide pool, to a portion of rock that is exposed to the air between tides, we see another and even more intense form of individuality, diversity, and unity. A rock face covered with acorn and goose barnacles, blue-shelled mussels, periwinkles, lichens, snails, brown sponges, finger limpets, and various kinds of seaweed forms a dense carpet of interlocking life that takes considerable focused attention to see fully. The longer we let our eyes poke around the profusion of life, the more we realize what diversity, individuality, and unity mean in nature. For instance, we see barnacles growing on top of and out of the openings of the mussel shells, but in the tiny crevices between the mussels and barnacles are also periwinkles, limpets, and snails of all sizes, some so small they look like a grain of sand and some as large as a barnacle but so well camouflaged it takes several minutes to distinguish them. (It is as if they *appear* only when we give them our undivided attention. By seeing and naming them, we create them, or, rather, we create them *for ourself*. Their world *is there* but not for you or me until we pay attention to it.) The longer we press our vision into the crevices of the rock face, the more different things we see. What appeared a half hour ago as a "mess" of scaly stuff has now become a highly differentiated world of species and individuals living a tightly knit, interconnected existence. Many of these individuals die to give life to others, and all of the living depend on both the life and death of the others.

A tide pool or rock face shows us on a small scale what is harder to see but everywhere present in all other aspects of the planet: unbelievable individuality, diversity, and complexity combined with astonishing networks of interconnectedness and interdependence. The first phenomenon comes home to us only when we spend time with the detail, the particularity, of another creature—look at the patterns on its body, notice the complexity of its physiology, learn something of its habits, appreciate its differences from others of its species. The second reality, the unity that knits various species and individuals together, emerges for us when we notice how interrelated and interdependent each is with the others. They not only feed off each other but their very hold to existence is by clamping onto, clinging to, other beings. They live on top of, in between, and inside one another.

Of course we human beings do as well. But raised and educated to believe we are separate, independent individuals, we forget that our own lives as well as the ongoing life of our species depend also on living on top of, in between, and inside other forms of life on our planet. These relationships, needless to say, are not always pleasant and harmonious; in fact, they are often just the opposite. That nature is red in tooth and claw, that survival involves eating and being eaten, is everywhere evident. And we obviously participate in this pattern—hunger, destruction, sacrifice, waste, death, pain, and suffering are intrinsic to this picture and therefore to our actions and lives as well. Whether the relationships on our planet be predatory, symbiotic, or harmonious (and nature displays all these types), each and every creature, including human ones, is, for good or for evil, intertwined with the life and death of the others. We are locked together on our planet into a common destiny. We cannot go it alone.

To summarize and move on: we have, in this chapter, compared and contrasted the classic and contemporary organic models, especially in regard to the sense of unity and difference that each projects. With the help of the common creation story we now have a way of thinking of unity and difference that addresses many of the problems of the classic model as well as goes far beyond it in richness, suggestiveness, and potential as a model for a cosmological, ecological theology. We now turn to substantive issues of how to reconceive Christian theology. For instance, how would this new model change the *way* we do theology? How would our sources and criteria of theology be different? We will consider these questions in the next chapter.

For Knowledge of God's Creation

Almighty and everlasting God, you made the universe with all its marvelous order, its atoms, worlds, and galaxies, and the infinite complexity of living creatures: Grant that, as we probe the mysteries of your creation, we may come to know you more truly, and more surely fulfill our role in your eternal purpose; in the name of Jesus Christ our Lord. Amen.
—The Book of Common Prayer

3 / METHODOLOGY

A Theology of Nature

When we begin to think of ourselves—and of God—in an ecological context, everything changes. To think of ourselves, our nature, and our role in the scheme of things from a cosmic, planetary perspective and to think of God as the One who is in, with, and under the entire process of the universe removes us from a narrow psychological or broader political viewpoint, the two other chief contexts in which Christian theology has recently been situated.[1] The cosmological perspective, however, is not novel; in fact, it is the oldest context in both the Jewish and early Christian traditions. This perspective has usually been qualified by a redemption or salvation faith; that is, because God has liberated us, we believe therefore that God is also the creator and redeemer of all that is.[2] It suggests a theology of nature: from our experiences of liberation from forms of oppression, both personal and political, we infer that God is the giver and redeemer of *all* life. A theology of nature stands in contrast to a natural theology, which also uses a cosmological perspective but does so in order to support the thesis that God can be known through the creation or, more generally, to find a consonance or harmony between scientific and theological knowledge. Natural theology tries to harmonize (or find points of contact between) belief and knowledge of the world; a theology of nature attempts to reconceive belief in terms of contemporary

65

views of the natural world. A theology of nature does not solicit the help of science to provide a basis for or to confirm faith, but uses the contemporary picture of reality from the sciences of its day as a resource to reconstruct and express the faith. A theology of nature, an understanding of all of the natural order, including human history, in light of divine goodness and power, is the main focus of this entire essay. This theology of nature will express divine goodness and power as well as our place in the scheme of things in terms of the view of reality coming to us from contemporary science, a view we have characterized in terms of the organic model.[3]

Before we proceed with a theological sketch of these matters, many important issues need attention. First, where does the project of reflecting on the model of embodiment as a way of expressing both divine and human reality fit into the planetary agenda, and how is this theology of nature in conversation with other theological projects, notably creation spirituality and natural theology? Second, what is the status of a theology of nature that attempts to remythologize Christian doctrine with the help of the organic model? It is a form of embodied knowing as is all metaphorical knowledge, and we will need to spell out the limits as well as the plausibility of this kind of knowing. Third, since the organic model on which this essay is based comes from an interpretation of postmodern science, we will need to justify this reading: Does science give us one "objective" view of reality, or is it, like other important human enterprises, a construction of reality?

This chapter is concerned with placing my small piece in the larger quilt, finding the right spot to sew it, seeing how it fits with the many other pieces. Or in the language of the academy, it is concerned with methodological issues, especially epistemological ones, the nature and limits of knowledge, including scientific and theological knowledge, as they pertain to this particular project. A central question will be: What is the status of remythologizing key Christian doctrines with the help of the model of embodiment, a model that comes from a reading of contemporary science?

Theology and the Planetary Agenda

Theology is often deceptively pretentious. Theologians talk about God and the world—in other words, about everything there is—and often do so as if they had privileged communication with the divine mind. In truth, of course, they are just human beings who have had experiences that they believe connect them with sacred powers, experiences they interpret in the language and categories of the religious communities in which they were raised or subsequently joined. The reason for mentioning this obvious point is to underscore that theologians, like everyone else, come from and live in limited, concrete contexts; if they contribute anything to the planetary agenda, it will be influenced by all the characteristics of their contexts. In other words, theologians (and scientists also, as we shall see) are *embodied*. They offer their bits of theological reflection qualified by their gender, race, class, sexual orientation, physical capabilities, not to mention geographic location, family of origin, personal choices, partner and childbearing histories, and so on. The list is not meant to diminish the contributions of theologians (or scientists), but only to relativize contributions that sometimes masquerade under the cloak of objectivity, absoluteness, or certainty.

Theologians have important offerings to make to the planetary agenda, but these are best made, I believe, in the spirit of collegiality. Each of us as theologians ought to be aware that, at most, we have an insight or two to add to the conversation concerning planetary well-being, and that other suggestions, although different from our own, might well be helpful.[4] The academy, including theology (which is now situated for the most part in the academy rather than the church), does not, generally speaking, operate in the mode of collegiality, but if we could agree that the planetary crisis that faces us all is sufficiently serious so as to mandate a new way of conducting our business, perhaps we would be willing to change. A collegial style would mean acknowledging a more or less common agenda for theological reflection, although one with an almost infinite number of different tasks. Broadly speaking, the encompassing agenda would be to deconstruct and reconstruct the central symbols of the Jewish and Christian traditions so as to be on the side of life and its fulfillment, keeping the liberation of the oppressed (including the earth and all its creatures) in central focus. That is so broad, so inclusive, an agenda that it allows for myriad ways to construe it and carry it out.

There are two direct implications of a collegial perspective. First, differences would not only have to be respected but sought out and applauded. With an agenda so broad and deep, no one person, group, religion, or one experience of oppression, can define or solve all the problems. Moreover, if the goal is the health of the planet and all its creatures, then the task is obviously not one that can be fulfilled simply by "taking thought," no matter how good or fine the thought is, but only as people's hearts and actions are changed at a daily rate and on a permanent level. Such changes can occur only in particular places, through diverse means (including economic, social, and political systemic changes), and in different religious and cultural traditions. The changes that are needed to replace a narrow anthropocentric sensibility with a cosmocentric one are immense; they are also diverse, and, therefore, the appreciation of different contributions, rather than reliance on a single perspective or solution, is mandatory. The goal is not utopia, but sustainability and livability: not the kingdom of God, but a decent life in community for all life-forms and the ecosystem on which they rely. The image to keep in mind is not the patterned quilt, but the crazy quilt, in which a patchwork of different pieces is sewn together somewhat haphazardly but nonetheless into a serviceable covering. The goal of the planetary agenda would be realized with such a cover for the needs of earth's creatures.

A second implication of a collegial theological style is advocacy. It is obvious that the goal of planetary well-being is different from "the interpretation of God's revelation," one version of the church theologian's task, or from "the pursuit of truth," a version of the academic theologian's task. A collegial theology is obviously interested, that is, concerned, biased, and caring, which distinguishes it from both the absoluteness of a stance within revelation and within (presumed) objectivity. An advocacy theology admits to being situated, concerned, and particular, to being *embodied*. Its focus is on praxis, on the consequences for those who live within various constructions, whether these be economic, political, familial, racial, or theological. With the help of the hermeneutics of suspicion and deconstruction, we now know that all thinking is a form of advocacy and the question is always, Whose good is being advocated? Who benefits? A cosmological, collegial perspective that promotes diversity and advocates planetary well-being is obviously different from a kind of advocacy that supports the redemption of those human beings who accept Jesus as savior or one that offers a truth available to all who search with open minds.

The emphasis on praxis and commitment, on a concerned theology, need in no way imply a lack of scholarly rigor or a retreat to fideism. Rather, it insists that one of the criteria of contemporary theological reflection—thinking about our place in the earth and the earth's relation to its source—is a concern with the *consequences* of proposed constructions for those who live within them. For centuries people have lived for the most part unknowingly within the constructs of Christian reflection. Some of these constructs have been liberating, but many others have been oppressive, patriarchal, and provincial. A planetary perspective would advocate, as all theologies have done, but would do so consciously and would argue for including much on earth hitherto excluded.

These brief comments on a cosmological Christian theology characterized by collegiality, diversity, and advocacy have been abstract. It is time to make them more concrete. Two outstanding contemporary forms of theology from a cosmological context demand our attention. An analysis, both appreciative and critical, of each of them will help us to see where the present project on the organic model fits into theological reflection that is in conversation with postmodern science.

Creation Spirituality

It has been said that most of us are right in what we affirm and wrong in what we deny; that is, we see one or two things clearly and hold them so deeply that we are often blind to other insights. If this is so, it speaks to our need for collegiality: openness to and appreciation of a variety of passionately held convictions. And this is true with the kind of cosmological theology associated with the names of Thomas Berry, Matthew Fox, Brian Swimme, and their followers.[5] Negatively, creation spirituality is a critique of a sin-centered, redemption-oriented interpretation of Christianity that focuses on guilt, sacrificial atonement, and otherworldly salvation. Positively, it is a celebration of cosmic evolution and splendor that we learn about in the common creation story and that provides us a sense of personal grandeur and responsibility as the only creatures who consciously know this story. Creation spirituality redresses centuries of an increasingly narrow focus of divine concern on human beings, especially Christian human beings, with the virtual elimination, at least in Protestant circles, of creation, which, at most, becomes the backdrop for redemption.[6] Moreover, creation spirituality, especially in the work of Berry and Fox, has given the planetary agenda a number of key insights necessary for cosmological health. These insights are expressed with poetic power and passion, for the goal is not only to illumine the mind but also to move the heart.

A number of these insights deserve our attention. Berry, a Passionist priest, cultural historian, and disciple of Pierre Teilhard de Chardin, provides us with some rich ones. His notion of a functional cosmology is central.[7] He claims, rightly I believe, that most contemporary people do not have a story of the cosmos that on a daily basis helps them understand how they and other created beings fit into the scheme of things. The Genesis myth used to be such a working cosmology but is no longer helpful for most of us. The common creation story, says Berry, is a narrative that all peoples on the earth can know about and affirm not only as their own story but the story of all other people and all other living creatures.[8] We can once again, he says, have a sense of belonging, not as the lords over creation, but as the ones in whom the universe has become conscious. As such, we should acknowledge a sense of personal grandeur, living as affectionate, intelligent, imaginative creatures in profound communion with all other creatures and with a sense of our special place in a marvelous universe.[9]

Creation spirituality, at its best (which is also its place of greatest weakness), gives us what I would call "a mystique of the earth," as epitomized in these words by Berry: "The universe, by definition, is a single gorgeous celebratory event."[10] He sees clearly the awesome mystery and splendor of our planet embodied in "the shape of the orchid, the coloring of the fish in the sea . . . and the pure joy of the predawn singing of the mockingbird."[11] In a moving passage he writes: "If we have a wonderful sense of the divine, it is because we live amid such awesome magnificence . . . If we lived on the moon, our minds and emotions, our speech, our imagination, our sense of the divine would all reflect the desolation of the lunar landscape."[12] And he can make us *feel* that awesome mystery, the sacred character of our habitat, which demands from us a "sense of courtesy toward earth and its inhabitants" and engenders in us the need to develop a capacity for wonder at the "numinous quality of everyday reality."[13] Anyone who reads Berry and is not moved to a deeper level of connection with and appreciation of our glorious planet must have a rather closed, dry soul.

But what Berry and other creation spirituality writers lack is a sense of the awful oppression that is part and parcel of the awesome mystery and splendor. The universe has not been for most species, and certainly not for most individuals within the various species, a "gorgeous celebratory event." It has been a story of struggle, loss, and often early death. To see the universe and especially our planet as "the primary mode of the divine presence," as Berry does, is to claim implicitly an optimistic arrow in the evolutionary story, a position that Berry's mentor, Teilhard de Chardin, embraced but that few if any scientists are willing to allow.[14] Creation spirituality suggests an ungrounded optimism, based in part on its reading of evolutionary history but also on an illumination model of how human beings change: to know the good is to do the good. If we learn about the common creation story and where we fit into the scheme of things, we *will* change.

Matthew Fox, also a Roman Catholic priest in orders, has tried recently to address the charge levelled against creation spirituality that its aesthetic perspective of celebrating the cosmos neglects the painful ethical issues of oppression and injustice.[15] His prescription for change, however, involves neither repentance, which is too reminiscent of redemption negativity, nor addressing the gross economic disparity between North and South America, the regions he focuses on. Rather, he suggests that by releasing "the mystic child" within each of us, we will *want* to share our wealth with others, spontaneously and naturally. He calls us to "imagine, for example, the rituals that could develop around letting go of $100 billion of our defense department budget" in favor of health, education, and toxic cleanup.[16] But, we must ask, what prompts people to let go of $100 billion in the first place? Is engaging in practices to release the wounded mystic child within first-world people sufficient? Once our celebrative, joyful spirits are free, *will* we share? Will we "agree on a 'preferential option for the poor' because a creation story instructs us that in our origins we are all poor . . . all born gratuitously into this vast cosmic dance"?[17] Deep in our souls many of us will whisper, no—I won't, we won't.

Creation spirituality, I believe, presents us with a picture not of how things are but how they should be: it is a utopian, eschatological vision and ought to be allowed to function that way. All utopian visions, including even some science fiction ones, play a prophetic role in presenting a critique of contemporary culture through the evocation of a paradise of joy, interrelatedness, and sharing.[18] Such visions provide a goal toward which transformative action can aim. We need such visions. But we also need to remind ourselves that they are utopias, not reality, a concession not made by the adherents of creation spirituality. Lacking that acknowledgment, creation spirituality can rightly be criticized for glossing over the profound pessimism (for most species and individuals) in evolutionary history as well as the deep reservoirs of evil in the human heart. A millennial dream of the human species, "joining the dance of all creation," once we have undergone an inner transformation by illumination from the common creation story, is not the world in which we live. Most life-forms, including human beings, live in a world characterized by brutal, deep, as well as subtle forms of oppression.

Nonetheless, the planetary agenda needs the contribution of creation spirituality. Its cosmological perspective, advocacy for the earth and all its life-forms, its poetic power and celebrative posture, are important aspects of planetary health. If seen as prescriptive (what should be) rather than as descriptive (what is), it beckons us not to rest in what is but to strive for what might be. Thomas Berry captures this change of sensibility well when he suggests we reflect on what it would be like to think of nature not as resource, recreation, or retreat, but as relative, the primary relative of us all, our mother and father, the source of our being and the being of everything else.[19] It would, indeed, be a profound—a utopian, eschatalogical—change.

Natural Theology

The cosmological theologies that we now turn to are only loosely and perhaps even wrongly included under the heading of natural theology, since " 'Natural theology' is traditionally that knowledge of God and the divine order which . . . reason can acquire without the aid of revelation," and no contemporary theology makes such a presumption.[20] The point of connection for contemporary cosmological theologies is knowledge and reason. While creation spirituality focuses on appreciating nature as sacred and advocating the well-being of all its creatures in poetic, passionate terms, natural theology as used here is concerned with understanding the natural order as manifesting purpose (strong version) or at least as being consonant or congruent with religious belief (weak version).[21] While the contemporary science and theology conversation is a wide-ranging, complex, and highly nuanced one with many players and positions, it is mainly concerned with the issue of credibility: How can one both be a believer and take the contemporary scientific view of reality seriously? How can one avoid the schizophrenia that has beset so many Christians of the modern era? On the one hand, their doctrinal tradition presents them with an anachronistic three-story or dualistic universe in which God is pictured as an external superperson intervening now and then in human and natural affairs. On the other hand, they live in a world characterized by the common creation story with its seamless fifteen-billion-year evolutionary history that allows for no external forces and in which human beings are not at the center. This is a serious concern, and the conversation that is taking place around it is exciting.[22] At the very least, theologians are claiming that credible theologies *must* take seriously the view of reality current in their day. *Not* to do so simply means that theology takes an outmoded view as its implicit understanding of reality. Thus, for instance, most popular theology and some ecclesiastical theologies still operate with a Newtonian, dualistic, atomistic view of reality in which individual human beings relate to an external, deistic God, with nature marginalized or nonexistent. So the question for theology is not worldview or not but *which* worldview?[23] Augustine's success was due to his doctrinal reformulations based on the view of reality current in his day—Neoplatonism; Thomas Aquinas created the medieval synthesis with the help of an Aristotelian worldview; the Deists of the eighteenth century worked with the picture of Newtonian science. In our day, process theology has taken postmodern science seriously, and many feminist theologies are informed by an ecological, evolutionary sensibility—reasons, I believe, why both of these movements strike many as the most viable current theological options. At any rate, the point at issue is that when the picture of reality undergoes a major paradigm shift, theology must attend to it.

I agree profoundly with this perspective. For the first time in several hundred years, the lessening of positivism in science and the growing awareness that science, like other significant interpretations of reality, is a construction, relying on paradigms, models, and metaphors, has made possible a serious, open conversation between theologians and scientists.[24] Moreover, the picture of reality coming to us from contemporary science is so attractive to theology that we would be fools not to use it as a resource for reimaging and reinterpreting Christian doctrine. My project will be centrally concerned with this very matter.

But there is another dimension to the credibility issue in the science and theology conversation: the attempt to show, one way or another, and to one degree or another, that the cosmic process itself manifests some trace of divine purpose. Needless to say in this day, several hundred years after David Hume and Immanuel Kant devastated the so-called arguments for the existence of God, these traces are often scarcely more than faint trails in the sand, but it is the need, the intention, to interpret cosmic history meaningfully that is important. It is the *how* and *why* questions: faced with the fifteen-billion-year evolutionary history of the universe, with space and time frames that boggle the mind, not to mention the waste, loss, and suffering of species on our planet, some theologians and scientists ask why and how it exists? How can I understand it and make sense out of it? What meaning does it have? Of course, such a question has moral and ethical dimensions, especially from an existential perspective (Why am I here? How is my life meaningful?), but, principally, the problem is an intellectual one—making sense out of an evolutionary history that can appear to be either indifferent to human concerns or, worse, malevolent in regard to them.[25] In other words, the enterprise is not just showing that reason and revelation, science and theology, are compatible (a weak version of natural theology), but justifying, as is the business of theodicy, the ways of the creator, if we now take creation to be the entire cosmic panorama.[26]

The seriousness of natural theology should not be underestimated. Most broadly, it is concerned with showing the continuity between creation and redemption; that is, to show that the God of redemption, the loving power who heals and saves the world and its creatures, is also the source of the entire cosmos and has been working in it from the beginning. Salvation is not a surd, but has been, to use Gordon Kaufman's phrase, the "creative serendipity" operative throughout the entire process.[27] A Christian perspective needs something like this, even though it is difficult if not impossible to establish scientifically. But one should not attempt to skirt what is essentially a faith issue (belief in a loving God) by commandeering the help of science. Some in the science-theology conversation try to secure the help of contemporary science in support of very faint traces of divine purpose in the sands of evolutionary time. This is a dangerous game, called physico-theology by one interpreter—basing theology on science—an enterprise with a long history of failure.[28] In the more extreme versions, as in the work of Pierre Teilhard de Chardin, an optimistic arrow, a teleological movement of the entire cosmos toward its fulfillment, is implicit within the process, becoming explicit in "Christogenesis," which completes the lower evolutionary processes, including human becoming.[29] There are many current attempts to find some meaning in evolutionary history; one of the most ingenious is the so-called Anthropic Principle.[30] One definition of it reads as follows: "Intelligent life, be it rare or common, could not have evolved in a physical universe constructed even a tiny bit differently; therefore, preexisting intelligence must have designed the cosmos."[31] The principle relies on a gap in scientific explanation (the why of the initial fine tuning), always a risky place for religion to stand, for science has in the past and undoubtedly will in the future close such gaps. Moreover, the "designer God" who emerges either starts up the whole show at the big bang or fine tunes it—a very limited God indeed, with a narrow job description by Hebrew or Christian standards.[32]

But there are other possibilities for finding significance in the cosmic process. One rich and thoughtful attempt is process theology, which uses the analogy of the human self to postulate a form of subjectivity and purpose throughout all of existence, from the lowliest bit of matter to God.[33] Process theology, with its deep appreciation for the intrinsic value of all entities in the natural order, is attractive to both ecologists and feminists, among others. Another important contribution, and a very light trace in the sand, is Gordon Kaufman's "creative serendipity," as a way of characterizing the surprising result of the evolutionary process. It is at most, he claims, a "proto-teleology," a retrospective view that does not provide any proof of purpose, divine or otherwise, but allows faith to take a step toward that view of things (while the evidence could also be interpreted otherwise).[34] I believe Kaufman is on the right track. If one intends to take scientific explanation seriously, then no teleological maneuvers should be considered. That is an old game, one that theologians have lost before, and there is no reason to suppose that the ground rules have changed. At the very most, we might be able to say that from where we stand now, retrospectively, the cosmic panorama is an amazing show: it generates wonder, surprise, and gratitude.

I would make several points from the foregoing analysis. First, as theologians, we should aim for coherence or compatibility between the scientific view and the interpretation of our basic doctrines.[35] That is the bottom line: a theology that avoids this task and settles for an outmoded view is irresponsible and will eventually be seen to be incredible. What we need, however, is compatibility with the picture of reality broadly embraced in our time, rather than a concern with either technical scientific issues or intramural scientific debates. As indicated before, however, the picture of reality, because it is a picture, is also open to interpretation (as in the reductionism versus holism debate).

Second, the notion of God in natural theology—both the weak and strong versions—is, from the perspective of the Jewish and Christian traditions, a thin and impersonal one. If the goal of natural theology is to find meaning or purpose in the beginning (why) and the process (how), then a designer God, a God whose main attribute is providing some purpose or structure, is the answer. The issue at stake, most broadly, is theodicy, and it can take an aesthetic form (justifying the whole panorama of creation as significant) or an existential one (justifying the pain of individual beings who are wasted by the process).[36] Both deistic and mystical understandings of God are possible from this perspective: God as the One who initiates the process and as the One who permeates its processes. What does not seem possible is the personal God of the Jewish and Christian traditions; in fact, a personal God is repudiated by many of the theologians in this conversation as incompatible with the postmodern view of reality.[37] This issue will be of central importance as we attempt to reconstruct the organic model for our time. I believe not only that the personal model is one of the central continuities of the Western religious tradition, the loss of which would signal a paradigm shift of such proportions as to end that religious tradition, but that it is possible to understand the personal model in a way that is compatible with (although not demanded by) contemporary science.[38]

Third, and of central importance, while the epistemological questions of why and how, aimed at satisfying our intellectual, aesthetic, and existential postures as Christians faced with the contemporary scientific view of reality are important, another question may be of equal if not greater importance: *What does this picture of reality suggest to us about the relation of God and the world, and what should we do, how should we act, in light of it?* Rather than taking the perspective of the beginning (the why) or the process (the how), I am suggesting that we stand where the fifteen-billion-year history has evolved—the present picture—and focus on the more practical knowledge problem of who God is, who we are, and what our responsibilities are as understood within this picture. This is the central project of my essay, which is not meant as a substitute for the why and how questions, but as a somewhat neglected and urgently needed addition.

One of the areas that is often lacking in the science-theology conversation is concern with issues of human and ecological oppression and injustice at a bodily rather than an existential level. Because the focus is usually on questions of meaning and purpose, the responses suggested appeal more to satisfying the inner rather than the outer person. Or, one could say that the liberation theologies and contemporary science have not so far become conversation partners, but what might happen if they did? Does a perspective that asks questions about the oppression of and injustice toward other human beings as well as other creatures have anything to gain by paying attention to science? Yes, I think it does. A theology of nature perspective, using the picture of reality coming to us from postmodern science as a resource for reimaging the relation of God and the world as well as our place in the scheme of things, will attempt to make that case.

Theology of Nature:
Remythologizing Christian Doctrine

While the attempt to see continuity between the Christian story of redemption and the cosmic story of the evolution of the universe is one that all Christians must support, it may be that a retrospective perspective—which is very ancient—is still the best one. That is, faith seeking understanding sees traces of divine purpose, love, and care in our cosmic story, as Christians have in other ages found them in pictures of reality current in their time. We, they, also find more than traces of evil, perversion, and seeming malevolence (the present version speaks of them in terms of the brutalities of natural selection), so that the end result is not evidence of purpose leading to belief but corroboration of faith arrived at in spite of evidence to the contrary.[39]

Lest this distinction sound like a retreat into fideism, I suggest we look at a similar stance by the biologist Stephen Jay Gould.[40] Gould's position, as I understand it, is that evolution displays no direction or purpose, no overriding push or pull toward some goal. It is not the "conventional tale of steadily increasing excellence, complexity, and diversity" that could be imaged by a ladder or a cone.[41] Rather, the appropriate model is a bush with many branches, most of which met with extinction in a way that was "utterly unpredictable and quite unrepeatable."[42] What brings about the incredible diversity (and what we consider levels) in evolution is not purpose but small and unpredictable changes operating in a contingent fashion. Adaptations are always developed for local environments; hence, cause is always local and specific, and, if a feature proves useful for later developments, that is just a happy accident for that species, as was the development of a sturdy fin in our ancestor fishes, which proved useful as a backbone later on land.[43] Gould claims that a sense of larger purpose or direction has no support. What happens happens in the details, at the local level through the interaction of innumerable factors, and hence anything that *does* happen might very well *not* have happened or happened otherwise. He uses the inspired example of the Jimmy Stewart movie, *It's a Wonderful Life*, to illustrate the point: small and unpredictable changes lead to vastly different results both in human development and in evolutionary history.

Many religious people find this conclusion unnerving since it appears to eliminate purpose (God) from the evolutionary process. But there is another possibility, a possibility that is the central thesis of this book: *it is indeed a wonderful life*. What has evolved (regardless of why or how it occurred) is complex, diverse, intricate beyond our wildest imaginations.[44]

From Where We Stand:
Christian Doctrine in Light of the Organic Model

We ourselves are a marvel beyond belief, not only because we did evolve but because of what and who we are—indeed, just a little lower than the angels (or perhaps just a little higher, given the present state of angelology). I am suggesting that from the point of view of both contemporary science and Christian reformulation, one valid and important place for the believer to stand is before the *present* picture of evolutionary history. We could focus on the *what* rather than the *why* or *how*: on what (who) we have become, both in our relations with other life-forms (our place in the cosmos) and our special responsibilities, rather than on how we got the way we are. The latter epistemological question has always fascinated the West, but a more practical kind of question perhaps ought to be: Who are we in the scheme of things, and what is required of us? Likewise, within this more practical framework, to say God is creator is not to focus on what God did once upon a time, either at the beginning or during the evolutionary process, but on how we can perceive ourselves and everything else in the universe as dependent upon God now, in terms of our cosmic story. What does it mean to say that God is both transcendent and immanent in relation to the world as presently conceived and imagined? How can we model this sense of unitary dependence of the universe on God as well as our proper place in the scheme of things in light of the present state of evolutionary history?

Moreover, and of utmost importance, whatever may have been the mechanisms of evolutionary history in the past, *evolution in the present and future on our planet will be inextricably involved with human powers and decisions.* Willy-nilly, whether we want it or not, the future of our planet has to a significant degree fallen into our hands. Natural selection is not the only or perhaps even the principal power on our planet now; cultural evolution, the ability to evolve into a sharing, caring human population living with other life-forms in a fashion that our planet can sustain, may be more important. And at this point, we can certainly introduce the notion of purpose, of direction. Those from the Christian tradition might well suggest that the future direction of evolution ought to be toward wider sympathetic inclusiveness with all forms of life, especially the most needy and vulnerable, understanding this direction as a contemporary reading of the paradigmatic Christian story—the destabilizing, inclusive, nonhierarchical vision of fulfillment for all of creation.[45] The various humanitarian and religious traditions will have directions, purposes, goals to suggest for the common future of our planet. The understandings of salvation from different cultural and religious communities suggest guidelines for the present and future of creation, whatever its past. None of these can be read off evolutionary history and can only be read back into it with a very light touch and with an equal—if not greater—attention to the radical contingency, deep mystery, and seeming indifference if not malevolence (from the perspective of any particular species or individual) of the process. But we can say, from where we now stand on our planet, both that it *is* a wonderful life (a diverse, rich, complex one) *and* that we have a part to play in its future.

The present essay, then, does not so much deny the value of other projects, those with traditional epistemological concerns, as it suggests that another legitimate, and limited, issue is also valid. We can emphasize that while creation spirituality is concerned with appreciating the cosmos and natural theology with understanding it, another concern is acting responsibly within it. While this essay will focus on the ethical or pragmatic concern, it will nevertheless rely on both appreciation and understanding as necessary prerequisites for appropriate action. That is, through remythologizing the doctrines of God and human beings in light of the picture of reality from contemporary science—through the use of the organic model as a way of reconceiving the relation of God and the world—the appropriate human stance vis-à-vis God and our planet will emerge. Remythologizing involves both appreciation and understanding; it is a form of embodied thought combining image and concept that calls forth both a feeling and a thinking response. It also implies an ethical response.[46] If one uses the model of the universe as God's body, if one appreciates and understands creation as organically interrelated, one would, or at least might, act differently toward it than if one used the model of creation as a work of art (one possible model from the Genesis story).[47] The assumption that what we appreciate and how we think influences how we behave is a very complex issue and has supporters and detracters on both sides (among them the Greeks versus Paul, the former rather optimistic about the correlation and the latter bemoaning that he knows the good but does not do it). Hence, it behooves us to be modest about any remythologizing project: it is indeed but one small voice in the planetary conversation.

It might help to situate my project if we compare it to a well-known similar one, that of Pierre Teilhard de Chardin. Teilhard's impressive achievements as a scientist and a theologian are not at issue here; rather, it is that aspect of his work concerned with internalizing the new scientific story that was just emerging in his time. He was one of the first involved in the contemporary science-theology conversation. While one aspect of his work was a strong natural theology to show the convergence of evolutionary and theological purpose, another, and I believe more important, contribution was his attempt to remythologize the new creation story from a Christian perspective.[48] What was special about his work and why in spite of continuing criticisms of it from both scientific and theological circles it continues to draw attention is that he felt deeply the need to reimagine Christian doctrine in terms of twentieth-century science and to see the new scientific story in Christian terms.[49] His achievement was essentially poetic, not scientific or theological (if theology is equated with conceptualization). If his project is understood as a thought experiment, a likely account, to help people internalize the new sensibility from a Christian perspective—how a Christian should feel and act in the awesome spatial and temporal dimensions of this story—then both the limitations and the distinctive contributions of his project become clear. Something of this sensibility is expressed when Teilhard writes: "Blessed be you, universal matter, unmeasurable time, boundless ether, triple abyss of stars and atoms and generations: you who by overflowing and dissolving our narrow standards of measurement reveal to us the dimensions of God. . . ."[50] Every revelation of the awesomeness of the universe as pictured by twentieth-century science became for Teilhard an occasion for celebrating God's sublimity as its creator. Teilhard's distinctive contribution was his attempt to internalize the new creation story from a Christian perspective in a series of often outrageous metaphors, such as, for instance, the bread and wine of the eucharist as embodying *in nuce* the entire universe: "There is but one single mass in the world: the true Host, the total Host, is the universe which is continually being more intimately penetrated and vivified by Christ."[51] Christ and matter, Christianity and evolutionary history, are reimagined together through the metaphor of the eucharist. My point is not that Teilhard's remythologizing of the new creation story was entirely successful; rather, it is that he attempted it at all.

Hopefully, the nature of my project, both its limitations and possible contribution, is becoming clearer. It is to embody the picture of reality from postmodern science in a model that will help us internalize its new sensibility in a way not just compatible with but enriched by Christian faith (a two-way project). In a way similar to Teilhard's project, it will try to embody the new creation story metaphorically, using the contributions of both contemporary science and Christian faith, for the organic model comes from and is enriched by both science and Christianity. Unlike some versions of natural theology that operate by reason alone (finding their material in the sciences) and unlike some theologies of nature that rely on faith alone (finding their material in revelation), our theology of nature will be dialectical. Theology of nature has sometimes been understood as the opposite of natural theology, as in this statement by Jürgen Moltmann: "Every theology of nature interprets nature in the light of the self-revelation of the creative God . . . the aim of our investigation is not what nature can contribute to our knowledge of God, but what the concept of God can contribute to our knowledge of nature."[52] Our position questions that dualism, for if one is interested in thinking holistically, as beings-in-a-world, a world of which God is the creator and redeemer, then one will search for a way to express, to model, that situation which will take both contributions seriously. The mutual influence of postmodern science and Christian faith can be seen in the model of the universe (creation) as God's body. Both can contribute to an understanding of the organic model in distinctive ways; in fact, as we will try to show, the model is a rich one precisely because of the interaction of the two kinds of organic discourse, scientific and Christian. Religious traditions, including Christianity, always have used and should continue to use the images, symbols, and concepts arising out of the common contemporary cultural field to express their most deeply held beliefs.[53] Needless to say, the use of these materials will change the faith. But to the extent that major religious models likewise influence culture, as in the case of the monarchical model's long and deep domination over the Western sensibility, Christianity's contribution to the contemporary organic model may also be important. In the model of the universe as God's body, not only does postmodern science help us understand the unity and diversity of the body in liberating ways, but divine embodiment makes sacred all embodiment: neither perspective alone is as rich as both together.

Reasons for Living within the Organic Model

We come, then, finally, to the thorny issue of the status of metaphors and models and especially the model we have chosen to work with, the universe as God's body, the organic model. Why choose this one? What criteria support it? Does it have the backing of reason, revelation, experience, tradition, or what? Is it valuable because it is useful, liberating, or rhetorically powerful? These age-old, complex questions cannot be dealt with easily or lightly, but already in this project some directions toward an answer have emerged. First, this essay is concerned with the body, embodiment. It takes as its point of departure, its site or point of view, the supposition that embodiment is basic. This is not a foundation, revelation, or inference from reason; rather, it is a wager, proposition, or experiment to investigate. I found in my own journey as a Christian, a feminist, and an amateur ecologist that the body kept emerging in different ways as an often neglected but very important reality, seemingly a basic one. Likewise, at least on one reading of postmodern science, the organic model has emerged as a central way to interpret the contemporary picture of reality. Hence, what we will say about criteria for ways of modeling the world will be heavily weighted in the direction of embodiment. Any argument for a model of reality that neglects, disparages, or negates embodiment (such as Cartesianism, Kantianism, and deconstruction, to a lesser extent) would be operating out of a fundamentally different paradigm than the one presupposed by this essay.

Second, criteria are multiple. This is necessarily the case if one is operating experimentally with a model to be investigated rather than a truth of revelation to be illustrated or a datum of science to be proven. The model of the universe as God's body obviously does not fall into either of the above categories. To take this discussion out of the stratosphere, let us ask why someone *would or might* adopt the organic model as a major way to interpret reality. (This is assuming a more or less conscious choice; millions have adopted the model unconsciously over the course of human history.) When one decides to live as if something is the case (which is what one does in adopting models, for as metaphors they are not descriptions but invitations to experimental living) there are usually many reasons for doing so, of many different sorts, and at many levels of consciousness. Life is complex, to say the least; why, then, should the credibility, persuasiveness, and power of a model by and in which to live be less so? Any one or even two reasons for living as if the world is organic, and as if we are all interrelated and interdependent—a view that has vast and potentially demanding consequences for how one conducts one's business—are surely inadequate. One would need multiple reasons, and that, I believe, is what is the case when we consciously embrace a model, in contrast to simply accepting the dominant one in our culture.

I shall suggest a few reasons that might persuade someone to adopt a model, particularly the organic one. Our supposition is that no one reason, one basis or foundation, exists for being willing to live according to the organic model, but a variety of reasons and feelings, as well as hunches and hopes, come into play.[54] Since we are embodied beings (not merely minds deciding in an abstract and disembodied way on truth) attempting to find satisfying, helpful, rich constructs within which to live our lives, we are likely to be persuaded to adopt a model only if it speaks to many different dimensions of our personal and social lives. It has to make sense not just to our minds, but to our bodies, our feelings, our needs, and even our hopes and dreams.

A sampling of some of these reasons includes our own embodied and cultural experience; the testimony of significant communities to which we belong; the view of reality current in our time; and the usefulness of a perspective, model, or construct for humane living. These four reasons are certainly not exhaustive; they are only meant to suggest a few important factors that might contribute to adopting this model. Let us look at each of them.

"Experience" is a word so fraught with misunderstanding, bad press, and dissension that introducing it without at least two chapters of qualifications and critiques by Kantians, Hegelians, deconstructionists, feminists and womanists, as well as Whiteheadians and empiricists, may be the height of folly. But the term will not disappear in spite of its slippery philosophical status, mainly because in its most basic sense experience simply means the act of living, which all creatures undergo. The controversy emerges when the question arises as to what we experience. From the perspective of our issue—what might persuade someone to adopt a model, especially the organic one?—I would make two points.

First, at the most basic level, experience is embodied; we are bodies that experience. Of course there is no such thing as "disembodied experience," and yet, curiously, the body is often forgotten. Those who think and write about the status of experience often seem to neglect this primordial level that connects our sophisticated mental probings into and in response to our environment with the amoeba's tentative reaching out and recoiling. Experience is *felt* experience, the experience of bodies at the most elemental level.[55] Experience begins with feelings of hot and cold, hunger and satiety, comfort and pain, the most basic ways in which all creatures live in their environments. We live here also and this basic level connects us in a web of universal experience making possible an ever-widening inclusive sympathy for the pains and pleasures of creatures like and unlike ourselves. While some would insulate us from our citizenship in this community of nature, separating off our experience as linguistic and hence qualitatively unlike that of other animals,[56] embodied experience links the cries of a hungry child and a wounded animal, the exhilaration we feel at the sight of a magnificent sunset and the soothing touch of a hand on a painful sore. Through our bodies, in their agonies and ecstasies that lie behind and beyond all linguistic expression, we are bound into a network of relations with our natural environment and experience ourselves as bodies with other bodies. Whatever else experience means, it includes bodily experience as a primordial reality, uniting us in ever-widening concentric circles with the entire planet in all its diverse, rich forms of embodiment.

Second, and of equal importance, experience is always embodied for human beings not only in relation to the natural world but also culturally, economically, sexually, socially, and so on. It is radically concrete: the sites of experience are particular forms of privilege or oppression as the various liberation movements have persuasively argued. Sites of experience are neither general nor neutral; they are highly specific and marked by various forms of power or lack of power. Embodiment for human beings is certainly a physical reality as we have underscored, but it is also a construction of culture, and even the physical dimension is a highly constructed reality.[57] Even physical reality is experienced differently depending on one's cultural, economic, racial, and gender situation. There is no experience-in-general nor any body-in-general, yet there is experience and there is body, both constructed and both particular. That we are embodied (all differently and constructed variously) and that we respond from our own experience (all differently contextualized) influence us as we reflect on adopting constructs within which to live our lives.

If the view of experience that sets a priority on physical and cultural embodiment is persuasive, then serious consideration of the organic model might follow. The view of experience suggested here supports adopting a model of reality that privileges the needs of bodies as well as their physical and cultural differences. Moreover, this view implies that an appropriate religious experience might be a natural affection for other creatures as manifestations or sacraments of the divine as well as a natural longing for union with God through these others.[58]

A second reason for adopting a particular construct or model is that it carries the testimony of the religious community in which one stands.[59] Other significant communities also influence one's decision, but religious communities in the past have functioned as primary interpretive traditions, and for many still do. Some people, of course, accept the doctrines of a religious community as absolute, believing that they have been revealed from on high, but there is also a reason to take seriously a historical, cultural tradition because it has molded one's society and one's own being. For most Westerners the important traditions are Jewish and Christian. They have given the West its identity for good and for bad, and many still find them personally nourishing.[60] Others believe that with radical revision, they can be prophetic means of liberating the oppressed. The point is that these traditions matter and rather than abandoning them for alternatives (such as Buddhism or Goddess religions, for instance), one might judge a construct or model in light of an interpretation of one's own formative tradition.[61] To take Christianity as an example, one interpretation of this tradition finds it to be a highly organic one, although ambivalently so, tending to stress the symbolic character of embodiment imagery rather than the physical base of the imagery. Nonetheless, it is a tradition that is open to a reconstruction of its organic model along lines more compatible with an ecological sensibility.

Another reason (one we have stressed repeatedly) for adopting a model is that it is compatible with the view of reality current in one's time. The organic model is one of the major ways that postmodern science is being interpreted. It has considerable scientific backing. While, as we have stressed, major scientific theories are constructs in a way not unlike other significant construals of reality,[62] including religious ones, nonetheless, scientific models have both a universality and a persuasiveness at least to most Westerners that few if any other constructs can claim. If one wants to live as a whole person in the world as understood in one's time, one needs to attend seriously to the picture of reality that is assumed at that time to be the way things are. Moreover, if that picture (as in the case of the organic model) is a highly attractive one, one that not only does the usual things that major models must do, such as give a comprehensive, coherent interpretation of relevant data, but is also illuminating, rich, and thought-provoking, then one has even more reason to consider adoption.

Finally, and of primary importance, one adopts a model because it helps to make things better. One has the hunch and the hope that it is good for human and other forms of life. In spite of evidence to the contrary, one dreams of a new age when all beings shall live together in peace and justice. Some models seem to help us both to envision and to work toward that hope more than others. To believe that a perspective or construct is meaningful and true because it is useful in the conduct of life is as old and honored a tradition as the view that one should accept it because it corresponds with an ideal, eternal reality. The first tradition is Aristotelian, privileging a pragmatic, practical, concrete view of truth, while the second is Platonic, insisting on an idealistic, abstract, speculative view. The first says that truth is concerned with the good life for the members of a community that they must define and work for, while the second claims that there is an ideal reality external to the world that is the standard against which all human understanding is judged.[63] Each has its merits. The Platonic tradition has the particular value of providing an ideal (a utopia, the kingdom of God) as a prophetic critique against all actual societies as well as a goal toward which to strive. The Aristotelian tradition, with its emphasis on practical reason, conversation in regard to the common good among the citizens of the *polis* (now the cosmos), and present, worldly goals of well-being for all members of a community, is gaining ground. It has always been attractive to the American pragmatic mind, but it also lies behind socialism, contemporary feminism, and many liberation movements.[64] As the catchphrase expresses it, we must not only understand the world but change it. Knowledge is not just a speculative matter but has a practical end: to make things better.

And this is certainly the case with models we adopt to understand the worlds within which we live. Is it, for instance, better to live as if the world is a machine with all parts externally related, each independently serving a specific function, and the whole maintained through outside forces driving the parts, or is it better to live as if the world is an organism with all parts internally related and interdependent, with each part also independent in its own concrete particularity, and the whole maintained through powers inherent in the various parts? In assessing a model for adoption, we do (or should) base our judgment on many factors, among them, our own concrete, embodied experience; the insights and beliefs of the communities commanding our deepest allegiance; the picture of reality current in our time; and *also* whether the model will help us live so that human beings and other creatures can thrive and reach some level of fulfillment. To say a model for living is meaningful and true because it is useful in this sense is not a lesser view of the matter. It assumes that our function as human beings on this planet is not mainly to think correct thoughts that correspond to some eternal set of verities, but to live appropriately and responsibly. Our reason, understood as a practical faculty, can assist us in this task. This assumption for many of us, myself included, extends as well to faith in God, which is not so much correct thoughts about God (ones that correspond to God's being), but appropriate, responsible action to help a planet, created and loved by God, be an adequate home for all its many creatures.[65] We are, in other words, called to a way of life, not to a set of beliefs, to a practical, mundane task involving our total embodied selves and oriented toward the fulfillment of (among other things) the basic, bodily needs of all creatures in the planetary community. We are not called to a speculative, abstract journey of enlightenment of our inner selves, which is basically indifferent to embodiment, our own and that of other beings.

In summary, I have suggested a few criteria (embodied experience, interpretive communities, the current picture of reality, and usefulness) that might be persuasive reasons for adopting a major model, especially the organic one. Taking all this into account, we still need to press the question of the status of a major construct such as the organic one. Is it a useful fiction? a given natural reality? a revealed absolute? a partial but inadequate truth? By promoting it as a worldview within which to live are we being utilitarians, empiricists, revelationists, or critical realists, to use some of the traditional epistemological positions? From the above discussion on reasons one might give for adopting a particular construct, it is evident that none of these positions is adequate alone, although we should include aspects of each of them in our answer. The reasons for adopting a construct are plural and multidimensional; the status of the adopted construct is the same. For example, the organic model is useful, based in reality (as currently understood), has connections with beliefs in some religious communities, and offers one important but only partial construct. Together these reasons might satisfy an interrogator, although she might still ask, "But is reality *really* organic, does it have the characteristics of an organism that you have spelled out?" As a metaphor or model of reality, the answer must always be a no and yes: no, of course it does not have these characteristics, since embodiment is a way of talking about reality (which can also be spoken of in many other ways); but yes, for the reasons given above, reality appears to be relatively patient in regard to accepting this construct or grid through which it is seen. If we always and only have constructs with which to interpret reality, then necessarily we have to answer the question in more or less terms—is reality more patient, open to, tolerant of this model or that one? The answer lies, I believe, in reasons such as the ones we have given for being persuaded to adopt a model. The answer, then, is finally a belief or a wager that reality is like this more than it is like that. And if enough of us were so to live, reality would *become* more like we believe. That is not a vicious circle, but a hope against hope. We can create reality—in fact, we do all the time with the constructs we embrace unknowingly. We can also create reality knowingly—and humanely—by living within models that we wager are true as well as good for human beings and other forms of life.

A Reading of Postmodern Science: Organism or Mechanism

Throughout this essay we have been assuming that the organic model is a plausible reading of contemporary science, but for many people science gives us only one view, the "objective" view. Unlike other human enterprises, science does not present us with constructions of reality, but reality in its true, unvarnished state. The typical Western attitude toward science is realistic, universal, and honorific: science alone tells us about reality; it gives us one, absolute view; and its results should be accepted without question.

But this does not appear to be the case. Within the scientific community itself there is considerable debate concerning the picture of reality emerging from postmodern science, a debate characterized by two camps: the unifiers versus the diversifiers, reductionism versus holism, or the machine versus the organic model.[66] Is the universe basically simple, reducible finally to one principle (the GUT, the Grand Unified Theory, or TOE, the Theory of Everything), or is it complex, intricate, and diverse, with many interrelated principles governing its behavior? Are human beings and other living organisms "nothing but" atoms and molecules? Can they be explained entirely in terms of physics and chemistry, or are higher-level concepts needed to account for their complexity and diversity?[67] It appears that both positions are possible readings. Molecular biologists and some cosmologists opt for the simple, unitary, "nothing but" position, and other biologists and cosmologists as well as ecologists claim that the intricacy, diversity, and complexity of the present universe demand a more holistic, multidimensional explanatory approach.

We have, then, two pictures, one that sees all reality atomistically, understandable in terms of terminology from physics and chemistry and eventually explained by one law (the GUT or TOE), versus another view that recognizes the validity of the first picture but claims that other additional levels are not so adequately explained. Both are models, not neutral, empirical descriptions; hence, judgment is involved. The first appeals to a sensibility that desires to reduce complexity to simplicity, to unlock the secret of the universe, while the second marvels at the intricacy, complexity, and surprise of an essentially mysterious universe. The first sensibility assumes that we can know a basically simple universe, which can be reduced to mathematics and perhaps to one underlying law, while the second sees us belonging to an unbelievably rich and diverse process and, at most, appreciating its complexity. Both are anthropomorphic, that is, imagined on models from human experience: the first sees human beings (and everything else) using the model of a machine with parts that can be separated, studied, and completely understood; the second sees human beings (and everything else) using the model of a body, with human beings as the self-reflexive part of the body.

The point to emphasize is that both positions are ideologies, both are readings. Reductionists are usually less ready to accept this qualification than are the supporters of organicism, in part because reducing matter to its smallest, most discrete parts has been a highly successful method of research, as in the spectacular DNA discoveries of the past several decades.[68] But it is a huge, unwarranted step to move from a method of research to a view of reality: scientific materialism, the metaphysical position that the true nature of an entity is manifest in its constituent parts (atoms and molecules), is not mandated by the reductionist research method. Scientific materialism is a faith and should be acknowledged as such.[69] Reductionism in its "nothing but" mode is a form of literalism, projecting one construct of reality as if it were the only one, forgetting the abstractive, selective, and partial nature of all constructions of reality—in other words, forgetting that all attempts to speak of reality are metaphorical.[70]

So we have a choice. We can stand with the unifiers before the utter simplicity and beauty of the one explanation of everything, the reduction of everything to its beginning at the moment of the big bang, and the subsequent reduction of all life to its simplest chemical components, *or* we can stand with the diversifiers who are dazzled by the rich diversity and complexity that galactic and biological evolution has produced over the last fifteen billion years and who revel in the interrelated, interdependent levels of the whole panorama of the universe.[71] *Or*, as a third and attractive option, we can accept reductionism as a successful method of research as well as the physical base of all levels of nonliving and living entities and, at the same time, opt for the holistic, organic view as the picture of reality or metaphysics with which theology should be in conversation. A holistic metaphysic can include the research methods of reductionism as well as its insistence on the primacy of matter, whereas a reductionist metaphysic cannot include the multilevelled complexity and diversity of holism in any way except to reduce the whole to its parts.[72]

It would seem, then, that there is a presumption in favor of holism over atomism, since the former can acknowledge the validity and necessity of the parts while the latter cannot do the same for the basic claims of holism. But this appeal to common sense, that the world is obviously rich, diverse, intricate, interrelated, and interdependent and cannot be reduced to its smallest constituent parts, does not save us from having to choose between constructs. The point is that we *do* have a choice, and since the choice is not between reality and a picture of reality, but between two pictures of reality, factors other than correspondence with reality must enter. One key factor is the meaning of scientific objectivity. It is common knowledge since Thomas Kuhn and his work on the theory-laden context within which science operates that science is a metaphorical enterprise at heart, that it is constructive and interpretive, and that therefore it is closer to philosophy and even theology than anyone thought fifty years ago during the heyday of positivistic science.[73] It is this acknowledgment that has made it possible to claim that reductionism or scientific materialism is not the only option in postmodern science, that holism is a credible reading as well. On what basis, then, does one make the choice? The answer must be held in abeyance as we dig more deeply into the issue of scientific "objectivity."

It is not only that scientific views of reality are metaphorical, as can clearly be seen in the mechanistic (machine model) and organismic (body model) views. They are also constructions from and by concrete human beings who occupy embodied sites, particular cultural, gender, racial, social, and economic settings. Thus, as Langdon Gilkey says, "The 'world' described by science is in part always a historical construct, different as the cultural 'minds' of different epochs and places differ."[74] Or as Stephen Jay Gould puts it, "Science, since people must do it, is a socially embedded activity."[75] When the gaze shifts from science to the scientist, it becomes immediately evident that his (or sometimes her) knowledge is embodied, as is all knowledge. While male critics such as Gilkey, Gould, and many others have insisted on this point, recent feminist critiques of scientific objectivity have done so with an intriguing result. They have raised the possibility that from a stronger view of objectivity might emerge an agenda for scientific research that took into account the well-being of human beings and the planet.[76] The argument is that scientific objectivity is weak due to the narrow cultural base of its practitioners and would be strengthened by opening the doors to scientists from diverse backgrounds. Present-day practicing scientists who are largely white, male, middle-class, and Western need to admit their partial, biased social location, a location that influences the deep complicity of their research agendas with the needs of the military/governmental/industrial complex to the exclusion of other needs. Scientists from other social locations (women as well as people of different racial, economic, and cultural backgrounds) could strengthen scientific objectivity by broadening its base, which would change what was considered important to research. If all views, including of course those of women (of whatever race or background) are biased, then acknowledging the limitations of particular social locations by opening the conversation to those from different locations could result in stitching together various partial perspectives so that a wider, deeper objectivity results. In other words, the issue of objectivity in science moves from the end, the testing of hypotheses, to the beginning, *who* is setting the scientific agenda, the research programs that will benefit some but not other members of society. The supposition is that the present weak objectivity is a cloak for research programs that benefit the powerful institutions at the expense of the less privileged. As Sandra Harding writes: "How are such institutions for 'observing nature' as Western science and technology in their daily practices causally connected to such other institutionalized practices as reproducing gender, marriage violence against women, racist educational systems, production for profit and the like?"[77] The question is *who* does science and *for whose* benefit? The feminist criticism accepts both the political and the empirical character of science; its criticism aims at a greater, not a lesser, objectivity for science by broadening the base of who participates in setting scientific agendas so that science might be emancipatory, liberating, beneficial for more people—and for the planet that supports us all.[78]

The important issue here is situated or embodied knowledge resulting in a stronger objectivity, and therefore the possibility of humane scientific projects. The "view from the body" is always a view from somewhere versus the view from above, from nowhere: the former admits to its partiality and accepts responsibility for its perspectives, while the latter believes itself universal and transcendent, thus denying its embodiment and limitations as well as the concrete, special insights that can arise only from particularity.[79] But when acknowledged, each embodied site can join with others in a network of partial perspectives in which the goal of the many bodies rather than of a few privileged ones will emerge as the priority agenda.[80] This embodied view of objectivity, one that operates from specific sites in order to be of benefit to a more inclusive circle of embodied beings, is at odds with some forms of traditional, Western (male) epistemology. Its two key notions are embodiment and praxis (versus disembodiment and theory): knowledge or truth is not concerned with neutral (read masked) abstractions corresponding to eternal verities but with situated, embodied sites of insight and need, oriented toward increasing inclusivity and betterment.

What all this comes to is acknowledging two related forms of embodiment: the embodied sites (cultural, gender, racial, economic locations) from which scientists tell us about the world and the embodied research agendas that direct their particular forays into the world. Both are concrete, particular, and partial as are all embodied projects—in other words, everything that human beings do. Hence, in order to gain any semblance of agendas beneficial to the many (many people, animals, plants, whatever), numerous sites must be included to allow for an inclusive agenda, one that in Donna Haraway's words would be "friendly to earthwide projects of finite freedom, adequate material abundance, modest meaning in suffering, and a limited happiness."[81]

We return now to the question raised earlier: On what scientific basis can one choose the holistic model, the organic model? The answer is on the basis of a stronger objectivity, a more inclusive view, a piecing together of various embodied research sites and agendas that will benefit more of the planet's creatures and supporting structures. The organic model, we are suggesting, acknowledges the well-being of both the whole and the parts; in fact, its view of unity and diversity is one that accords well with the notion of a stronger objectivity, that is, the benefit of the many as possible only through attending to a number of different embodied sites. This position does not deny the reductionistic, atomistic approach as a research method, but it accepts an organic picture of reality at the ideological or metaphysical level. This model, I believe, will help us more than the reductionist model to function with a stronger objectivity, one that will consider not just my well-being or the well-being of my kind, but the well-being of the various embodied sites or centers of interest and need that comprise the planet. Of course, this includes diverse human embodied sites, but it also can and should include the embodied sites of all other creatures as well.

* * * * *

To summarize: the organic model we are suggesting pictures reality as composed of multitudes of embodied beings who presently inhabit a planet that has evolved over billions of years through a process of dynamic change marked by law and novelty into an intricate, diverse, complex, multilevelled reality, all radically interrelated and interdependent. This organic whole that began from an initial big bang and eventuated into the present universe is distinguished by a form of unity and diversity radical beyond all imagining: unity that is characterized not by sameness but by seemingly infinite differences and diversity that is marked not by isolation but by shared atoms over millennia as well as minute-by-minute exchanges of oxygen and carbon dioxide between plants and animals. All of us, living and nonliving, are one phenomenon, a phenomenon stretching over billions of years and containing untold numbers of strange, diverse, and marvelous forms of matter—including our own. The universe is a body, to use a poor analogy from our own experience, but it is not a human body; rather, it is matter bodied forth seemingly infinitely, diversely, endlessly, yet internally as one.

Is this a model within which to live on planet earth for the twenty-first century? Is this also a model with which Christians might express the relation of God and the world? Is this a model that will help us gain an appropriate sense of our place in the scheme of things as well as reimagine the immanence and transcendence of the Western God? It might well be. It is certainly worth some serious reflection. We will first consider where we fit from the perspective of the common creation story bracketing the deeper theological and christological dimensions. This will help us to see ourselves in a sober, mundane, and realistic light.

If I were alone in a desert
    and feeling afraid,
I would want a child to be with me.
For then my fear would disappear
    and I would be made strong.
This is what life in itself can do
because it is so noble, so full of pleasure
    and so powerful.
But if I could not have a child with me
I would like to have at least a living animal
at my side to comfort me.

Therefore,
let those who bring about wonderful things
in their big, dark books
take an animal
to help them.
The life within the animal
will give them strength in turn.
    For equality
gives strength, in all things
and at all times.

                                        —Meister Eckhart

4 / ANTHROPOLOGY

At Home on the Earth

*A*n ecological theology based on the model of embodiment is a theology of space and place. It is a theology that begins with the body, each and every body, which is the most basic, primary notion of space: each life-form is a body that occupies and needs space. A theology of embodiment takes space seriously, for the first thing bodies need is space to obtain the necessities to exist—food, water, air. Space is not an empty notion from an ecological perspective ("empty space"), but a central one, for it means the basic world that each and every creature inhabits. Finding our niche, our space, which will provide the necessities for life, is the primary struggle of all life-forms, including human ones. Many cannot find the needed space or are edged out from occupying it by stronger individuals.

Space is an earthy, physical, lowly category unlike time, which is a peculiarly human, often mental, and sometimes grand notion.[1] (To be sure, in postmodern physics space and time are on a continuum and must be considered together, but from an ecological perspective, our ordinary separation of the two is still a functional notion.) In Christian thought space has often been connected with "pagan" fertility, earthy religions that celebrate the rebirth of life in the spring after its wintry death. The eternal return of the earth's physical cycle is contrasted with the historical movement toward the eschatological fulfillment of creation in the kingdom of God, a fulfillment beyond earthly joys. In space versus time, the old dichotomy of nature versus history is played out. The dichotomy is certainly not absolute, for history takes place in nature and nature itself has a history, as the common creation story clearly demonstrates, but for the past several hundred years at least, the focus and preference of Western thought has been on history to the detriment of nature. We can scarcely overstate the importance of time and history in relation to evolutionary development, both biological and cultural. We *are*, everything *is*, only as it has become and is becoming through the complex machinations of temporal development.[2] However, since this essay deals with bodies and their most basic needs, it will focus on a neglected necessity for bodies: space. For us, now, space should become the primary category for thinking about ourselves and other life-forms. Let us look at a few reasons why this ought to be the case.

First, space is a levelling, democratic notion that places us on a par with all other life-forms.[3] As the self-conscious, responsible form of life on our planet, we enjoy more than this status, but we need to begin our anthropology (who we are in the scheme of things) with the basics. The category of space reminds us not only that each and every life-form needs space for its own physical needs, but also that we all exist together in one space, our finite planet or, in terms of our model, within the nurturing matrix of God's body. We are all enclosed together in the womblike space of our circular planet, the indispensable space from which we derive all our nourishment. With the notion of space, the peculiar kind of differentiation and unity that characterizes contemporary science takes on new meaning and depth. Each and every life-form needs its own particular space and habitat in which to grow and flourish. This includes, of course, human beings who need not only food, water, and shelter, but loving families, education, medicine, meaningful work, and, some would include, music, art, and poetry. Spaces are specific and different for the billions of species on our planet; hence, the notion of space helps us to acknowledge both the basic necessity of all life-forms for space to satisfy their physical needs as well as the specific environments needed by each life-form, given their real differences. And yet, all these differences and special needs must be satisfied within one overarching space, the body of our planet. We are united to one another through complex networks of interrelationship and interdependence, so that when one species overreaches its habitat, encroaching on that of others, sucking the available resources out of others' space, diminishment and death must occur at some point. This process of natural selection has been going on since the beginning of the earth and has resulted in the rich, diverse planet we presently inhabit. The issue now, however, is whether one species, our own, has encroached so heavily on the space, the habitats of other species, that serious imbalance has occurred. As the dominant species for several hundred years, we have forgotten the primary reality of planetary space: it is limited and therefore attention to the primacy of space for other life-forms entails a levelling move toward egalitarianism. We need to remember that at a basic level all life-forms are the same: all need a space for the basics of life.

The second reason we need to turn from a historical (temporal) to a natural (spatial) perspective is because space highlights the relationship between ecological and justice issues. The crisis facing our planet is, in a sense, temporal: How much time do we have to preserve the possibility of life in community? But the reason that time matters is because we are misusing space. Theoretically, we have plenty of time, at least the five billion years of our sun's life, but we may only have a few hundred because of what we have done and continue to do to our plants, trees, water, and atmosphere. We are ruining the space, and when this occurs, justice issues emerge centrally and painfully. When good space—arable land with clean water and air, comfortable temperatures and shade trees—becomes scarce, turf wars are inevitable. Wars have usually, not just accidentally, been fought over land, for land is the bottom line. Without good land, none of the other goods of human existence is possible. Geography, often considered a trivial subject compared to the more splendid history (the feats of the forefathers), may well be *the* subject of the twenty-first century. Where is the best land and who controls it? How much good space is left and who is caring for it? Justice for those on the underside, whether these be human beings or other vulnerable species, has everything to do with space. In a theology of embodiment, space is the central category, for if justice is to be done to the many different kinds of bodies that comprise the planet, they must each have the space, the habitat, they need.

The third reason that we ought to focus on nature rather than history, on space rather than time, is that we need to realize that the earth is our home, that we belong here, that this is not only our space but our *place*. Christians have often not been allowed to feel at home on the earth, convinced after centuries of emphasis on otherworldliness that they belong somewhere else—in heaven or another world. That sojourner sensibility has faded with the rise of secularism, but it has not been replaced with a hearty embrace of the earth as our only and beloved home. Rather, many still feel, if not like aliens or tourists, at least like lords of the manor who inhabit the place but do not necessarily consider it their only, let alone beloved, home. Christian theologies as well as works of spirituality have not encouraged meditation on the beauty, preciousness, and vulnerability of the earth and its many creatures. The profound ascetic strain within the tradition that has feared tooclose association with human bodies has extended this as well to other animals and the body of the earth. But what if we were not only allowed but encouraged to love the earth? What if we saw the earth as part of the body of God, not as separate from God (who dwells elsewhere) but as the visible reality of the invisible God? What if we also saw this body as overlain by the body of the cosmic Christ, so that wherever we looked we would see bodies that are incorporated into the liberating, healing, inclusive love of God? Would we not then feel obliged to love the earth and all its many bodies? Would it not be the first duty of those who not only belong to the earth but know we belong to it? If the earth is an aspect of God's body, and if the paradigmatic story of Christianity is that the Word became flesh to liberate, heal, and include all who are needy, then Christians have a mandate to *love* the earth. God, in the model of the universe as God's body, makes her home in the universe (and in our planet) and gives us, we believe, in the story of Jesus of Nazareth some clues as to how we should live in our home. The most basic clue is to *love it*, for that is what the liberating parables, the healing stories, and the eating practices in different ways suggest. We belong to the earth; it is not only our space, but our place, our beloved home.

But we are reaching beyond where we ought to begin. An embodiment anthropology must start with who we are as earthly, physical creatures who have evolved over billions of years as pictured by postmodern science. This is a modest, humble beginning but one with enormous consequences for how we view both our status and our responsibilities. Reflections on our place in the scheme of things will provide clues to where we belong, our proper place, and hence from the perspective of contemporary science, what improper behavior might be. Thus, this chapter will focus on fleshing out the place (space) of human beings, not primarily from a Christian or even a religious perspective, but from the broad parameters of evolutionary biology. This will be a mundane view, the earthly, physical, bodily view, which should be a significant element in any interpretation of the status of human beings as well as of our wrongdoing.

Our Place in the Scheme of Things

The first step in a theological anthropology for our time is not to follow the clues from the Christic paradigm or even from the model of the universe as God's body, but to step backward and ask, Who are we in the scheme of things as pictured by contemporary science? Who are we simply as creatures of planet earth, quite apart from our religious traditions? That is not a question Christians have usually asked, believing that theological anthropology had little relationship to so-called secular views of human nature. Failing to ask that question, however, has often meant that Christian reflection on human existence has been "docetic": human beings come off as a little lower than the angels—not fully human. We have not seen ourselves as mundane, as being of this world, of the earth, earthy. We have defined our duties primarily in relationship to God (First Great Commandment) and secondarily in relationship to other human beings (Second Great Commandment), but seldom in relationship to the earth, its creatures and its care. A first, sobering step, therefore, is to look at ourselves from the earth up, rather than from the sky down. The postmodern scientific picture of reality will by no means tell us all we need to know about ourselves, but it will give us a base in reality (as understood in our time), so that whatever else we say about ourselves from the perspective of belonging to the body of God, a body overlain by the cosmic Christ, will be grounded, literally rooted, in the earth.

As we begin this task, let us recall the central features of the contemporary scientific view of reality. At its heart is the common creation story. In broad strokes, the story emerging from the various sciences claims that some fifteen billion years ago the universe began with a big bang that was infinitely hot and infinitely concentrated. This explosion eventually created some hundred billion galaxies of which our galaxy, the Milky Way, is one, itself containing billions of stars, including our sun and its planets. From this beginning came all that followed, so that everything that is is related, woven into a seamless network, with life gradually emerging after billions of years on our planet (and probably on others as well), and evolving into the marvelously complex and beautiful earth that is our home. All things living and all things not living are the products of the same primal explosion and evolutionary history and hence interrelated in an internal way right from the beginning. We are distant cousins to the stars and near relations to the oceans, plants, and all other living creatures on our planet.

We need to highlight several features of this story as we consider how it might help reformulate a postmodern theological anthropology, that is, who we are in the scheme of things. First of all, the world here is the universe, beside which the traditional range of divine concern—mainly with human subjects—dwindles, to say the least. In this view, God would relate to the entire fifteen-billion-year history of the universe and all its entities and inhabitants, living and nonliving. On the universe's clock, human existence appears a *few seconds* before midnight. This suggests, surely, that the whole show could scarcely have been put on for our benefit; our natural anthropocentrism is sobered, to put it mildly. Nevertheless, since it took fifteen billion years to evolve creatures as complex as human beings, the question arises as to our peculiar role in this story, especially in relation to our planet.

A second feature of the new picture is its story character: it is a historical narrative with a beginning, middle, and presumed end, unlike the Newtonian universe, which was static and deterministic. It is not a realm belonging to a king or an artifact made by an artist, but a changing, living, evolving event (with billions of smaller events making up its history). In our new cosmic story, time is irreversible, genuine novelty results through the interplay of chance and law, and the future is open. This is an unfinished universe, a dynamic universe, still in process. Other cosmologies, including mythic ones such as Genesis and even earlier scientific ones, have not been historical, for in them creation was finished. At the very least, this suggests that in our current picture God would be understood as a continuing creator, but of equal importance, we human beings might be seen as partners in creation, as the self-conscious, reflexive part of the creation that could participate in furthering the process.

A third characteristic of the common creation story is the radical interrelatedness and interdependence of all aspects of it, a feature of utmost importance to the development of an ecological sensibility. It is one story, a common story, so that everything that is traces its ancestral roots within it, and the closer entities are in time and space, the closer they are related. The organic character of the universe in no sense, however, supports a levelling or simplifying direction, that is, a lack of individuation. Precisely the opposite is the case. Whether we turn to the macrocosm or the microcosm, what we see is an incredibly complex, highly individuated variety of things, both living and nonliving. No two things, whether they be two exploding stars or the stripes on two zebras, are the same; individuality is not just a human phenomenon—it is a cosmic one. At the same time, however, the exploding stars and the zebras are related through their common origin and history. The implications of this feature of the universe for theologial anthropology are immense. The common character of the story undercuts notions of human existence as separate from the natural, physical world; or of human individuality as the only form of individuality; or of human individuals existing apart from radical interdependence and interrelatedness with others of our own species, with other species, and with the ecosystem. As physicist Brian

Swimme puts it, "No tribal myth, no matter how wild, ever imagined a more profound relationship connecting all things in an internal way right from the beginning of time. All thinking must begin with this cosmic genetic relatedness."[4] Were this feature of the scientific picture to become a permanent and deep aspect of our sensibility, it would be the beginning of an evolutionary, ecological, theological anthropology that could have immense significance in transforming how we think about ourselves as well as our relations and responsibilities toward other human beings, other species, and our home, planet earth.

A fourth feature is the multilevelled character of the universe, from the flow of energy in subatomic reality to the incredibly complex set of levels that comprise a human being. One critical aspect of this complexification is increasing subjectivity or the ability to experience and feel. Whatever we might or might not want to say about subjectivity in atoms or rocks, it surely increases as we progress to animals and to its present culmination in human self-consciousness. On the one hand, this means that no absolute distinction exists between the living and the nonliving, for life is a type of organization, not an entity or substance. As Ian Barbour reminds us, the chemical elements in our hands and brains were forged in the furnaces of the stars. On the other hand, the higher levels should not be reduced to or understood entirely in terms of the lower levels, as reductionists claim. What is significant, however, for a theological anthropology is not only the continuity from the simplest events in the universe to the most complex, but also their inverse dependency, which undercuts any sense of absolute superiority. That is, the so-called higher levels depend on the lower ones rather than vice versa. This is obviously the case with human beings and plants; the plants can do very nicely without us, in fact, better, but we would quickly perish without them. But it is also the case with aspects of our earth that we have until recently taken for granted, such as clean air and water. This very important point needs to be underscored: *The higher and more complex the level, the more vulnerable it is and dependent upon the levels that support it.* For theological anthropology, this is a very sobering thought, especially for a tradition that has been accused of advising human beings to subdue and have dominion over all other created beings.

It has profound implications for reconceiving the place of human beings in the scheme of things.

Finally, the common creation story is a public one, available to all who wish to learn about it. Other creation stories, the cosmogonies of the various world religions, are limited to the adherents of different religions. Our present one is not so limited, for any person on the planet has potential access to it and, as a human being, is included in it. This common story is available to be remythologized in different ways by any and every religious tradition, and hence is a place of meeting for the religions, whose conflicts in the past and present have often been the cause of immense suffering and bloodshed as belief is pitted against belief. Moreover, various ancient organic creation stories can enrich the common story. What this common story suggests is that our primary loyalty should not be to nation or religion, but to the earth and its creator (albeit we would understand that creator in different ways). We are members of the universe and citizens of planet earth. Again, were that reality to sink into human consciousness all over the world, not only war among human beings but ecological destruction would have little support in reality. This is not to say that they would disappear, but those who continue such practices would be living a lie, that is, living in a way not in keeping with reality as currently understood.

Who are we, then, according to the common creation story? According to the major characteristics of that story, human beings are radically other than what either the Christian tradition, especially since the Reformation, claims we are or what secular, modern culture allows. These two views differ in critical ways, with the religious picture focusing on the importance of human beings, especially those who accept Jesus Christ as savior, whereas the secular picture elevates individualism, consumerism, and technology. In both cases, however, the focus is on human beings and individual well-being. In light of the common creation story, however, this is a narrow vision indeed. Yet so profoundly does it reflect a part of the post-Enlightenment consciousness that we, for the most part, accept it as natural, that is, as the proper order of things.

But, according to contemporary science, the religious/secular/ modern picture of human reality is a lie, a very large and dangerous lie. According to the common creation story, we are not the center of things by any stretch of the imagination, although in a curious reversal, we are increasingly very important. That is, even as the sense of our insignificance deepens when we see our place in an unimaginably old and immense universe, nonetheless, at least on our tiny planet at this time, because of the wedding of science and technology, we are in a critically important position. We have the knowledge and power to destroy ourselves as well as many other species *and* we have the knowledge and the power to help the process of the ongoing creation continue. This means, in a way unprecedented in the past, that we are profoundly responsible.

The several characteristics of the common creation story we have highlighted suggest, then, a decentering and a recentering of human beings. From this story we learned that we are radically interrelated with and dependent on everything else in the universe and especially on our planet. We exist as individuals in a vast community of individuals within the ecosystem, each of which is related in intricate ways to all others in the community of life. We are especially dependent on the so-called lower forms of life. We exist with all other human beings from other nations and religions within a common creation story that each of us can know about and identify with. The creation of which we are a part is an ongoing, dynamic story that we alone (we believe) understand and hence have the potential to help continue and thrive or let deteriorate through our destructive, greedy ways. Our position in this story is radically different than it is, for instance, in the king/realm story, one of the major models in Western religion. We are decentered as the only subjects of the king and recentered as those responsible for both knowing the common creation story and helping it to flourish. In this story we feel profoundly connected with all other forms of life, not in a romantic but in a realistic way. We are so connected, and hence we had better live as if we were. We feel deeply related, especially, to all other human beings, our closest relatives, and realize that together we need to learn to live responsibly and appropriately in our common home.

In light of this story, the model of the human being seeking its own individual salvation, whether through spiritual or material means, is not only anachronistic to our current sense of reality but dangerous. We need to think holistically, and not just in terms of the well-being of human beings. We need to move beyond democracy to biocracy, seeing ourselves as one species among millions of other species on a planet that is our common home.[5] That is not the only context in which we need to view ourselves, but it is an important, neglected perspective. Our loyalty needs to move beyond family, nation, and even our own species to identify, in the broadest possible horizon, with all life: we *are* citizens of planet earth.

Such identification is not sentimental; it does not emerge merely from a fondness for charming panda bears or baby seals. It is simply the truth about who we are according to the contemporary picture of reality. We are profoundly interrelated and interdependent with everything living and nonliving in the universe and especially on our planet, and our peculiar position here is that we are radically dependent on all that is, so to speak, "beneath" us (the plants on land and the microorganisms in the ocean as well as the air, water, and soil). At the same time we have become, like it or not, the guardians and caretakers of our tiny planet. In a universe characterized by complex individuality beyond our comprehension, our peculiar form of individuality *and* interdependence has developed into a special role for us. We are the responsible ones, reponsible for all the rest upon which we are so profoundly dependent. No longer should we speak of ourselves as children, especially in a religious context, as the passive, needy children of a loving, all-powerful father who will take care of us and our planet. Nor can we continue to act like willful, brash adolescents out of control, as we have been doing in the modern story of scientism, militarism, individualism, and consumerism. We need to become who we really are, neither the possessor nor principal tenant of planet earth, but responsible adults, the only species on the planet that knows the common creation story and can assume our role as partners for its well-being. We no longer have an excuse, the excuse of ignorance, for the story unfolding before our eyes over the last hundred years has revealed our place in the whole. This proper place has decentered and recentered us: we are no longer the point of the whole show, as Western culture and the Christian tradition have often implied, but we have emerged as bearing heavy responsibilities for the well-being of the whole, responsibilities that will be difficult and painful to carry out.

Theological anthropologies emerging from this understanding of human being can and will vary greatly, given the tradition, social context, and kinds of oppression experienced by different communities and individuals. The context with which we are dealing is the broadest one possible—the human being as species. It is, nevertheless, but *one* context, not the only one. But were it to become a feature of theology for the planetary agenda, it would contribute some of the following notes: a focus on gratitude for the gift of life rather than a longing for eternal life; an end to dualistic hierarchies, including human beings over nature; an appreciation for the individuality of all things rather than the glorification of human individualism; a sense of radical interrelatedness and interdependence with all that exists; the acceptance of responsibility for other forms of life and the ecosystem, as guardians and partners of the planet; the acknowledgment that salvation is physical as well as spiritual and hence, that sharing the basics of existence is a necessity; and, finally, the recognition that sin is the refusal to stay in our proper place—sin is, as it always has been understood in the Jewish and Christian traditions, living a lie.

We began our theological anthropology with the place of human beings as seen in the common creation story rather than as a reflection of divine reality, understood either from revelation or from fundamental theology. It is important to underscore that this is a modest thesis that is not directly concerned with the liberation and salvation of the outcast and the oppressed—in other words, with the heart of Christian faith, as I understand it. The focus has been on our empirical, cosmic setting as earthlings (although that setting has significant implications for understanding salvation in our time, as we have seen). This setting has been for the most part neglected in recent theology and needs to be recalled and reinterpreted. Christian theologians will want to say more and other things about who we are, but we need to begin with our planetary citizenship.

It is a modest thesis, but given the great differences between the understanding of our proper place in post-Reformation Christianity and the common creation story, theological reflection conducted in terms of the new story would have revolutionary results. Once the scales have fallen from our eyes, once we have seen and believed that reality is put together in such a fashion that we are profoundly united to and interdependent with all other beings, everything is changed. We see the world differently, not anthropocentrically, not in a utilitarian way, not in terms of dualistic hierarchies, not in parochial terms. We have a sense of belonging to the earth, of having a place in it, and of loving it more than we ever thought possible.

In conclusion, it is precisely this sense of belonging, of being at home, that is perhaps the heart of the matter. It is the heart of the matter because it is the case—we *do* belong. As philosopher Mary Midgley writes: "We are not tourists here . . . We are at home in this world because we were made for it. We have developed here, on this planet, and we are adapted to life here . . . We are not fit to live anywhere else."[6] Postmodern science allows us to regain what late medieval culture lost during the Reformation and during the rise of dualistic mechanism in the seventeenth century—a sense of the whole and where we fit in it. Medieval culture was organic, at least to the extent that it saw human beings, while still central, as embedded in nature and dependent upon God. For the last several centuries, for a variety of complex reasons, we have lost that sense of belonging. Protestant focus on the individual and otherworldly salvation, as well as Cartesian dualism of mind and body, divided what we are now trying to bring back together and what must be reintegrated if we and other beings are to survive and prosper. But now, once again, we know that we belong to the earth, and we know it more deeply and thoroughly than any other human beings have ever known it.[7] The common creation story is more than a scientific affair; it is, implicitly, deeply moral, for it raises the question of the place of human beings in nature, and calls for a kind of praxis in which we see ourselves in proportion, in harmony, and in a fitting manner relating to all others that live and all the systems that support life.[8]

To *feel* that we belong to the earth and to accept our proper place within it is the beginning of a natural piety, what Jonathan Edwards called "consent to being," consent to what is. It is the sense that we and all others belong together in a cosmos, related in an orderly fashion, one to the other. It is the sense that each and every being is valuable in and for itself, and that the whole forms a unity in which each being, including oneself, has a place. It involves an ethical response, for the sense of belonging, of being at home, only comes when we accept our proper place and live in a fitting, appropriate way with all other beings. It is, finally, at a deep level, an aesthetic and religious sense, a response of wonder at and appreciation for the unbelievably vast, old, rich, diverse, and surprising cosmos, of which one's self is an infinitesimal but conscious part, the part able to sing its praises.

Sin:
The Refusal to Accept Our Place

The common creation story gives us a functional, working cosmology. It gives us a way of understanding where we fit.[9] It tells us that we belong and where we belong: it is both a welcoming word celebrating our grandeur as the most developed, complex creatures on our planet to date and a cautionary word reminding us that we belong in a place, not all places, on the earth. In the words of James Gustafson, human beings are thus reminded of "their awesome possibilities and their inexorable limitations."[10] The Genesis myth no longer functions for most people as a working cosmology, as a framework providing a sense of both space and place, grandeur and groundedness, possibilities and limitations, for the conduct of daily living. The Genesis myth, rich and profound as it still can be shown to be,[11] does not strike most people as a working model or construct within which the ordinary events and details of their lives can be understood. Moreover, the creation story that does function, at least implicitly, in Western culture is one heavy with otherworldly overtones, seeing human beings as resident aliens on the earth. But the common creation story has for many people immediate credibility upon first hearing.

"So this is where I, we, fit, not as a little lower than the angels but as an inspirited body among other living bodies, one with some distinctive and marvelous characteristics and some genuine limitations. I am of the earth, a product of its ancient and awesome history, and I really and truly belong here. But I am only one among millions, now billions of other human beings, who have a place, a space, on the earth. I am also a member of one species among millions, perhaps billions, of other species that need places on the earth. We are all, human beings and other species, inhabitants of the same space, planet earth, and interdependent in intricate and inexorable ways. I feel a sense of comfort, of settledness, of belonging as I consider my place in this cosmology, but also a sense of responsibility, for I know that I am a citizen of the planet. I have an expanded horizon as I reflect on my place in the common creation story: I belong not only to my immediate family or country or even my species, but to the earth and all its life-forms. I *do* belong to this whole. I know this now. The question is, can I, will I, *live* as if I did? Will I accept my proper place in the scheme of things? Will *we*, the human beings of the planet, do so?"

This little meditation has led us into the second major contribution of the common creation story to a theological anthropology: not only does it give us a functional cosmology but also a grounded or earthly notion of sin. One of the advantages of starting our reflections on human existence with our possibilities and limitations as seen in light of the common creation story is that it keeps them from being overstated or spiritualized. In this story we are not a little lower than the angels, nor the only creatures made in the image of God: our particular form of grandeur is in relation to the earth and derived from it—we are the self-conscious, responsible creatures. Likewise, in the common creation story, we are not sinners because we rebel against God or are unable to be sufficiently spiritual: our particular failing (closely related to our peculiar form of grandeur) is our unwillingness to stay in our place, to accept our proper limits so that other individuals of our species as well as other species can also have needed space. From the perspective of the common creation story, we gain a sober, realistic, mundane picture of ourselves: our grandeur is our role as responsible partners helping our planet prosper, and our sin is plain old self-ishness—wanting to have everything for ourselves.

We need to press more deeply into the issue of sin, both what we can learn about it from the common creation story and how this view is both like and unlike the classical understanding of sin in the Christian tradition. We need also to reflect on what an ecological view of sin means in a number of different contexts—in relation to other human beings (us versus us), other animals (us versus them), and nature (us versus it). But before delving into these matters, we need to ask why God has been left out of the contexts to be considered. Sin in the Christian tradition has usually been, first of all, against God; it is in our reflections also, for in the model of the universe (world) as God's body, sin against any part of the body *is* against God. Our model helps us to keep theology earthly; it helps us to avoid abstraction, generalization, and spiritualization. To anticipate what we will say in subsequent chapters, an incarnational theology always insists that both sin and salvation are earthly matters—fleshly, concrete, particular matters having to do with disproportion and well-being *in relation to* the forms of God's presence we encounter in our daily, ordinary lives: other bodies. Sin against the many different bodies—the bodies of other people, other animals, and nature—*is* sin against God in the model of the world as God's body.

What is the relation of an ecological view of sin with the classical Christian view? It deepens rather than contradicts it. The classical view can be summarized with the phrase "living a lie," living out of proper relations with God, self, and other beings. Sin, in the Hebrew and Christian traditions, is a relational notion, having to do with the perversion of fitting, appropriate attitudes and actions in relation to other beings and the source of all being. Sin is, therefore, thinking, feeling, and acting in ways contrary to reality, contrary to the proper, right relations among the beings and entities that constitute reality. Some interpretations of sin in Judaism and Christianity, such as legalism or personalism (sin as breaking God's law or offending the divine majesty), do not, I believe, point to what is most profound in these traditions. Sin is not just breaking divine laws or blaspheming God; rather, it is living falsely, living contrary to reality, to the way things are. (And yet, breaking divine laws and blaspheming God are *symptoms* of living falsely, of failing to accept one's place as limited. The limits of law and humility before the divine glory are signs pointing to our proper, realistic place in the scheme of things.)

An autobiographical point might make the point clearer. When I was first introduced to Christian theology as a college student, I recall being deeply impressed with its view of sin—it struck a chord of authenticity in me—while I remained quite unmoved by the various traditional interpretations of redemption. The classical understanding of sin focuses on wanting to be the center of things, and I already knew deeply that longing. Augustine calls it "concupiscence," literally, insatiable sexual desire but, more broadly, wanting to have it all, whatever the all is. In other words, sin is limitless greed. As a privileged member of the world's elite, I was an easy target for this view of sin. While as a female in the American fifties I perhaps lacked an overbearing sense of my own self-worth—or sin understood as pride—yet by class and race I fit the pattern of the voracious Western appetite for more than my share: I was an "ecological" sinner. The Augustinian interpretation, in focusing on the bloated self, the self that wants it all, the self that refuses to share, highlights the ecological dimension of sin. From this perspective, selfishness is the one-word definition of sin—at least for us first-world types.[12]

To say that sin has an ecological dimension means that we must view beings, organisms, in relation to their environment. The environment of all beings, according to our model of the universe as God's body, is the "divine *milieu*": we live and move and have our being, along with all other beings, in God. Therefore, sin or living a lie will be living disproportionately, falsely, inappropriately within this space, refusing to accept the limitations and responsibilities of our place. Moreover, this space, place, has been further defined and qualified for Christians by the cosmic Christ, the embodied life paradigmatically expressed in the liberating, healing, inclusive ministry of Jesus of Nazareth. But in order to ground living rightly in the earth, in our mundane relations, let us step back from the divine *milieu* as our environment and consider an ecological view of sin within a more lowly environment: our relations with other human beings, other animals, and the natural world.

Us versus Us:
Living a Lie in Relation to Other Human Beings

This section need not be long because the evidence of disproportionate space and place of some human beings in contrast to others—the rich and poor within nations and between nations—is everywhere and growing.[13] If the most basic meaning of justice is fairness, then from an ecological point of view, justice means sharing the limited resources of our common space.[14] From the perspective of the one home we all share, injustice is living a lie, living contrary to reality, pretending that all the space or the best space belongs to some so that they can live in lavish comfort and affluence, while others are denied even the barest necessities for physical existence. The disproportion here, epitomized in the billionaires versus the homeless, the standard of living of the first-world versus third-world countries, the swollen stomachs of starving people versus obesity in others, forces us to think concretely and physically about sin.[15] The common creation story deepens the classical view of right relations in regard to members of our own species: it suggests that loving our neighbor must be grounded in mundane issues of space, turf, habitat, land. Every human being needs an environment capable of supporting its sustenance and growth. While this might at first appear to be a minimalist view, reducing human beings to the physical (animal?!) level, it is precisely the minimum that those individuals and nations bloated with self, living the life of insatiable greed, refuse to recognize. It is far easier as well as less costly to one's own life-style to offer spiritual rather than material goods to the poor. The ecological view of sin refuses to raise its eyes above the minimalist view, insisting that justice among human beings means first of all adequate space for basic needs. It also means, for some, staying in their own proper, limited place.

While our analysis of ecological sin will focus on the more neglected areas of our relations with other animals and nature, proper relations with our nearest and dearest kin, our own species, must be first in consideration and importance. Some environmentalists, most notably deep ecologists, claim that human beings as one species among many million, perhaps billion, are of no special importance.[16] Their needs for space, for land, for nourishment should not take precedence over the needs of all other species. This radical egalitarianism gives the assumption of a split between ecological and justice issues a theoretical base. It is not simply that space on our planet is limited and we must share it; it is also the case, say some, that we do not deserve any special space or more space than, say, the polar bear or giant sequoia trees. Undoubtedly on some scales of reckoning, we do not deserve it, but try telling this to the parent of a starving child, and all we have done, in the minds of many, is widen the abyss separating justice and ecological issues.

The issue on which to focus when we consider justice versus ecological issues is not our species versus other species, but *some members* of our species versus other members. While it is certainly the case that the human population is too large and encroaches on the habitats of other species, lumping human beings all together as *the* ecological problem masks the profound justice issues within our population. Those to whom this essay is addressed—we well-off Westerners—need to admit that the first lie we live is in relation to others of our own kind. *The* ecological sin is the refusal of the haves to share space and land with the have nots. It has been shown that human populations stabilize when the standard of living improves; hence, it is not only our gross numbers encroaching on other species' populations that is the problem but the disproportionate way in which space is controlled by some humans to the disadvantage of others. Over the long haul, stabilizing the human population at a sustainable level is primarily a justice issue among human beings. Thus, justice issues *within* the human species have a direct effect on environmental issues between our species and other species. Simply put, we need to do some housecleaning as a first step. Until we rectify gross injustices among human beings, in other words, begin our ecological work at home, we will have little chance of success abroad, that is, in relation to other species and the planet as a whole.

Us versus Them:
Living a Lie in Relation to Other Animals

The ecological view of sin deepens when we realize that other animals, beside human ones, must have space, and that they too have a place. The common creation story not only tells us that we are related to the physical bodies of all other animals but also gives detail and depth to this statement. While there are tens of billions of known kinds of organic molecules, only about fifty are used for the essential activities of life. Molecules are essentially identical in all plants and animals. "An oak tree and I are made of the same stuff. If you go back far enough, we have a common ancestor."[17] If some degree of intimacy is true of us and oak trees, it is astonishingly true of us and other animals.[18] We not only *are* animals but we are genetically very similar to all other animals and only a fraction of difference away from those animals, the higher mammals, closest to us. And yet one would scarcely suspect this from the way animals are conventionally regarded as well as used in our culture. While most people now have or pretend to have a raised consciousness in regard to the needs of all human beings for the basic necessities of life, the same cannot be said for attitudes about other animals. This is not the place for a review of human use and misuse of animals as manifest in pleasure hunting, excessive meat eating, the fur trade, circuses and traditional zoos, vivisection, cosmetic animal testing, and so on.[19] But even listing a few of our more callous practices in regard to animals illustrates our degree of insensitivity to their needs, wishes, and feelings. In fact, it is by suppressing any thought that they might have needs, wishes, or feelings, in other words, that they are *anything like us* (or we like them—the more valid evolutionary comparison) that we can continue such practices with good, or at least numbed, consciences.

What does it mean to live a lie in relation to other animals? What is ecological sin in regard to them? The common creation story helps us answer this question specifically by providing a realistic picture of who we are in relation to other animals, both our profound intimacy with them and our important differences from them. We recall that one of the special features of this story is the way both unity and diversity are understood: the interrelationship and interdependence of all living things as well as the distinctive individuality and differences among living forms. Embodied knowing, paying attention to concrete differences, is a necessary step in embodied doing, behaving appropriately toward other life-forms, each of whom has special characteristics and needs. The common creation story helps us to move into a new paradigm for responding to our fellow animals, one in which we appreciate the network of our interdependence with them as well as their real differences from us. In the conventional model, the model that views them as resources or recreation, as something to serve us or amuse us, we can appreciate neither our profound closeness nor our genuine differences: they are simply "other." The new paradigm, however, presses us into a much more complex, highly nuanced relationship with other animals, one that refuses either a sentimental fusion or an absolute separation. In this paradigm we are neither "a species among species" nor "the crown of creation." Who, then, are we?

One way to answer this question is to focus on the characteristic that has usually separated us totally and irrevocably from all other animals: our intellect. We are rational, linguistic, logical beings and therefore unlike all other animals. Various studies of incipient language and reasoning powers in some higher mammals have questioned this assumption, so that few would any longer agree with Immanuel Kant's inflated view of man [sic]: "As the single being on earth that possesses understanding, he is certainly titular lord of nature, and, supposing that we regard nature as a teleological system, he is born to be its ultimate end."[20] Nonetheless, few probably agree either with philosopher Mary Midgley that mathematical rationality in human beings is not necessarily superior to practical reason in a mother elephant as she cannily maneuvers to protect her young.[21] While Kant saw a human being as a thinking thing with no relation to body, many of us still see other animals as bodily things with no mind or spirit. Our common creation story tells us that neither position is the case: We are on a continuum with them as they are with us; it is not us versus them but us *and* them, for the roots of human nature lie deep within those others we call animals.[22] Who we are, then, is in some sense who they are: whatever we are and have is based in and derived from those others. Nor is it self-evident that the characteristic we have chosen to distinguish ourselves from the other animals, namely rationality, is worthy of being elevated above all others. As Midgley comments, "Being clever is not obviously so much more important than being kind, brave, friendly, patient, and generous . . . ."[23] Dualism—separating reason and feeling—is part of the impasse to thinking in a connected, relational way about animals, because we lock animals into the feeling category. Rationality, however, is not just cleverness, and intelligence includes a structure of preferences, a priority system based on feeling. The higher animals have deep, lasting preferences, and hence a type of practical reason.

We are like other animals in complex ways; we are also different from them—and they from one another—in complex ways.[24] We have simplified our relationship with other animals by focusing on one human characteristic, a kind of rationality divorced from feeling, which has allowed us to put ourselves on top, with other animals as inferior to us and radically different from us. The operating model here is the ladder, with rationality at the top and ourselves as its sole possessor. Everything that does not possess rationality is alien, including our own feelings and bodies as well as other animals, plant life, and the earth. But what if the evolutionary model were the bush rather than the ladder, a model much closer to what the common creation story tells us. A bush does not have a main trunk, a dominant direction of growth, or a top. There is no privileged place on a bush; rather, what a bush suggests is *diversity* (while at the same time interconnectedness and interdependence, since all its parts are related and all are fed by a common root system). The bush model helps us to appreciate different kinds of excellence, each of which is an end in itself. In this model other animals are not defined by their *lack* of rationality. "Is there nothing to a giraffe except being a person *manqué*?"[25] Asked positively, would a dolphin think that we could swim, a dog be impressed with our sense of smell, or a migrating bird be awed by our sense of direction?[26] We are profoundly and complexly united with other animals as well as profoundly and complexly different from them and they from each other. The more we know in detail about other species, the more this abstraction will take on reality and power. Even to learn about one other species, for instance, following the research of a naturalist who has devoted her life to studying the lowland gorillas or fruitbats or caterpillars, will raise consciousness regarding the deep as well as subtle ways that animals resemble and differ from one another.

What such study often does is return us to a state of wonder, curiosity, and affection that we as children had for other animals. Children often possess wide powers of sympathy for injured animals, demonstrating a natural affection for members of other species that we need to develop rather than squelch. The young of different species play together in a mixed community that, unfortunately, gets rather thoroughly sorted out by adulthood.[27] But we can make at least a partial return to this mixed community by way of a "second naïvete," a way that involves educating ourselves on our genuine, deep, and concrete forms of interrelatedness with other life-forms.[28]

The study of similarities and differences among animals (including ourselves) also presses us to refuse easy notions of egalitarianism between ourselves and other animals as a solution to our historic insensibility toward them.[29] If equality has proven to be problematic in valuing differences among human beings, tending toward universalism or essentialism in its integration of the minority into the majority's assumptions, it is even more questionable a category to help us live appropriately with other animals. "Speciesism" is not just a prejudice against other animals that can be rectified by treating them like human beings; rather, it is the refusal to appreciate them *in their difference*, their differences from us and from each other that require, for instance, special and particular habitats, food, privacy, and whatever else each species needs to flourish.

Who are we, then, in the scheme of things in relation to other animals? What does it mean to live a lie in relation to them? The common creation story tells us that we are like and unlike them; that special forms of similarity and difference unite and divide us from them and each of them from one another. We need to develop a sensibility that appreciates some of these most central ways in which we are united and different. Living a lie in relation to them means, the common creation story tells us, lumping the other animals all together in an inferior category judged by our own superior intellect; separating ourselves from them as alien creatures with whom we have no intrinsic relationships; and, most especially, numbing ourselves to their real needs, preferences, and ability to feel pain so that we can continue to use them for our own benefit.

Refusing to live this lie will not make life easier or better for us—at least not in the short run. It will complicate it. If the resources of our planet are already strained in dealing with the needs of the human population, a large proportion of whom go hungry daily, how, why should the rights of other animals be included? Again, the issue of space is central, for increasingly, it is not hunting that is decimating other animal species, but loss of habitats due to our excessive population and the voracious life-style of some of us. But the common creation story tells us that space must be shared. It tells us that life on our planet evolved together and is interdependent in complex ways beyond our imagining; it deepens our understanding of who "family" is and the needs of different family members. At the very least it tells us that we cannot live alone, that for utilitarian reasons we need to live truthfully, rightly, appropriately with our kin, the other animals. But the work of naturalists—as well as the wonder and pleasure we felt as children and our own children feel for other animals—makes us ask: Do we not also *want* them as our companions?[30] Do we not also delight in them and value them, not just for their usefulness to us, but in their differences as well? Is wonder at the sublimity of a whale or the intricacy of an ant colony a marginal, dispensable part of human existence that few of us care about?[31] It all depends on how you define our most distinctive characteristic, as rationality or wonder?

Wonder may well be what is special about us from the perspective of the common creation story. We are the creatures who *know* that we know. Many creatures know many things; intelligence is not limited to human beings. But the ability to step back, to reflect on *that* we know and *what* we know—in other words, self-consciousness—may well be our peculiar specialty. As Annie Dillard notes, "The point is that not only does time fly and . . . we die, but that in these reckless conditions we live at all, and are vouchsafed, for the duration of certain inexplicable moments, to know it."[32] To live at all and to know it: these are the roots of wonder. I was distinctly and peculiarly human when, at age seven, I thought with terror and fascination that someday I would not "be" any longer. In that thought was contained not only consciousness of life but self-consciousness of it: it is a wonder to be alive but it is a deeper wonder to know it. Knowing that we know places special possibilities and responsibilities on us. Self-consciousness is the basis of free will, imagination, choice, or whatever one calls that dimension of human beings that makes us capable of changing ourselves and our world. The issues around this area in regard to limitations and possibilities are enormous and beyond dealing with in this essay.[33] The point relevant to our concerns is that in relation to other animals, our ability to wonder, to step back and reflect on what we know, places us in a singular position: our place in the scheme of things may well be to exercise this ability. To be sure, the distance that self-consciousness gives us has many aspects. A technological, rational dimension, one that can be used both for the destruction and preservation of our planet and its creatures, allows us to assess the results of various kinds of knowledge. But we are more likely to put this knowledge to work on the side of the well-being of the planet if we are moved by a deeper dimension of self-consciousness. That dimension is one close to the root meaning of wonder as surprise, fascination, awe, astonishment, curiosity: we are the ones capable of being amazed by life. *It is a wonder.* The common creation story deepens that wonder in us, not only through knowing that it has occurred at all on this planet, but also by knowing the complex, diverse, intricate way it has developed, eventuating in the truly wonder-filled creatures that we are. It is indeed a "wonderful life." One of the most profound lessons we can learn from the common creation story is appreciation for life, not just our own, but that of all the other creatures in the family of life. We are the ones, the only ones on our planet, who know the story of life and the only ones who know that we know: the only ones capable of being filled with wonder, surprise, curiosity, and fascination by it. A first step, then, toward a healthy ecological sensibility may well be a return, via a second naivete, to the wonder we as children had for the world, but a naivete now informed by knowledge of and a sense of responsibility for our planet and its many life-forms. To know that we know places special burdens on us: it means, as we will suggest in later chapters, being designated as God's partners. On our planet we are the self-conscious aspect of the body of God, the part of the divine body able to work with God, the spirit who creates and redeems us, to bring about the liberation and healing of the earth and all its creatures. We know that we know: we have a choice to act on behalf of the wonderful life that we are and that surrounds us.

Us versus It:
Living a Lie in Relation to Nature

John Muir, the eminent American naturalist, wrote at the end of his life: "I only went out for a walk and finally concluded to stay until sundown, for going out, I discovered, was actually going in."[34] This summarizes a life-long conversion to the earth, the realization that one *belongs* to the earth. It is not natural for most of us to believe, let alone feel, that we belong to nature, to realize that by going out we are actually going in. Susan Griffin, poet and ecofeminist, eloquently expresses our complex in-and-out relationship with nature: "We know ourselves to be made from this earth. We know this earth is made from our bodies. For we see ourselves. And we are nature. We are nature seeing nature. We are nature with a concept of nature. Nature weeping. Nature speaking of nature to nature."[35] We are the self-conscious ones who can think about, weep for, and speak of nature, but we are also one in flesh and bone with nature. It is this dual awareness of both our responsibility for nature and our profound and complex unity with it that is the heart of the appropriate, indeed necessary, sensibility that we need to develop.

The proper balance of this dual awareness in relation to nature, specifically in relation to the earth, the land, may be even more difficult than in relation to other people and other animals, for we have a clearer notion of the ways we are both united to and distinct from them than we do with such things as oceans, plants, and land. Most Westerners tend to objectify nature so totally that human beings are essentially distinct from it. But for the contemporary movement called deep ecology, bent on converting us from *ego*centricity to *eco*centricity, human beings are essentially one with nature. We see here two extremes.[36]

Nonetheless it is instructive, given how difficult it is for most of us to identify with nature, to listen to deep ecology remembering, once again, that the planetary agenda is a conversation of many voices. The limitations of any position should not blind us to its insights. The central insight of deep ecology is, as one of its founders Aldo Leopold puts it, that we are "fellow-voyagers with other creatures in the odyssey of evolution," just "plain citizens" of the biotic community.[37] We are not special: humanism is an error of egocentricity, for we live with other species in an "ecological egalitarianism," as one among many. But deep ecology presses us to acknowledge more than egalitarianism; it wants us to *feel* our deepest, physical connections with and dependence on the earth. This is its greatest asset as well as limitation, for in identifying us ever more deeply with nature, deep ecology tends to blend us into nature, which is problematic in a number of ways.

But first let us learn how this perspective can help us identify with the earth, with the land and especially its plants, waters, and atmosphere. The value of deep ecology is that it insists we are not merely connected to nature but that all its parts, including ourselves, intermingle and interpenetrate. The Amazon rainforest is not just important to our well-being; it is, literally, our external lungs without which we will not be able to breathe. Deep ecology assumes profound organicism, a reliance on the model of body absolutely and totally. This organic model is not distinguished by diversity but rather by the fusion of its many parts.[38] The danger of a position based on this model may already be evident, but since the value of deep ecology is not, I believe, in its conceptual adequacy but in its poetic power to make us feel unity, let us listen to a few of its most able spokespersons.

Richard Nelson, anthropologist and essayist, writes of his experience on a remote Northwest island off the Pacific coast. "There is nothing in me that is not of earth, no split instant of separateness, no particle that disunites me from the surroundings. I am no less than the earth itself. The rivers run through my veins, the winds blow in and out with my breath, the soil makes my flesh, the sun's heat smolders inside me. A sickness or injury that befalls the earth befalls me. A fouled molecule that runs through the earth runs through me. Where the earth is cleansed and nourished, its purity infuses me. The life of the earth is my life. My eyes are the earth gazing at itself."[39]

Gary Snyder, poet and deep ecologist, comments on his poem, "Song of the Taste": "All of nature is a gift-exchange, a potluck banquet, and there is no death that is not somebody's food, no life that is not somebody's death . . . We all take life to live . . . The shimmering food-chain, food-web, is the scary, beautiful condition of the biosphere . . . Eating is truly a sacrament."[40]

The following credo by poet Robinson Jeffers is often quoted by deep ecologists: "I believe the universe is one being, all its parts are different expressions of the same energy, and they are all in communication with each other, therefore parts of an organic whole . . . It seems to me that this whole alone is worthy of the deeper love."[41]

Some may, however, object to the extreme fringe as expressed in a comment such as the following: "Deep ecology . . . requires openness to the black bear, becoming truly intimate with the black bear, so that honey dribbles down your fur as you catch the bus to work."[42]

At its best deep ecology helps us to enlarge our sense of self—that is, what we include in our definition of who we are.[43] A narrow self-definition includes only one's nearest and dearest: family and friends, or at most, one's tribe or nation. A broader self-definition takes in not only all people but some of the higher or more interesting animals (at least the poster ones, such as dolphins or snow leopards). But a cosmological self-identification acknowledges that we are part and parcel of everything on the planet, or, as Alan Watts puts it, "the world is your body."[44] Only as we are able both to think and feel this enlarged definition of self will we be able to begin to respond appropriately and responsibly to the crises facing our planet. Deep ecology makes an important contribution, for it radicalizes us into a new way of looking at the earth in which we are decentered as masters, as crown, as goal, and begin to feel empathy in an *internal* way for the sufferings of other species. As Aldo Leopold comments, "For one species to mourn the death of another is a new thing under the sun."[45] It is indeed new and requires an expanded self-identification, a sense that I care about another species in a way analogous to the way I care about those near and dear to me. I do not merely regret the loss, but I feel it and weep for it. Can we also expand this sense of self to include ecosystems and even the planet?[46] When we read of the pollution of the oceans or the destruction of rainforests, do we feel grief for the earth itself, for that beautiful blue-green living marvel of a planet spinning alone in space?

We are a part of the whole, deep ecology insists, and we need to internalize that insight as a first step toward living truthfully, living in reality. A question, however, that rises immediately is *which* part are we? just any part? no particular part? Deep ecology is based on the classic body model of a single organism, a model made more extreme by a view of ecological unity in which living things are so profoundly interrelated and interdependent that they are, in effect, one. The result is a merging of parts, "an oceanic fusion of feeling," that denies the diversity, individuality, and complexity of life-forms that have emerged from evolutionary history, and is a weak basis for an environmental ethic.[47] The organic model based on the common creation story does not fuse all the parts; difference and individuality are central ingredients of this picture. Ecofeminists have been especially concerned to deny fusion and insist that the "loving eye" pays attention to the independence and difference of the other.[48] It is a kind of knowing that acknowledges the others in the world "as being independent, different, perhaps even indifferent to humans. Humans *are* different from rocks in important ways, even if they are also both members of some ecological community."[49]

Unless this difference is acknowledged — including the *indifference* — and acknowledged in relation to the particularity and peculiarity of this and that species, this and that ecosystem, there is no solid basis for an environmental ethic. A statement by one deep ecologist indicates the problem with an ethic based on the fused self: "Just as we need no morals to make us breathe . . . [so] if your 'self' in the wide sense embraces another being, you need no moral exhortation to show care . . . ."[50] No "oughts" are necessary, for care flows "naturally" from the expanded self. The sentimentality and danger of this view are evident: Even parents and lovers, whose sense of self certainly does embrace the child or the beloved, can and do engage in outrageous acts of emotional and physical destruction toward the other. What is missing from deep ecology is a developed sense of *difference*. An environmental ethic in regard to nature—the land, ecosystems, the planet—must be based on knowledge of and appreciation for the intrinsic and particular differences of various species, biotic regions, oceanic ecosystems, and so on. We need to learn about these differences and make them central in our interaction with the environment. A sense of oneness with the planet and all its life-forms is a necessary first step, but an *informed* sensibility is the prerequisite second step. Aldo Leopold, a deep ecologist who does not fall into the fusion trap, is on the right track when he tells us that we need a land ethic, an ethic toward the land that no longer sees it "like Odysseus' slave-girls" as still property, as "still strictly economic, entailing privileges but not obligations."[51] The intrinsic value and independence of the land, not our sense of oneness with it, is the basis of living rightly in relation to it. A land ethic that aims "to preserve the integrity, stability, and beauty of the biotic community" is an example of living appropriately on the land, refusing to live the lie that we are the conquerors, the possessors, the masters of the earth.[52] A land ethic deals with the issue of space—the prime issue for an environmental anthropology—in its broadest and deepest context. *The* space, the ultimate space, as it were, that we all share, is the land, oceans, and atmosphere that comprise the planet. The complex question that faces us is how to share this space with justice and care for our own species, other species, and the ecosystems that support us all. How can we live with the others that inhabit this space appropriately and justly, realizing we have a place, but not all places, that we need space but cannot have the whole space?

Our reflection on sin in three contexts—as living a lie in relation to other human beings, other animals, and nature—has highlighted space as a central category for an ecological anthropology. In each case we have insisted that the attention to difference, even though we acknowledge and feel profound unity with these others, is central. We close these thoughts with two more that lead into the rest of the book: We *are* different in the common creation picture, for we are the self-conscious ones that can care for the others; and we *are* different in the model of the body of God as qualified by the cosmic Christ, for we are called to be the liberating, healing, sharing self-conscious ones. In other words, our special-ness in the common creation story takes a particular turn in the Christian story, and it is to this that we now turn.

In the following chapters we will move beyond what the common creation story tells us about our place in the scheme of things by deepening, qualifying, and radicalizing it. We will see ourselves as living also in the body of God, a body that in the Christic paradigm is characterized by God's liberating, healing, and inclusive love. Each of these contexts—the common creation story, the body of God, and the Christic paradigm—tells us important things about ourselves and where we fit. Each contributes to a functional cosmology for Christians living in an ecological era.

Goodnight God
I hope that you are having
a good time being the world.
I like the world very much.
I'm glad you made the plants
and trees survive with the
rain and summers.
When summer is nearly near
the leaves begin to fall.
I hope you have a good time
being the world.
I like how God feels around
everyone in the world.
God, I am very happy that
I live on you.
Your arms clasp around the world.
I like you and your friends.
Every time I open my eyes
I see the gleaming sun.
I like the animals—the deer,
and us creatures of the world,
the mammals.
I love my dear friends.

—Danu Baxter, four-and-a-half years old

5 / THEOLOGY

God and the World

**A Meditation on Exodus 33:23b:
"And you shall see my back;
but my face shall not be seen"**

When Moses in an audacious moment asks of God, "Show me your glory," God replies that "no one can see me and live," but he does allow Moses a glimpse of the divine body — not the face, but the back (Exodus 33:20-23). The passage is a wonderful mix of the outrageous (God has a *backside*?!) and the awesome (the display of divine glory too dazzling for human eyes). The passage unites guts and glory, flesh and spirit, the human and the divine, and all those other apparent dualisms with a reckless flamboyance that points to something at the heart of the Hebrew and Christian traditions: God is not afraid of the flesh. We intend to take this incarnationalism seriously and see what it does, could, mean in terms of the picture of reality from postmodern science. Were we to imagine "the Word made flesh" as not limited to Jesus of Nazareth but as the body of the universe, all bodies, might we not have a homey but awesome metaphor for both divine nearness *and* divine glory? Like Moses, when we ask, "Show me your glory," we might see the humble bodies of our own planet as visible signs of the invisible grandeur. Not the face, not the depths of divine radiance, but enough, more than enough. We might begin to see (for the first time, perhaps) the marvels at our feet and at our fingertips: the intricate splendor of an Alpine forget-me-not or a child's hand. We might begin to realize the extraordinariness of the ordinary. We would begin to delight in creation, not as the work of an external deity, but as a sacrament of the living God. We would see creation as bodies alive with the breath of God. We might realize what this tradition has told us, although often shied away from embracing unreservedly: we live and move and have our being *in* God. We might see ourselves and everything else as the living body of God.

We would, then, have an entire planet that reflects the glory, the very being—although not the face—of God. We would have a concrete panorama for meditation on divine glory and transcendence: wherever we looked, whether at the sky with its billions of galaxies (only a few visible to us) or the earth (every square inch of which is alive with millions of creatures) or into the eyes of another human being, we would have an image of divine grandeur. The more we meditated on these bits of the divine body, the more intricate, different, and special each would become. Such meditation is a suitable way for limited, physical creatures with lively imaginations such as ourselves to contemplate the divine being. It is enriching for it does not occur only at one place but everywhere and not just in one form but in an infinite myriad of forms. It is neither otherworldly nor abstract, but is a this-worldly, concrete form of contemplating divine magnificence. It is a way for limited, physical beings like ourselves to meditate on divine transcendence in an immanent way. And it is based on the assumption, central to the Christian tradition, that God not only is not afraid of the flesh but loves it, *becomes* it.

If we are allowed, indeed, invited as Moses was to see God's glory in the divine back, then we experience not only awe as we meditate on the wonders of our planet but also compassion for all bodies in pain. If God is available to us in bodies, then bodies become special. The metaphor of the world as God's body knits together the awe we feel for the magnificent intricacy and splendor of all the diverse kinds of bodies *and* the pain we feel for a suffering human or animal body. We cannot in good conscience marvel with aesthetic delight at the one and not identify with the pain of the other: bodies are beautiful and vulnerable. If God is physical, then the aesthetic and the ethical unite: praising God in and through the beauty of bodies entails caring for the most basic needs of all bodies on the planet. If God is physical, then the divine becomes part of the everyday, part of the pain and pleasure of bodily existence.

We begin to see a new way of imagining and expressing divine transcendence and immanence. It is not a model of transcendence in which God is king and the world is the realm of a distant, external ruler who has all power and expects unquestioned obedience from his subjects, human beings.[1] Nor is it a model of immanence in which God the king once entered the world by becoming a servant in the form of one human being. Rather, it is a radicalization of both divine transcendence and immanence. The model of the universe as God's body radicalizes transcendence for *all* of the entire fifteen-billion-year history and the billions of galaxies is the creation, the outward being, of the One who is the source and breath of all existence. In the universe as a whole as well as in each and every bit and fragment of it, God's transcendence is embodied. The important word here is "embodied": the transcendence of God is not available to us except as embodied. We do not see God's face, but only the back. But we *do* see the back.

The world (universe) as God's body is also, then, a radicalization of divine immanence, for God is not present to us in just one place (Jesus of Nazareth, although also and especially, paradigmatically there),[2] but in and through all bodies, the bodies of the sun and moon, trees and rivers, animals, and people. The scandal of the gospel is that the Word became flesh; the radicalization of incarnation sees Jesus not as a surd, an enigma, but as a paradigm or culmination of the divine way of enfleshment.

We are suggesting, then, that the model of the universe as God's body is a way of expressing both radical transcendence *and* immanence, but in a fashion that limits our perception and knowledge to the back of God. In other words, we are dealing here with a model or metaphor, not a description: the universe as God's body is a rich, suggestive way to radicalize the glory, the awesomeness, the beyond-all-imagining power and mystery of God in a way that at the same time radicalizes the nearness, the availability, the physicality of divine immanence. In this one image of the world as God's body, we are invited to see the creator *in* the creation, the source of all existence in and through what is bodied forth from that source. And yet, as we contemplate divine transcendence immanently in the bodies of all things and creatures, we know what we see is the back, not the face, of God. The very recognition and acceptance of that limit gives us permission, as the Hebrew psalmists also felt, to revel in the many embodiments divine transcendence takes: the clouds and winds, thunder and water, deer and young lambs, midwives and mothers, kings and shepherds. Everything can be a metaphor for God, because no *one* thing *is* God. The body of God is not the human body nor any other body; rather, all bodies are reflections of God, all bodies are the backside of divine glory.

Radicalizing the incarnation, therefore, by using the model of the universe as God's body is neither idolatry nor pantheism: the world, creation, is not identified or confused with God. Yet it is the place where God is present to us. Christianity's most distinctive belief is that divine reality is always mediated through the world, a belief traditionally expressed in the Chalcedonian formula that Christ was "fully God, fully man." For our time when we understand human existence in continuity with all other forms of life and hence must think of our relation to God in an ecological context, that mediation is appropriately radicalized and expanded to include the entire cosmos. In both instances, the Word is made flesh, God is available to us only through the mediation of embodiment. We are offered not the face of God, but the back. God is neither enclosed in nor exhausted by the body shown to us, but it is a body that is given.

It is enough and it is a body. "It is enough" acknowledges that for those who are persuaded to live within this model, it provides guidance and significance to life, a way of being in the world. Those who wager on this construct believe it tells them something about the way things are; in other words, that it gives them intimations of how God and the world are related. That intimation is suggested by the metaphor of body. "It is a body" suggests content, substance, for what it means to live within this particular construct. It places a premium on the physical, the lowly, the mundane, the specific, the vulnerable, the visible, the other, the needy, for all these words describe aspects of bodies of various kinds. No body, no material form, is absolute, eternal, general, abstract, otherworldly, self-sufficient, invincible, or invisible. Bodies in the universe, in all their differences, share some characteristics that suggest a focus, an area of concern, for those who would live within the construct of the body of God. At one level our model—the universe as God's body—moves us in the direction of contemplating the glory and grandeur of divine creation, an aesthetic awe at unending galactic wonders, while at another level it moves us in the direction of compassionate identification with and service to the fragile, suffering, oppressed bodies that surround us. The model embraces both the guts and the glory, both the mud and the mystery—or, more precisely, suggests that the peculiar form of divine glory available to us, if we live within this model, is *only* through the guts, the mud. Incarnationalism, radicalized, means that we do not, ever, at least in this life, see God face to face, but only through the mediation of the bodies we pay attention to, listen to, and learn to love and care for.

We have used Exodus 33: 20-23b as a meditation to help us reflect on some of the most important dimensions of the model of the universe as God's body within a Christian context. In the rest of this chapter and the next, we will analyze the model in more formal terms. First, we will look at five major models within the Christian tradition for understanding the relationship of God and the world: the deistic, the dialogic, the monarchical, the agential, and the organic. We will conclude that combining the organic (the world as the body of God) and the agential (God as the spirit of the body) results in a personal and ecological way of reimagining the tradition's Lord of creation in terms compatible with contemporary science. In the next chapter we will turn to the Christic paradigm as the place where, within that tradition, we gain some guidance on the "shape" of the body, the forms or patterns with which to understand divine immanence. This paradigm suggests a trajectory or direction for creation. It is not one that we find in evolutionary history, but from our wager of faith in the liberating, healing, and inclusive teachings, life, and death of Jesus of Nazareth, we *can* read it back into natural, historical, and cultural evolution as a way to express its goal. We will suggest that the model of the body of God, when seen within a Christic framework, can serve as a unifying metaphor, encompassing in scope both creation and salvation—the liberation, healing, and fulfillment of all bodies. We will also ask in what ways the model of God as spirit of the body is a continuation and a revision of the tradition's understanding of divine transcendence and immanence as expressed in its trinitarian formula.

Major Models of God and the World

The First Vatican Council (1870) expressed a view of the relation of God and the world that is, with some variations, a common one in major creeds of various Christian churches since the Reformation:

"The Holy, Catholic, Apostolic, Roman Church believes and confesses that there is one true and living God, Creator and Lord of Heaven and earth, almighty, eternal, immense, incomprehensible, infinite in intelligence, in will, and in all perfection, who, as being one, sole, absolutely simple and immutable spiritual substance, is to be declared really and essentially distinct from the world, of supreme beatitude in and from himself, and ineffably exalted above all things beside himself which exist or are conceivable."[3]

What drives this statement is the passion to remove God from any real connection with the world—"really and essentially distinct from the world" sums it up. In fact, it is difficult to imagine how a God so described could have a genuine, significant relationship with anything outside the divine reality.[4] And yet the Christian tradition has insisted that God not only created the world but admired it and loved at least its human creatures sufficiently so that when they "fell," God became one of them, suffering and dying to redeem them from their sins. The two images of God—one as the distant, all-powerful, perfect, immutable Lord existing in lonely isolation, and the other as the One who enters human flesh as a baby to eventually assume the alienation and oppression of all peoples in the world—do not fit together. Jesus as the immanent, loving image of God is a surd, an enigma, against the background of the distant, exalted, incomprehensible deity. In its credal statements on God and Jesus the tradition attempts to express this view of radical transcendence and radical immanence: the totally distant, "other" God, exalted and perfect, entered into human flesh in Jesus of Nazareth, so that this one man is fully divine and fully human. In the worldview current in first-century Mediterranean times and operable through the Middle Ages, that way of radicalizing and relating transcendence and immanence had some credibility; but it does not in our time. This view seems neither sufficiently radical (God is transcendent only over our world and especially human beings and immanent only in one human being) nor believable (it assumes a dualistic view of reality with God dwelling somewhere external to and exalted above the world and yet entering it at one particular point).

What other options are there for relating God and the world? The principal criteria guiding our analysis and critique of various options will be the radicalization of divine transcendence and immanence as well as those mentioned earlier (embodied experience, usefulness, and compatibility with Christian faith and the contemporary picture of reality). We will suggest that the model of God the spirit, the giver and renewer of her body, the universe, is one that is compatible with readings of both Christianity and postmodern science. A couple of brief comments about this proposal are necessary before setting it in the context of other traditional and contemporary models. First, it is a personal model of God, assuming that we will inevitably imagine God in our image, but to do so with the notion of spirit rather than self, soul, or mind suggests that divine agency is concerned not only with human beings but with all forms of life: God's spirit is the breath of life in all lifeforms. Second, recalling our discussion of the face and back of God, the model of God as spirit of his body, the universe, implies that both terms, *spirit* and *body*, are backside terms: they are both metaphors. Spirit is not really God, while body is a metaphor, nor is spirit closer to divine reality; rather, they are both forms of God's visible being, ways of expressing immanent transcendence and transcendent immanence suitable for creatures like us who are inspirited bodies. The depth and mystery of God are not available to us in this or any other model: the glory of God is only reflected in the world and then in a dim and distorted mirror. It is this dim, distorted mirror that we attempt to model.

We will have much more to say about our model, but with this sketch in mind let us look briefly at some alternatives in order to place the model within a broader context.[5] First, the deistic model, the simplest and least satisfying one, arose during the sixteenth-century scientific revolution. It imagines God as a clockmaker who winds up the clock of the world by creating its laws and then leaves it to run by itself. The model has the advantage of freeing science to investigate the world apart from divine control but essentially banishes God from the world. It is, sadly, the view of many contemporary scientists as well as Christians, with the qualification that some Christians allow periodic, personal interventions of God in times of crisis such as natural disasters, accidents, and death. The view encourages an irresponsible, idolatrous attitude in the scientific community, allowing it to claim for itself sole rights both to interpret and to dispose of the world. On the part of Christians it encourages an interventionist, God-of-the-gaps view of divine activity.

The second view of God and the world, the dialogic one, has deep roots in both Hebrew and Christian traditions: God speaks and we respond. It has been a central view within Protestantism and was highlighted in twentieth-century existentialism. In its contemporary form the relation between God and the world is narrowed to God and the individual: the I-Thou relation between God and a human being. As seen, for instance, in the writings of Søren Kierkegaard or Rudolf Bultmann, this position focuses on sin, guilt, and forgiveness and has the advantage of allowing for a continuous relationship with God, but does so at the expense of indifference to the natural and social worlds. The dialogic position assumes two tracks, religion versus culture (the latter including scientific knowledge and all social institutions such as government, the economy, the family), with each left to run its own affairs.[6] God and the human being meet, not in the world, whether of nature or culture, but only in the inner, internal joy and pain of human experiences. Liberation theologies have protested the focus on individual (usually white, male, Western, affluent) alienation and despair, insisting that God's relation to the world must include the political and social dimensions as well.

The monarchical model, the relation of God and the world in which the divine, all-powerful king controls his subjects and they in turn offer him loyal obedience, is the oldest and still the most prevalent one.[7] It is both a personal and a political model, correcting the impersonalism of the deistic model and the individualism of the dialogic. It also underscores the "godness" of God, for the monarchical imagery calls forth awe and reverence, as well as vocational meaningfulness, since membership in the kingdom entails service to the divine Lord. But since all power is controlled by the king, issues of human freedom and theodicy are highly problematic. Moreover, and most critical for our concerns, the king is both distant from the natural world and indifferent to it, for as a political model it is limited to human beings.[8] The continuing power of this model in liturgical use is curious, since contemporary members of royalty scarcely call up responses of awe, reverence, and obedience, but its nostalgic appeal, as evidenced in the gusto with which we all sing Christmas carols that are rife with this imagery, cannot be underestimated. Any model that would attempt to criticize or partially subvert it ought to look carefully at the main reason for its attraction: it is the only model that attempts to dramatize divine transcendence. Nonetheless, the model of God as king is domesticated transcendence, for a king rules only over human beings, a minute fraction of created reality. The king/realm model is neither genuinely transcendent (God is king over one species recently arrived on a minor planet in an ordinary galaxy) nor genuinely immanent (God as king is an external superperson, not the source, power, and goal of the entire universe).

A fourth model, the agential, also has strong backing in the Hebrew and Christian traditions. Here God is assumed to be an agent whose intentions and purposes are realized in history, especially human history. It has been revived during this century as a way of talking about divine purpose throughout the entire span of cosmic history.[9] The analogy that is often used in this model to explain divine action in the world is the human self realizing its purposes through its body: God is related to the world and realizes the divine intentions and purposes in the world, in a way similar to how we use our bodies to carry out our purposes.[10] This view of divine action has the advantage of internalizing divine action within cosmic processes; however, since these actions are one with the processes, it is difficult if not impossible to differentiate divine action from evolutionary history. Moreover, since the human being is the prototype for divine action, the human body emerges implicitly as the model for God's body, suggesting anthropomorphism: God is understood as a superperson with a high degree of control over the world in a way similar to our control over the actions of our bodies. Finally, at least in its contemporary form, the model has been advanced largely to satisfy intellectual puzzles: How might we imagine divine action in an internal rather than an external, supernatural fashion? The classic agential model, which is at heart personal (God as father, mother, lord, lover, king, friend), God as actor and doer, creating and redeeming the world, has profound ethical and liturgical dimensions, while the contemporary version does not. But if the model were God as spirit (breath, life) of the body (the world, universe) rather than the mind or self that directs and controls creation, the ethical and liturgical dimensions might reemerge.

The agential model should, I believe, be joined with the fifth and final major model, the organic, for either alone is lacking in light of our criteria but together they suggest a more adequate model. The organic model is the one on which this essay is focused: the world or universe as God's body. However, alone, that is, apart from the agential model, which suggests a center of being not exhausted by or completely identified with the world or universe, the organic model is pantheistic. The world is, becomes, divine. Christian thinking, with its ancient commitment to a transcendent deity who created a world distinct from himself has had, as we have seen, a highly ambivalent relationship to the organic model.

Two recent instances of serious reconsideration of it, both under pressure from the view of reality in postmodern science and both combining agency and organism, are process theology and the work of Teilhard de Chardin. Process thought moves toward a social view of agency (every entity or actual occasion is an agent, including God), while Teilhard suggests a more traditional view of God as the supreme agent guiding the evolutionary process toward more and more complex, unified agents.[11] The process version of organicism emphasizes the interdependence and reciprocity of all agents, with God as one among many, though the preeminent one, while Teilhard's version gives a greater role to divine purpose and direction. These are both exciting, provocative proposals with profound implications for an ecological sensibility. Process ontology, with its insistence on the agency or subjectivity of all entities, provides a basis for the intrinsic value of every created being, living and nonliving. Teilhard's view also underscores the value of each and every aspect of evolutionary reality, although in a more traditional sacramental mode. All things are being transformed through their processes of natural growth toward the divine source and goal of their existence.[12] Both of these variations on the organic model are pan*en*theistic, not pantheistic; in both, divine transcendence and immanence are radicalized, with Teilhard expressing the radicalization mythologically and process theology conceptually. In differing degrees both are credible, persuasive readings of postmodern science and Christianity.

My essay is a continuation and development of these projects at the metaphorical level. While Teilhard certainly did work poetically and mythologically, as I have suggested, his images were rather esoteric (Omega Point, noogenesis), referring to parts of the process of evolutionary teleology. Process theologians, although conceptually oriented, have also suggested some powerful metaphors, notably A. N. Whitehead's notion of God as the Great Companion. They have also revived a limited use for the model of the world as God's body.[13] Both process theology and Teilhard are radical revisionings of the relation of God and the world; however, neither suggests an overall *model* for reimaging that relation.

Spirit and Body

My essay undertakes such a task, although with a profound debt to the organic and agential models of Teilhard and process theology. The agential model preserves transcendence, while the organic model underscores immanence. Alone, the agential model overemphasizes the transcendent power and freedom of God at the expense of the world. Alone, the organic model tends to collapse God and the world, denying the freedom and individuality of both. But if the model were that God is related to the world as spirit is to body, perhaps the values of both the agential and organic models could be preserved.

Two related issues, however, face us immediately. The first is the suitability of *any* personal language for God as being compatible with contemporary science. The second, assuming that we can provide reasons for retaining agential language, is the *kind* of personal imagery that is most appropriate. The dilemma set by these issues is an acute one: the Hebrew and Christian traditions are profoundly and, I would argue, indelibly agential; yet postmodern science, as we have seen, does not appear to permit any purpose or agency apart from local causation. This dilemma has caused some theologians to retreat from personal language for God except in worship.[14] The implication is that personal language does not really refer to God but is necessary for liturgical purposes, while the proper way to speak of God in the context of postmodern science is impersonally. One unfortunate result of this position is a willingness to continue to use traditional metaphors for God such as God as lord and father (since they are "only" liturgical images), without working toward more appropriate ones.

This approach permits, I believe, too strong a control of science over theology. If it can be shown that *all* personal metaphors are incompatible with postmodern science, the case becomes stronger. But since little reconstructive work on such models has been attempted, the images in question are traditional ones, not necessarily all personal ones. I agree that the monarchical, triumphalistic, patriarchal imagery for God is impossible to square with an evolutionary, ecological, cosmological framework. Even some of the more intimate models—God as mother (and father), lover, and friend—need to be balanced by other, less anthropocentric ones.[15] But are all personal models worthless, discordant, incongruous from the perspective of contemporary science? Moreover, if we do discard them all and speak of God only or principally in impersonal terms, can we any longer pretend that we still belong within the Western religious paradigm? Finally, is not the refusal to imagine God in personal terms a gesture in the direction of disembodiment: *we* are embodied agents, and is it not therefore natural and appropriate, as the outermost contemporary evolutionary phylum, to imagine our creator "in our image"?

The major model we are investigating in depth is the combined agential-organic one of the universe (world) as God's body, a body enlivened and empowered by the divine spirit. We have dealt in some detail with the organic aspect of the model, the universe as God's body, but what of the agential or personal aspect, the spirit? To begin framing an answer to this question, we need to start with ourselves as the concrete, embodied beings we are. We are embodied personal agents, and if we are not to be surds or outcasts in the world, we need to imagine God's relationship to the world in a way that includes us, that makes us feel at home. Mechanistic, impersonal models exclude us; personal, organic ones include us. If the history of the universe and especially the evolutionary history of our planet makes it clear that we do, in fact, belong here and that evolution has resulted in self-conscious beings, then does it not make sense to imagine the relationship between God and the world in a manner that is continuous with that evolutionary history, especially if, as we shall suggest, there is a way of modeling personal agency that also touches one of the deepest traditions of Christian thought?

That tradition is of God as spirit—not Holy Ghost, which suggests the unearthly and the disembodied, nor initially the Holy Spirit, which has been focused largely on human beings and especially the followers of Christ, but the spirit of God, the divine wind that "swept over the face of the waters" prior to creation, the life-giving breath given to all creatures, and the dynamic movement that creates, recreates, and transcreates throughout the universe.[16] Spirit, as wind, breath, life is the most basic and most inclusive way to express centered embodiment. All living creatures, not just human ones, depend upon breath. Breath also knits together the life of animals and plants, for they are linked by the exchange of oxygen and carbon dioxide in each breath inhaled and exhaled. Breath is a more immediate and radically dependent way to speak of life than even food or water, for we literally live from breath to breath and can survive only a few minutes without breathing. Our lives are enclosed by two breaths—our first when we emerge from our mother's womb and our last when we "give up the ghost" (spirit).

Spirit is a wide-ranging, multidimensional term with many meanings built upon its physical base as the breath of life. We speak of a person's spirit, their vigor, courage, or strength; of team spirit, the collective energy of people at play; of the spirit of '76 or the spirit of Tienanmen Square, the vitality, grit, and resolution of a people banding together in a common cause to oppose oppression; of a spirited horse or the spirit of a sacred grove—animals, trees, and mountains can also have spirit.[17] All these connotations are possible because of the primary meaning of spirit as the breath of life: "Then the Lord God formed man [sic] from the dust of the ground and breathed into his nostrils the breath of life" (Gen. 2:7). Bracketing the sexism of the Genesis 2 creation story, it nonetheless suggests the prime analogy of this essay: the dust of the universe enlivened by the breath of God. Each of us, and each and every other part of the body as well, owes our existence, breath by breath as we inhale and exhale, to God. We "live and move and have our being" in God (Acts 17:28). Indeed we do. That is, perhaps, the most basic confession that can be made: I owe my existence at its most fundamental level—the gift of my next breath—to God. God is my creator and recreator, the One who gives and renews my life, moment by moment, at its most basic, physical level. And so does everything else in creation also live, moment by moment, by the breath of God, says our model.

We are suggesting, then, that we think of God metaphorically as the spirit that is the breath, the life, of the universe, a universe that comes from God and could be seen as the body of God. Both of these terms, *spirit* and *body*, are metaphors: both refer properly to ourselves and other creatures and entities in our experience of the world. Neither describes God, for both are *back*, not *face*, terms. Nonetheless, even with these qualifications, questions abound. Let us look at a few of them. Why choose *spirit* rather than other personal, agential terms such as *self*, *mind*, *heart*, *will*, *soul*, and the like? Does spirit language for God make sense in terms of postmodern science and the Christian tradition? Does contemporary science substantiate such language, or does it accommodate or allow it? Can Christians use the model of God as embodied spirit, and, more pointedly, in a transcendent sky-God tradition, is it pantheistic? Does it collapse God and the world?

One reason for suggesting spirit as the way to speak of divine agency is that it undercuts anthropocentrism and promotes cosmocentrism. Only a human being has a mind or self, whereas spirit, while able to include mind and self, has a much broader range. Most attempts to use the body metaphor in regard to God rely on the analogy of mind/body: God relates to the world as the mind (self) relates to the body. Not only does this form of the analogy involve difficult, often dualistic, arguments concerning the mind/body correlation, but, just as important for our considerations, it implies that divine activity in relation to the world is primarily intellectual and controlling: God is Mind or Will.[18] This is an old, deep tradition in the Hebrew and Christian traditions as manifest in Wisdom and Logos theologies: God creates the universe as its orderer, as the One who gives it direction, limits, and purpose. The emphasis is on the work of the mind, the work of intelligence and control. It is precisely this concern that surfaces in the ancient enterprise of natural theology: the need to answer the questions of why and how. But a spirit theology suggests another possibility: that God is not primarily the orderer and controller of the universe but its source and empowerment, the breath that enlivens and energizes it. The spirit perspective takes seriously the fecundity, diversity, range, and complexity of life and of life-supporting systems. It does not claim that the divine mind is the cause of what evolutionary theory tells us can have only local causes; rather, it suggests that we think of these local causes as enlivened and empowered by the breath of God. A spirit theology focuses attention not on how and why creation occurred either in the beginning or over the evolutionary aeons of time, but on the rich variety of living forms that have been and are *now* present on our planet. The breath of God enlivening each and every entity in the body of the universe turns our attention to a theology of nature, a theology concerned with the relationship of God and our living, breathing planet. The principal reason, then, for preferring spirit to alternative possibilities is that it underscores the connection between God and the world as not primarily the Mind that orders, controls, and directs the universe, but as the Breath that is the source of its life and vitality. The connection is one of *relationship* at the deepest possible level, the level of life, rather than *control* at the level of ordering and directing nature. And since, as we recall, our tendency is not only to model God in our image but to model ourselves on the models with which we imagine God, the metaphor of breath rather than mind might help us to support, rather than control, life in all its forms. Thus, in a spirit theology, we might see ourselves as united with all other living creatures through the breath that moves through all parts of the body, rather than as the demilords who order and control nature.

But is this model commensurate with twentieth-century science? If one understands the spirit of God as the source of the dynamic vitality of the universe and especially as the breath of all life-forms, then our focus is not on the purpose or direction of divine activity but on our dependence on God as the present and continuing creator. Our concern is not primarily intellectual but aesthetic and ethical: wonder and awe at the immensity, richness, and diversity of creation as well as gratitude and care for all its forms of life. Our response to this model is as grateful recipients of life rather than puzzlers over its mysteries. Contemporary science does not mandate or even imply such a model, but it is commensurate with an organic interpretation of its story. Since we and all other creatures and entities are in some sense inspirited bodies (even trees and oceans move with the winds), then if we were to think of God as in some sense continuous with this evolutionary history, one way to do so would be as the spirit of the entire body of the universe. This is not, of course, a scientific description nor is it a theological one; rather, it is a way of thinking about God and the world that makes sense in terms of postmodern science. It allows us to understand ourselves who have evolved into spiritual, embodied creatures as neither freaks nor surds in our world. It also allows us to think of God as the source of our being, the source of all being, not as the one who intervenes from the outside to initiate creation, patch it up, or direct it, but as the one who supplies us with the breath for all the incredible rich, teeming fecundity and variety of life.

It is a model of God and the world that focuses on "the wonderful life" that has emerged from evolutionary history, rather than on the divine ordering of the process. It does not attempt to enter into scientific discussions on the how and why of that history, but suggests that if one is *already* a person of faith (which cannot be arrived at or substantiated by postmodern science), then the picture of reality as an organic whole, a body, dependent on and sustained by the spirit of God, is one that fits with, is appropriate to, evolutionary history. This theology of nature is not a natural theology: it does not say that the scientific story gives evidence (even the tiniest bit) for belief in this or any other model of God and the world. All it says is that this way of conceiving of God and the world makes more sense in terms of the scientific picture than alternatives such as the deistic, dialogic, and monarchical models.

But this is enough. A theology of nature does not ask for scientific proof, only for a picture to help us think and act holistically about God, ourselves, and our world.

Where does this model stand in regard to the Christian tradition? We can answer that question on one level simply and forthrightly by recalling the theme of the 1991 World Council of Churches assembly in Canberra, Australia: "Come, Holy Spirit— Renew the Whole Creation," or the affirmation from the Nicene[19] Creed: "I believe in the Holy Spirit, the Lord and Giver of Life." While the spirit of God, now the Holy Spirit, has often played a lackluster role in relation to the Father and the Son in Christian trinitarian thought, its credentials in both the Hebrew Scriptures and in the New Testament are more than solid.[20] The motif that runs throughout is the spirit as the source of life and the renewer of life: a theology of the spirit focuses on God as the creator and redeemer of life. The trajectory begins with the spirit of God hovering over the waters of chaos and breathing life into living beings; the spirit renews creation in the gift of baptism, the second birth; and fulfills it in the eschatological vision of all creation in harmonious union. One of the great assets of the model is precisely its amorphous character in contrast to the highly human, personal, and androcentric nature of Father and Son: spirit is not necessarily human, personal (though it is relational), or male. In fact, it often has been designated female; but it may be best that, for once in Christian reflection, we let God be "it."[21] "It" (the divine spirit) roams where it will, not focused on the like-minded (the fathers and the sons—or even the mothers and daughters), but permeating, suffusing, and energizing the innermost being of each and every entity in creation in ways unknown and unknowable in our human, personal categories.[22]

The joining of the spirit that gives life to every creature with the Holy Spirit that renews all creation suggests a connection between Christian theology and the two forms of evolution— biological and biocultural. Creation, the gift of the spirit, could be seen as the action of God in the aeons of evolutionary development, which has resulted in the wonderful life we see about us as well as in ourselves. (This is a retrospective reading of creation in evolutionary terms.) In the model of the universe as God's body, divine incarnation is not limited to redemption but is everywhere evident in the bodies that live through the breath of the spirit. Within this model of the universe as God's body, God's presence and action are evident as the breath of life that gives all bodies, all forms of matter, the energy or power to become themselves. This understanding of divine action in light of evolutionary development focuses on *empowerment*, not direction. It does not claim that God is guiding the process in general or in particular; rather, it suggests that *all* life, regardless of which individuals or species prosper, is dependent upon God. God's creative action is not intermittent or occasional; on the contrary, it is continuous and universal, for without the sustaining breath of God, all the wonderful life, including our own, would fade and die. The "purpose" of creation from this perspective, however, is not human beings (or any other species), but the fecundity, richness, and diversity of *all* that is bodied forth from God and sustained in life by the breath of God. Needless to say, creation in this picture involves enormous waste, suffering, and death for all kinds of bodies—to suggest anything less or different is sentimental and false to the contemporary scientific picture of reality.

In Christian theology, however, the spirit of God is also the Holy Spirit, the spirit shaped and made known in the Hebrew Scriptures as well as in the life, teachings, and death of Jesus of Nazareth and the community that formed around him. Moreover, evolution is not only biological; with self-conscious creatures it enters a historical, cultural phase. At this point divine purpose can be spoken of within the evolutionary process in a new and special way. It is not only empowerment of but also a *direction* for all that teeming life, a direction expressed by Christians in the stories, images, and ideas of the Hebrew people, its paradigmatic founder Jesus, and all the lives and understandings of disciples over the centuries. The guide for interpreting that direction is called the Holy Spirit, and it works *through* human beings: we become the mind and heart as well as the hands and feet of the body of God on our planet. Christians claim that God has been in the natural process as its creator and sustainer (the spirit of the body) since the beginning, but now that process has been given a particular direction (a "new creation") characterized by inclusive love, especially for the vulnerable and oppressed. For Christians, the spirit has been qualified or given shape and scope by the Holy Spirit and is a direction or purpose for life that depends on our cooperation as God's partners.

Hence, we can say that God's action as the spirit of the body is twofold. The spirit is the source of life, the breath of creation; at the same time, the Holy Spirit is the source of the renewal of life, the direction or purpose for all the bodies of the world—a goal characterized by inclusive love.

One central issue remains in regard to our model of God as the spirit of life bodied forth in the universe: Is it pantheistic? This is a complex issue in Christian theology with intricate historical dimensions we cannot settle here. Nonetheless, the criteria for models of God and the world operative in this essay— commensurability with postmodern science as well as our own embodied experience and the well-being of our planet—cause us to lean toward an interpretation of Christian faith that accommodates this model. Since the model is commensurate with contemporary science, mirrors our own experience as embodied spirits, and connects us at the basic level of life-giving breath with all other life-forms on our planet, we are encouraged to look to those traditions within Christianity that emphasize the spirit in similar ways. These traditions can be characterized as neither theist nor pantheist, but pan*en*theist: "God is not exhausted by finite beings, not even all finite beings, yet God is *in* all finite creatures and apart from God there is nothing; nor is God 'apart' from anything."[23] This description of a panentheistic view of the relation of God and the world is compatible with our model of God as the spirit that is the source, the life, the breath of all reality. Everything that is is *in* God and God is *in* all things and yet God is not identical with the universe, for the universe is dependent on God in a way that God is not dependent on the universe. We joined the agential and organic models in order to express the asymmetrical and yet profoundly interrelational character of the panentheistic model of God and the world: while we, as members of the body, are radically dependent upon the life-giving breath from the spirit, God, as the spirit, is not so dependent upon the universe. Pantheism says that God is embodied, necessarily and totally; traditional theism claims that God is disembodied, necessarily and totally; panentheism suggests that God is embodied but not necessarily or totally. Rather, God is sacramentally embodied: God is mediated, expressed, in and through embodiment, but not necessarily or totally. It is, as we recall, the back and not the face of God that we are allowed to see.

Panentheism is, I would suggest, a strong motif in both Hebrew and Christian traditions that take seriously the mediation of God to the world.[24] These traditions deny, on the one hand, a picture of God as an external superperson (or Unmoved Mover) distant from and alien to the world and, on the other hand, a view of God as immediately available to the mind of human beings or as identified with natural processes. Rather, the panentheistic tradition is found in all those passages in the Hebrew Scriptures that mediate the divine presence through human words and acts as well as natural phenomena and in the New Testament in its central declaration that "the Word was made flesh" in Jesus of Nazareth. In all these instances, mediation and incarnation are central and, therefore, are open to, or ought to be open to, the embodiment of God, especially in its panentheistic form of the world (universe) as God's body and God as its spirit.

To sum up: we have suggested that God as the embodied spirit of the universe is a personal/organic model that is compatible with interpretations of both Christian faith and contemporary science, although not demanded by either. It is a way of speaking of God's relation to all matter, all creation, that "makes sense" in terms of an incarnational understanding of Christianity and an organic interpretation of postmodern science. It helps us to be *whole* people within our faith and within our contemporary world. Moreover, the model does not reduce God to the world nor relegate God to another world; on the contrary, it radicalizes both divine immanence (God is the breath of each and every creature) and divine transcendence (God is the energy empowering the entire universe). Finally, it underscores our bodiliness, our concrete physical existence and experience that we share with all other creatures: it is a model on the side of the well-being of the planet, for it raises the issue of ethical regard toward *all* bodies as all are interrelated and interdependent.

Creation:
Production, Procreation, or
Procreation-Emanation?

The Genesis creation story, however, does not suggest that the world is God's body; rather, the world and its creatures are products of God the Maker, the Craftsman, the Architect, the Sculptor. Whether one looks at Genesis 1 or 2, at the sweeping narrative of how God called into being the heavens and the earth, the seas and their teeming creatures, the land and its many animals and plants or at the more homey, domestic story of the molding of Adam and the other animals from the earth (and Eve from Adam's rib), the mode of creation is by word or by hand. In the first story, through the word ("Let there be . . . ") God creates an aesthetic panorama ("it was very good"); in the second, God sculpts forms from "the dust of the ground." Creation is production and as such it is external to God; it is also totally dependent on God for its existence. Many Hebrew Scripture scholars seem united in the opinion, however, that it is not the externality, the production aspect of the Genesis account, that is critical, but the dependence of all forms of existence on God the creator.[25] If dependence, rather than externality, is the critical feature of the tradition's creation sensibility, then we might consider options other than the production model, which has several problems.[26]

The production model emphasizes the beginnings of creation rather than its continuing, ongoing character; it can speak of divine transcendence only in an external way, making it difficult to affirm the immanence of God; and it is intellectual or aesthetic, implying a dualistic hierarchy of mind and body. A procreation model of creation, on the other hand, says, simply, that the world comes from, is formed from, God rather than out of "nothing" or out of some material other than God. Lest the reader immediately recoil in horror at the thought of the universe as bodying forth from God, let us briefly consider the alternatives. "Out of nothing" (*ex nihilo*) is not in Genesis or even in the Bible (except for a cryptic mention in the book of Maccabees). Rather, it is an invention of the early church fathers to underscore the transcendence of God. But, we might ask, does it also allow for divine immanence, as an adequate model of God and the world should? "Out of some material other than God" suggests that there is another creator, the one who made *this* material, thus undercutting radical dependence of all of reality on God. "Out of God" claims that whatever *is* is in and from God, but it does not say that God is identified with or reduced to what is bodied forth. It claims that we live and move and have our being in God, but not vice versa. A metaphor to express this source of all life is not the Architect who constructs a world, but the Mother who encloses reality in her womb, bodying it forth, generating all life from her being.[27]

Before continuing, let us recall once again that we are dealing with models, not descriptions. Models are to be judged not by whether they correspond with God's being (the face is not available to us), but by whether they are relatively adequate (in other words, more adequate than alternative models) from the perspective of postmodern science, an interpretation of Christian faith, our own embodied experience, and the well-being of our planet and all its life-forms. We *only* have models, and the Genesis story of the external Maker who produces an artifact is not, simply because of its age and status in the tradition, anything other than a model. What we must ask of all models is their relative adequacy on the basis of some agreed-upon criteria. I am suggesting that in light of the criteria operative in this essay, some version of the procreation model of creation is preferable to production models.

To make this suggestion more concrete, let us look at how the procreation model deals with the problems raised by the production model. On the issue of the beginnings of creation versus its continuation, a procreation (organic, growth) model has potential for expressing the ongoing character of creation in ways a production model does not. In the production model, creation is complete, finished, static; what is crafted is seen as an artifact that may be pleasing or beautiful, but it does not change. A procreation model, however, sees creation as emerging from God, as a body (in the case of the evolving universe, billions of bodies) that grows and changes. But our model, we recall, is not only or merely organic; it is also agential. Hence, it combines the procreation model with another in the tradition, the emanationist, in which the life-giving energy of creation emanates from its divine source.[28] The model, therefore, is not a pure procreation one in which the world is seen as God's child (reproduction) rather than as God's construction (production), but is a combination of the procreative and emanationist models: God bodies forth the universe, which is enlivened and empowered by its source. God is not the parent of the child, but the life of the body; our model does not highlight biological generation, but the dependence of all life on God. It borrows from the procreative model its physicality and from the emanationist model its continuing and profound connection with its source of life. Children grow up, move away, and can sever connections with those who gave them life, so the procreation model, while expressing powerfully the bodily base of creation, cannot capture its continuing dependence.[29] An emanationist model not only insists that all life derives from God, but that it continues to do so; thus, the dynamic, changing, evolving body that is all reality does not grow away from God, but in, through, and toward God.

Emanationist models of creation have a dialectical character: creation comes from God, attains partial separation, and returns to its source. Theologies influenced by these models, however, have often been idealistic, that is, centered in the mind, not the body, seeing the second phase, the partial separation, as a "fall" or a lesser state from the first or the third.[30] But if the emanationist model is combined with the procreative or the organic, this tendency is undercut, for the second phase is nothing less than God's *own* embodiment. It is not a lesser stage but, in fact, the only one we can know anything about. It is the back of God and wonderful beyond all imagining: it is the universe. Hence, we suggest that a procreative-emanationist model of divine creation is commensurate with the continuing creation of postmodern science, its story of the evolving history of the universe. It is a model rich in suggestive power for expressing the profound dependence of all things on God, their basic bodily reality, and their changing, growing character.

The model is also helpful when we turn to the issue of divine immanence as well as transcendence in relation to the world. The production model of the tradition has been heavily invested in protecting the transcendence of God, but has often done so by stressing divine control. In other words, transcendence was equated with so ereignty: it meant dominion over.[31] The result is to separate God and the world; God becomes the external Lord over the world. The monarchical and deistic models of God and the world both rely on this view of transcendence, and it has been one of the most problematic legacies of the Hebrew and Christian traditions in innumerable ways. Moreover, it does not help promote an ecological sensibility.

Divine transcendence need not mean God's external sovereignty over the world. A procreative-emanationist model of creation focuses our attention on a transcendent immanence, or an immanental transcendence. That is, it keeps our eyes on what we can see and touch and know: the universe as God's body with God's spirit as its enlivening breath is the place that we turn to learn of *both* divine transcendence and immanence. While transcendence can mean "to exist apart from the material universe," it can also mean "surpassing, excelling or extraordinary."[32] In the model of the universe as God's body, we look for divine transcendence not apart from the material universe, but in those aspects of the material universe that are "surpassing, excelling or extraordinary." This suggests that the universe could be a way to meditate on divine transcendence in a concrete, embodied way. In the model of the universe as God's body, we are invited to see the extraordinary in the ordinary, to see the surpassing wonder of divine transcendence in the smallest and largest dimensions of the history and present reality of the universe, especially our planet. Whereas in many models of divine transcendence, we must ink in either concrete but shallow terms (the domesticated transcendence of the political models—God as king, lord, master over human gs) or radical but abstract terms (God as omnipotent, omniscient, al, infinite, and so on), in our model we can think concretely *and* lly. We are asked to contemplate the visible universe, God's s the place where the surpassing, extraordinary character of resence is to be found. The universe in its age, size, complexsity, history, and beauty is the locus for our imagination to power in regard to what divine transcendence could, n. It serves as a deep reflecting pool of divine magnifiandeur. To contemplate what we know of the universe, ordinary ordinariness of a butterfly's wing to the ordiariness of the Milky Way, is beyond all our capacities the longer we reflect on either of these phenomena, ith wonder we become. This mode of appreciating nce, the concrete, radical way, is what I have characterized as the mediating, incarnational way of the Hebrew and Christian traditions. Psalm 104 is an excellent example: "O Lord my God, you are very great. You are clothed with honor and majesty, wrapped in light as with a garment. You stretch out the heavens like a tent, you set the beams of your chambers on the waters, you make the clouds your chariot, you ride on the wings of the wind, you make the winds your messengers, fire and flame your ministers" (1-4). One looks to the *world* to discover the glory of God, for as Gerard Manley Hopkins put it, "The world is charged with the grandeur of God."[33] Only now, the world is the universe: the common creation story has given us a more magnificent, more awesome, way to speak of that grandeur. In this concrete picture we have a more radical metaphor of divine transcendence than either the domesticated or abstract models of transcendence can give us. The universe as God's body gives us a concrete way of meditating on divine transcendence; a meditation that knows no end, for we can never imagine such transcendence to its finish or limits. It will, the longer we contemplate its wonders, whether at the microscopic or the macroscopic levels (as well as the middle level of cows, pine cones, and caterpillars), call forth more and more depths to the meaning of divine transcendence.

To contemplate divine transcendence as radically and concretely embodied means, of course, that it is not one thing: divine transcendence, in this model, would be *in* the differences, in the concrete embodiments, that constitute the universe. It is not the oneness or unity that causes us to marvel at creation, but the age, size, diversity, complexity that the common creation story tells us about. If God in the procreative-emanationist model is not primarily the initiator of creation (the simplicity of the big bang), but the empowering, continuing breath of life throughout its billions of years of history and in each and every entity and life-form on every star and planet, then it is in the *differences* that we see the glory of God. God is many, not one, for the body of God is not one body (except as *a* universe), but the infinite number of bodies, some living and some not, that are the universe. To know God in this model is to contemplate, reflect on, the multitude of bodies in all their diversity that mediate, incarnate, the divine. Once again, there is no way to God except by way of the back. Or to put it in more traditional terms, there is no way to divine transcendence except immanently.

Finally, the procreative-emanationist model does not support a dualistic hierarchy of mind and body as does the production model. The latter depends upon an intellectual/aesthetic context: creation is of the mind, not the body. The production model obviously fits masculine and the procreation model feminine gender construction: " 'higher,' metaphysical or spiritual or *ex nihilo* creation and 'lower' or 'lesser' physical, natural or elemental creation."[34] In the first model, creation derives from a source that is itself disembodied (but presumably mental and agential), while in the second, creation is born of a physical source (but perhaps only physical). The procreative-emanationist model suggests that creation is from a physical source (it is God's body), but also from the life-giving center of the divine body (the spirit of God). This model is not dualistically hierarchical: there is no mind directing the body, but rather a body suffused with the breath and power of life. It also does not privilege the intellect over the body nor reduce creation to physicality alone. The model refuses the stereotypes of masculine versus feminine creation, one from the mind, the other from the body, claiming that neither alone is adequate even to our own human, creative experience, let alone as a metaphor of divine creation. What we see in evolutionary history is neither extreme, but a continuum of matter that gradually over billions of years becomes brain (mind) in varying ways and degrees. We have suggested that spirit is a way of expressing the enormous range of this development, at least from the inchoate gropings of an amoeba to the reflective self-consciousness of a human being (the term, of course, does less well with quarks and with God).

To review and summarize: we began this chapter with a meditation from Exodus 33: "And you shall see my back; but my face shall not be seen." The motifs in this passage have been central to our reflections on a model for expressing the God-world relationship in our time. This organic-agential, procreative-emanationist, body-spirit model underscores creation as the continuing, dynamic, growing embodiment of God, a body given life and power for the evolution of billions of diverse entities and creatures. This body is but the backside of God, not the face; it is the visible, mediated form of God, one that we are invited to contemplate for intimations of divine transcendence. It is a concrete, radical, immanental embodiment of God's glory, magnificence, and power. We see this transcendent immanence, this immanental transcendence, in the intricate veins of a maple leaf supplied with the water of life, in the pictures from space of our blue-green marble of a planet, and in the eyes of a hungry child.

"And in the eyes of a hungry child": the model presses us not only to marvel at the wonders of the diverse, complex universe and especially our planet, but also to identify with—and suffer with—bodies in pain. If God is physical, if the universe is God's body, then the beauty and the vulnerability of bodies, the aesthetic and the ethical, unite. And it is this issue to which we turn in the next chapter. We will suggest that the paradigmatic Jesus of Nazareth in his identification with the oppressed—and the extension of this identification in the "cosmic" Christ—is one tradition's way of making creation as the body of God even more concrete and more radical than suggested so far. For this tradition (and others as well) will suggest what certainly cannot be read off or even imagined from the story of evolution or even from the model of the world as God's body: the goal or purpose of creation is love.

As we conclude this chapter, we must remind ourselves once again that we are dealing with models, not descriptions, and also that all models have limitations, including, of course, the one we have put forward. The organic-agential model, the world as the body of God, God as the spirit of the body, has several limitations: it focuses attention on bodily existence and needs; it pertains most appropriately to living creatures (and only by somewhat far-fetched, anthropomorphic analogies to other entities—certainly stars and rocks but also lichen and viruses, not to mention atoms and quarks); it says little about the point of all this breath and breathing—all the life that the spirit empowers. The question, however, is this: Does such a model help us to see some things we need to pay attention to both as Christians and as people of the twenty-first century? For instance, does the model of the world as God's body deepen the insight of the common creation story in a way that helps Christians to remythologize the relation of God and the world for our time? Does it help us to see what the immanence and transcendence of God might mean in an ecological context? Does it also help us to see all other bodies on our planet as incarnations of God, each one both beautiful and vulnerable? If this theology—this way of speaking of God and the world—does deepen the ecological context, then, we ask next: How does the Christic paradigm further deepen—as well as radicalize—the context within which we understand our place in the scheme of things?

As Christ teaches us we pray:

Eternal Spirit,
Earth-maker, Pain-bearer, Life-giver,
Source of all that is and that shall be,
Father and Mother of us all,
Loving God, in whom is heaven:
The hallowing of your name echo through the universe!
The way of your justice be followed by the peoples of the
*   earth!*
Your heavenly will be done by all created beings!
Your commonwealth of peace and freedom sustain our hope
*   and come on earth.*
*   With the bread we need for today, feed us.*
In the hurts we absorb from one another, forgive us.
In times of temptation and test, strengthen us.
From trials too great to endure, spare us.
From the grip of all that is evil, free us.
For you reign in the glory of the power that is love, now
*   and for ever.*
*   Amen.*

—From the New Zealand/Maori Anglican liturgy

6 / CHRISTOLOGY

The Body of God

"*A*nd the Word became flesh and lived among us" (John 1:14a). The scandal of uniqueness is absolutized by Christianity into one of its central doctrines, which claims that God is embodied in one place and one place only: in the man Jesus of Nazareth. He and he alone is "the image of the invisible God" (Col. 1:15). The source, power, and goal of the universe is known through and only through a first-century Mediterranean carpenter. The creator and redeemer of the fifteen-billion-year history of the universe with its hundred billion galaxies (and their billions of stars and planets) is available only in a thirty-year span of one human being's life on planet earth. The claim, when put in the context of contemporary science, seems skewed, to say the least. When the world consisted of the Roman Empire (with "barbarians" at its frontiers), the limitation of divine presence to Jesus of Nazareth had some plausibility while still being ethnocentric; but for many hundreds of years, well before contemporary cosmology, the claims of other major religious traditions have seriously challenged it. In its traditional form the claim is not only offensive to the integrity and value of other religions, but incredible, indeed, absurd, in light of postmodern cosmology. It is not remotely compatible with our current picture of the universe.

But the scandal of uniqueness is perhaps not the central claim of Christian faith. In the model of the universe as God's body, the important motifs are "became flesh" and "lived among us." It is the statement of faith that God is embodied and embodied paradigmatically as one of us, a human being, that is critical. It is not the exclusive claim that matters, for one would assume that the source, power, and goal of the universe, its life and breath, its enlivening energy, would be embodied in many forms through its vast reaches. Rather, it is both the concrete, physical availability of God's presence ("became flesh") and the likeness to ourselves, a human being ("lived among us") that matter.

In this chapter, we will suggest that the model of the world (universe) as God's body might, for Christians, be understood in "shape" and "scope" through the Christic paradigm. That is, from the story of Jesus of Nazareth and his followers we can gain some sense of the forms or patterns with which Christians might understand divine immanence. That story, both in its beginnings and its history, suggests a shape to the body; needless to say, other religious traditions would propose very different shapes, and even within Christianity, many variations exist. The shape suggested is obviously a construction, not a description, and is persuasive only in light of a range of criteria. This shape provides a purpose or goal for creation—something we could not find in evolutionary history. From the paradigmatic story of Jesus we will propose that the direction of creation is toward inclusive love for all, especially the oppressed, the outcast, the vulnerable. This paradigm suggests a trajectory for creation, one that we cannot read off evolutionary history but, from our wager of faith in the destabilizing, nonhierarchical, inclusive life, teachings, and death of Jesus of Nazareth, we can read back into natural, historical, and cultural evolution as its goal. Such a sweeping assertion will have to be carefully examined and qualified so as to limit it to the modest, metaphorical statement it is meant to be.

In addition to a shape to the body of God, we can also speak of its scope from a Christian perspective. What is the range of God's inclusive love? It is for *all* of creation and especially for the oppressed, needy creatures. Within a Christic framework, the body of God encompasses all of creation in a particular salvific direction, toward the liberation, healing, and fulfillment of all bodies. Thus, we can speak of the "cosmic" Christ, a metaphor for the scope of the body of God within a Christian framework. This scope or range is a retrospective perspective: from the standpoint of faith in the presence of God in the paradigmatic story of Jesus, though by no means only here, we wager the hope that the inclusive love of God is unlimited. Needless to say, such an assertion raises issues of evil and theodicy, issues that, in light of the workings of natural selection in evolution, are painful to contemplate and seemingly impossible to deal with satisfactorily. As Ivan in *The Brothers Karamazov* rightly claims, one innocent dead infant makes a compelling case against God.

In this chapter, then, we deepen, make more concrete, and in an important sense counter, what the common creation story tells us and even what the model of the world as God's body suggests. For the shape and scope of God's body as well as the significance of the common creation story is, for Christians, revealed in the Christic paradigm to be love. Neither the radical interrelatedness and interdependence of the common creation story nor the inspirited organicism of the world as God's body can tell us that liberating, healing, and inclusive love is the meaning of it all. But that is how Christians read the story of Jesus.

Finally, to conclude the present as well as the previous chapter, we will bring together the various aspects of our analysis of the model of God as spirit of the body, the universe, by viewing the model in light of the tradition's trinitarianism. While trinitarian reflection has had a number of purposes in Christian history, its greatest asset has probably been its value as a way to imagine divine transcendence and immanence in a unified manner. As suggested earlier, the Christian tradition has had great difficulty with this issue, often projecting a transcendent sky-God who becomes immanent only at the point of Jesus of Nazareth. This transcendent God is available to other human beings principally through the work of the spirit of Christ, that is, by means of the sacraments and the reading of Scripture. The rest of creation is more or less neglected in this view linking divine transcendence and immanence. We will suggest a different picture, one that agrees with the tradition that transcendence is available to us only immanently, only through the mundane, the physical, the bodily—but a body that is not limited to Jesus of Nazareth. It is a kind of trinitarian reflection that emphasizes both the mystery of God (the face or "first person") and the visible physicality of God (the body or "second person"), both the radical transcendence and the radical immanence of God. The mystery and the mud, the invisible and the visible, are mediated by the spirit ("third person"), the dynamic life and breath that moves in all things. Once again, the Christic paradigm will give a particular shape to this reflection: immanence does not mean simply overcoming the spatial distance of transcendence but the radicality of love for the vulnerable and the oppressed, the embodied God identifying with all suffering bodies.

The Shape of the Body:
The Christic Paradigm

In this and the following sections on the shape and scope of the body, we will be suggesting two interrelated moves in regard to christology: the first is to relativize the incarnation in relation to Jesus of Nazareth and the second is to maximize it in relation to the cosmos. In other words, the proposal is to consider Jesus as paradigmatic of what we find everywhere: everything that is is the sacrament of God (the universe as God's body), but here and there we find that presence erupting in special ways. Jesus is one such place for Christians, but there are other paradigmatic persons and events—and the natural world, in a way different from the self-conscious openness to God that persons display, is also a marvelous sacrament in its diversity and richness.

But if knowing and doing are embodied, are concrete and particular, as we have assumed throughout this essay, then we must begin with the story of Jesus, not with everything that is. We stand within particular historical, cultural communities and see the world through those perspectives. We gain our hints and clues, our metaphors of reality, through formative traditions that we also are called upon to re-form. Our first step, then, is to read the central story of Christian faith from the perspective of the organic model. The Christic paradigm must precede the cosmic Christ; the hints and clues for an embodied theology should arise from the particular, concrete insights and continuities of the tradition's basic story. This in no way privileges Scripture as the first or last word, but only as the touchstone text that Christians return to as a resource (not *the* source) for helping them to construct for their own time the distinctiveness of their way of being in the world.[1]

Christianity's Distinctive Embodiment: Inclusion of the Neglected Oppressed

The point at issue is *distinctive embodiment*; that is, what does, could, Christian faith have to say that is special, important, different, illuminating about embodiment—in relation to God, to ourselves, and to the natural world? Religious traditions will say many and different things about embodiment, and, as scholars have reminded us, Eastern, Goddess, and Native traditions, to mention a few, may say more and better things than does the Christian tradition. The question, however, for those of us who choose to remain Christian is, What does, can, the Christian faith contribute to an embodied theology, to an ecological sensibility? Our tradition and its theologians are not called upon to say the whole thing or the one thing; that presumption is a holdover from universalism and essentialism, which refuse to acknowledge the limitations of physical, cultural, historical—as well as religious—embodiment. Christianity is but one attempt, from a particular, concrete location, to speak of the unspeakable—reality. Its constructions are limited and partial, as are all constructions; nevertheless, they can and should be offered to the planetary agenda of our day as a voice in the conversation, a piece in the quilt. Like all other contributions, they will be judged by a variety of criteria, including their compatibility with the current view of reality from postmodern science, their fit with one's embodied (physical, cultural, historical) experience, and the value of the insights for planetary well-being.

What does Christian faith, and especially the story of Jesus, have to offer in terms of a distinctive perspective on embodiment? What is the shape that it suggests for God's body, the universe, enlivened by the breath of God's spirit? Christianity is *par excellence* the religion of the incarnation and, in one sense, is about nothing but embodiment, as is evident in its major doctrines. In another sense, as we noted earlier, Christianity has denied, subjugated, and at times despised the body, especially female human bodies and bodies in the natural world. This is not the place for a treatise on the sorry history of Christianity's treatment of bodies or even on the rich complexities of various incarnational theologies such as those of Paul, John, Irenaeus, certain medieval mystics, and so on. I want to make a more simple, direct proposal: *The story of Jesus suggests that the shape of God's body includes all, especially the needy and outcast.*[2] While there are many distinctive features of the Christian notion of embodiment, in an ecological age when the development of our sensibility concerning the vulnerability and destruction of nonhuman creatures and the natural environment is critical, we ought to focus on one: the inclusion of the neglected oppressed— the planet itself and its many different creatures, including outcast human ones. The distinctive characteristic of Christian embodiment is its focus on oppressed, vulnerable, suffering *bodies*, those who are in pain due to the indifference or greed of the more powerful. In an ecological age, this ought to include oppressed nonhuman animals and the earth itself.

We need to pause and consider this suggestion, for it is shocking by conventional human standards. Until recently, most people found the notion that the earth is vulnerable, that its many species as well as the ecosystems supporting life are victims, are oppressed, absurd. And many still do. Many will even deny that the destabilizing love that we see in Jesus' parables, which overturns the conventional dualisms of rich and poor, righteous and sinner, Jew and Gentile, should include the dualism of humans over nature. And yet a cosmological or ecological perspective demands this radicalization of divine love: God's love is unlimited and oriented especially toward the oppressed—whoever the oppressed turn out to be at a particular time. The definition of who falls into this group has changed over the centuries, most recently focusing not on the spiritually poor, but the physically poor, those oppressed through the deprivation of bodily needs or through discrimination because of skin color or gender. Thus, the liberation theologies based on oppression due to poverty, race, or gender (and their interconnections) have arisen to claim that the gospel of Jesus of Nazareth has a preferential option for the poor, the poor in body, those whose bodies and bodily needs are not included in the conventional hierarchy of value. These are bodies that are devalued, discarded, and destroyed; these are bodies that can claim no intrinsic value in themselves but are of worth only because they are useful to others. In the organic model, bodies are basic, we have suggested, and how they are treated—how they are fed and housed, valued in their differences, honored in their integrity—is the primary issue. One of the most fundamental aspects of the story of Jesus, the love that overturns conventional dualistic hierarchies to reach out to the outcast and the victim, ought, we suggest, be extended to another dualistic hierarchy, that of humanity over nature. Nature is the "new poor," and in an embodiment, organic perspective, this means bodily poverty.

It is important to be clear about this suggestion of nature as the new poor. It does not mean that the "old poor"—poor human beings—are being replaced, or that every microorganism is included in God's love in the same way as human beings are.[3] It does, however, suggest that nature is the "also" poor, and that even microorganisms have their place in creation, a place that is not merely their usefulness (or threat) to human beings. There are two interrelated issues in the notion of nature as the new poor. The first is nature's value as such and to God; the second is its relation to human beings as well as what human beings are presently doing to nature. A statement from the World Council of Churches on the meaning of the phrase "the integrity of creation" is helpful here: "The value of all creatures in and for themselves, for one another, and for God, and their interconnectedness in a diverse whole that has unique value for God, together constitute the integrity of creation."[4] This definition underscores the *intrinsic* value that each living being has in and for itself as a creature loved by God as well as the *instrumental* value that living beings have for one another and for God as parts of an evolutionary, weblike creation.[5]

Intrinsic versus instrumental value is the critical issue. It means, quite simply, that other creatures as well as our planet as a whole were not created for our benefit, as we have already learned from the common creation story. Therefore, when we consider some part of it solely in terms of usefulness to ourselves as, for instance, in the metaphors of "silo" (food), "laboratory" (experimental material), "gymnasium" (recreation), or "cathedral" (spiritual uplift), we transgress "the integrity of creation."[6] Nature as the new poor does not mean that we should sentimentalize nature or slip into such absurdities as speaking of "oppressed" mosquitoes or rocks. Rather, nature as the new poor means that *we have made nature poor*. It is a comment not about the workings of natural selection but of human sin. It is a hard, cold look at what one part of nature, we human beings, have done to the rest of it: we have broken the integrity of creation by the excesses of our population and life-style, by our utilitarian attitude toward other creatures as well as toward our own vulnerable sisters and brothers, by our refusal to acknowledge the value of each and every aspect of creation to itself and to God. Nature is not necessarily and as such poor; it is so only because of *one* species, our own, which threatens the vitality and viability of the rest of nature. To say that the inclusive love of Jesus' destabilizing parables ought to be extended to nature does not, then, imply a sentimental divine love for each and every cell or bacterium. Rather, it brings to mind the righteous judgment of the Creator whose body, composed of many valuable, diverse forms, is being diminished on our planet by one greedy, thoughtless, albeit self-conscious and hence responsible, part of that body— ourselves. It means that nature needs to be liberated and healed because *we* have enslaved it and made it sick. This perspective claims that in the twentieth century on our planet, human beings have caused nature to be the new poor in the same way that a small elite of the human population has created and continues to create the old poor—through a gross imbalance of the haves and have-nots. Those "other" people (the old poor) and nature (the new poor) are, in both cases, there "for our use."

Of course, all aspects of creation—including human beings— have instrumental as well as intrinsic value (we all live on top of, in between, and inside each other), but this cannot mean within the Hebrew and Christian traditions that *any* aspect of creation is nothing but fuel or fodder for others. The recognition of intrinsic value means, at the very least, that when we use other creatures for our benefit, we do so with humility, respect, and thanksgiving for these other lives. Moreover, to add nature as the new poor to God's inclusive love does not mean that each and every cell, elephant, or Douglas fir will thrive and prosper any more than it means that each and every poor human being does. In our complex world of natural selection, fortune and misfortune, human freedom as well as sin, nothing could be further from reality. It might mean, however, that *we* would look at nature with new eyes, not as something to be misused or even just used, but as our kin, that of which we are a part, with each creature seen as valuable in itself and to God. Indeed, we might see nature in our time as the new poor of Jesus' parables.

A cosmological and theocentric perspective—valuing the natural bodies around us because they are intrinsically worthwhile in themselves and to God, rather than for our purposes—is conventionally alien to us, but so is the overturning of the other hierarchies in the message of Jesus.[7] The central claim of the gospel is, then, not only that the Word became flesh, but the particular shape that flesh took—one that presented a shock to our natural way of considering things in terms of value to ourselves. And for us to admit that nature is the "new poor" is also a direct affront to our anthropocentric sensibility. Our first response, in fact, might well be that such a radical perspective, a theocentric-cosmological one, is useless in light of the ecological crisis we face, where increasing numbers of poor, needy people *must* use the natural environment to provide for their own basic needs. We do not need to add yet another category of the oppressed, especially that of nature. But the shape of the body of God from a Christian perspective suggests otherwise. That shape, we have suggested, is given its basic outlines from one of the central features of Jesus' ministry—his destabilizing parables that side with the outcast. Extended to the natural world, to our planet and its many nonhuman creatures, the parabolic ministry of Jesus names a new poor, which is by definition poor in body, for those creatures and dimensions of our planet are primarily body. An incarnational religion, a bodily tradition, such as Christianity, should not have to strain to include the natural world and its creatures, for they epitomize the physical. They are, as it were, the *representative* bodies.[8]

If we press this issue still further in light of other motifs in the ministry of Jesus—his healings and eating practices—we can develop our theme more deeply. Jesus' healing ministry has often been an embarrassment to the church, especially in light of the church's spiritualization of salvation; moreover, the healings appear to fall into the category of miracles and thus suggest a breaking of natural laws. But they are unmistakably central in all versions of Jesus' ministry, as central as the parables. As a symbol of focused concern, of what counts, the healing stories are crucial. We have suggested that in the organic model the body is the main attraction, and the healing stories seem to agree. Whatever else one wants to say about them, they focus attention on bodily pain and bodily relief. Since Christians understand Jesus of Nazareth as at least paradigmatic of God, that his ministry is a place to gain hints and clues about divine concern, then the centrality of the healing stories stands full square against any minimizing of the body. Bodies *count*, claims the healing ministry of Jesus, in the eyes of God. This perspective, of course, fits very well indeed with an ecological sensibility. It suggests that redemption should be enlarged to salvation: redemption means to "buy back" or "repay" through, for instance, a sacrifice, whereas salvation means healing or preserving from destruction. The first applies only to human beings who have offended (sinned) and hence need to be rescued through a substitutionary act of reconciliation, while the second can include the natural order, which, along with human beings, needs to be healed and preserved.

The healing metaphor for salvation is a modest claim. It does not suggest ecstatic fulfillment of all desires but rather preservation from destruction or, at most, the restoration to adequate bodily functioning. If the parables are the deconstructive phase of Jesus' ministry, overturning the oppressive, dualistic hierarchies, then the healing stories are the middle or reconstructive phase, not promising the kingdom but only what in ecological terms is called "sustainability," the ability to function in terms of bodily needs. The healings are a modest statement in light of the radical character of the parables. And yet, in another sense, at least in a cosmological or ecological context, they deepen the radicality of the parables, for they imply that bodily health and well-being is a priority of the gospel—and given the inclusiveness of the parabolic message and its bias toward the needy, this must mean not just human bodies but other vulnerable ones as well.

A third characteristic aspect of Jesus' ministry, his practice of eating with sinners, might be called the *prospective* phase, in contrast to the *deconstructive* (parables) and *reconstructive* (healing) dimensions. This practice was as much a scandal to Jesus' contemporaries as were the destabilizing parables and the miraculous healings.[9] It is also, although for different reasons, scandalous to an ecological era. It suggests that *all* are invited to the banquet of life. In the stories of Jesus feeding the multitudes as well as in his unconventional invitations to the outcasts to share his table, two motifs emerge. First, whatever food there is, be it only a few loaves, should be shared and, second, is the hope of abundance, of a feast that satisfies the deepest hungers of all creatures, of all creation. One could say there is a minimal and a maximal vision: the exhortation that the basic needs of all creatures, including the most needy, be met from available resources, and the faith that the deepest needs will also be met in the future. By focusing on food, which, along with breath, is the most immediate and necessary component of bodily health, the motif of God's love for all, especially the outcast and the vulnerable, is deepened and radicalized. Moreover, the food imagery includes, without any additional explanation or rationalization, the nonhuman creatures and the plants of our planet. Food is basic to all life and is, increasingly, a symbol of the planet's crisis: the exponential growth of the human population and the life-style of some in that population at the expense of all other living things. So, this one metaphor of food includes not only what is most basic but also what is deepest. The eating practices and feeding stories of Jesus not only suggest a survival strategy for the diversity of life-forms, but also project a vision when all shall gather at one table—the lion, the lamb, and human beings—and eat their fill. It is a vision of salvation as wholeness, characterized not by the overcoming of differences, but by their acceptance and inclusion. Such visions have a prophetic edge, for they serve both as a critique of current practices as well as a goal toward which to strive. They are not, then, so much about the future as about the present; they propose an alternative to the present, not necessarily realizable but at least as giving a direction toward which to aim.

Jesus' eating stories and practices suggest that physical needs are basic and must be met—food is not a metaphor here but should be taken literally. All creatures deserve what is basic to bodily health. But food also serves as a metaphor of fulfillment at the deepest level of our longings and desires. The church picked up and developed the second, metaphorical emphasis, making eating imagery the ground of its vision of spiritual fulfillment, especially in the eucharist. But just as the tradition focused on the second birth (redemption), often neglecting the first birth (creation), so also it spiritualized hunger as the longing of the soul for God, conveniently forgetting the source of the metaphor in basic bodily needs. But the aspects of Jesus' ministry on which we have focused—the parables, healings, and eating stories—do not forget this dimension; in fact, Jesus' activities and message, according to this interpretation, are embarrassingly bodily. The parables focus on oppression that people feel due to their concrete, cultural setting, as servants rather than masters, poor rather than rich, Gentile rather than Jew; the healing stories are concerned with the bodily pain that some endure; the eating stories have to do with physical hunger and the humiliation of exclusion. None of these is primarily spiritual, though each assumes the psychosomatic unity of human nature and can serve as a symbol of eschatological fulfillment—the overcoming of all hierarchies, the health and harmony of the cosmos and all its creatures, the satiety of the deepest groanings and longings of creation.

Our focus, however, has been on the bodily basics, because the major established traditions within Christianity (except for sectarian, monastic, and now liberation theologies) have neglected them, and because it allows us to include human as well as planetary well-being. The shape, then, of God's body from some central motifs in the ministry of Jesus is one that includes the rich diversity of created forms, especially in regard to their basic needs for physical well-being. *The body of God must be fed.*

But even this exhortation, let alone the fulfillment of creation's deepest longings, is difficult, perhaps impossible, to bring about. We have suggested that the distinctive feature of a Christian view of embodiment is inclusion of the outcast and the oppressed. This is a scandal by conventional human standards and (here the issue deepens and darkens) in light of the process of natural selection in evolutionary biology. In neither framework do the vulnerable get the basics, let alone any glory.

Evolution and Solidarity with the Oppressed

We have looked at this scandal in terms of conventional human standards, but what of natural selection? What consonance can there possibly be between Christianity's inclusion of the outcasts of society, as well as our extension to include our vulnerable planet and its many creatures, and biological evolution, in which millions are wasted, individuals are sacrificed for the species, and even whole species are wiped out in the blinking of an eye? Does not the Christian overturning of hierarchies, the healing of bodies, and the concern with basics of life for all seem like an absurdity — or, at least, hopelessly naive? Is there any fit between the distinctive embodiment perspective of Jesus' ministry and the common creation story? The answer is both yes and no; there is both consonance and dissonance.

Jesus voiced the yes in the stories we have of his life and death: human beings can *choose* to side with the vulnerable and the outcast. Evolution is not only or solely biological; it is also historical and cultural. Once evolutionary history reaches the human, self-conscious stage, natural selection is not the only operative principle, for natural selection can be countered with the principle of solidarity.[10] The notion of siding with the vulnerable is not the sole insight of Christianity by any means. All human beings, despite the historically dismal record of slavery, oppression of women and homosexuals, and genocide, just to name a few of our more heinous crimes against the vulnerable, have, nonetheless, the option of deciding differently — and sometimes do. That is, once evolutionary history reaches the self-conscious level, other principles can function as to which individuals and species live and thrive. Cultural evolution can expand ethical regard to include more and more others besides the dominant males of a culture: women, people of all races and classes, the physically challenged, gays and lesbians — and even animals and the earth. This is a democratizing tendency that counters the fang and claw of genetic evolution as well as its two basic movers, chance and law. Human choice, the expansion of who survives and prospers, can and has enlarged the pool, so that, for instance, the physically challenged are not necessarily cast aside as they would be if only genetic selection were operative. Enlarging the pool, however, is often a minimal step, for we all know that equality for all does not follow. Ethical regard is practiced differently for African-Americans than for whites and for gays and lesbians than for heterosexuals.

Nonetheless, once the scales have fallen from our eyes and we recognize that human beings have reached a plateau where both choice and power are involved in who lives and how well they live, we see that cultural evolution is as (if not more) important than natural selection—at least on this planet at this time. We now know that natural selection is not the only principle: something else is possible. We know that the recognition of the intrinsic value of other life-forms is an alternative. Some form of this insight is evident in the practice of most cultures and religions, though which life-forms count varies enormously. The point is that some do; that is, *all* life-forms are not simply grist for the biological mill, as natural selection holds. The issue becomes, then, where one draws the line in terms of intrinsic value. The model of the universe as God's body, composed of billions of different bodies, implies that all are valuable. The theocentric-cosmocentric view implicit in the organic model is radically inclusive: God loves the entire creation and finds it valuable. The Christic paradigm suggests a further shaping of the body, with particular attention to those parts of the body that hitherto have been excluded by human sin. In this reading, Christianity intensifies a cultural process we find in many different forms and places in human history: a radicalization of intrinsic value that is counter to the principle of natural selection (and this occurred, of course, centuries before those principles were known).

Solidarity with the oppressed, then, becomes the Christian form of both consonance with and defiance of the evolutionary principle. It is consonant with it because it claims that there is a next stage of evolution on our planet, one that is not primarily genetic but cultural: the necessity, for survival and well-being, for all life-forms to share the basic goods of the planet. It is defiant of it because it suggests that the principle needed for this to occur is not natural selection or the survival of the fittest, but the solidarity of each with all. We have reached the point where war, ecological destruction, sexual and racial discrimination, poverty and homelessness, are counterproductive to planetary well-being. We have also reached the point where we realize that the interrelationships and interconnections among all forms of life are so deep, permanent, and mysterious that the various species of plants and animals need one another. But solidarity of each with all should perhaps remain at this utilitarian level: we *need* each other to survive. The scandal of Christianity goes further: it insists on solidarity with the outsider, the outcast, the vulnerable. Does not this make Christian faith a surd, if not absurd, in view of postmodern science, rather than merely counter to it? Would not the planet be better off without these "outcast" types?

At this point, I believe we have no choice but to admit that the radical inclusiveness that is at the heart of Christian faith, especially inclusion of the oppressed, is not compatible with evolution, even cultural evolution. For as we have seen, its view of sinful human nature deepens the notion of the ecological sinner: the bloated self refusing to share. Hence, even the best of cultural evolution, from a Christian perspective, is lacking, for we "naturally" construct our worlds to benefit ourselves, including only those who are useful to us. Christian solidarity with the oppressed, therefore, will have some special, peculiar characteristics that are both counterrevolutionary and countercultural. One form will entail resistance to evil or the liberation of the oppressed, and another will involve suffering with those who, nonetheless, suffer. The first form is the primary one, what we have discussed under the rubric of the embodiment ministry of Jesus—his parables, healings, and eating practices that attempt in deconstructive, reconstructive, and prospective ways to free suffering bodies and fulfill their needs. The second form, the suffering of God—and ourselves—with those who, nonetheless, suffer, recognizes that irremediable, unconscionable, unremitting, horrific suffering *does* occur both to individuals and to whole species, suffering that is beyond our best efforts to address and seemingly beyond God's as well.

In both forms of Christian solidarity with the oppressed, the active and the passive, liberation and suffering, the cross and resurrection of the Christic paradigm are central to an embodiment theology. The death of our natural, sinful preference for hierarchical dualisms that favor the wealthy, healthy, well-fed bodies is a necessary prerequisite in the embodiment ministry of Jesus. His parables, healing stories, and eating practices demand our deaths—just as the practice of his embodiment ministry also brought about his own death. Neither biological nor cultural evolution includes this radical next step of identification with the vulnerable and needy through the death of the self. What is clear in the New Testament stories of the Christic paradigm is that for those who respond to its call, the way of solidarity with the oppressed will demand the cross (in some form or another). What is less clear, but hinted at, is that *bodies*, all suffering bodies, will live again to see a new day. Regardless of the difficulty of imagining what resurrection might mean, then or now, what is clear is the focus on the body, the physical basis of life. Faith in the resurrection of the body is the belief that the spirit that empowers the universe and all its living forms is working with us, in life and in death, to bring about the well-being and fulfillment of all the bodies in creation. Resurrection of the body puts the emphasis where it should be in an ecological theology: on the physical basis of life. As often as Christianity has forgotten and repudiated that basis, its most ancient and treasured belief in the resurrection of the body reminds it of its denial of the physical.

Natural Evil and Human Sin within a Wider Horizon

It is within the context of solidarity with the oppressed through liberation and suffering that we can also see the thorny issue of natural evil in a new light. This context diminishes the importance of natural evil while increasing the importance of another kind of evil, human sin. If Christian discipleship is shaped by solidarity with the needy, including nature as the new poor, then natural evil is not limited to what happens to me and mine, and sin becomes the limitation of one's horizon to the self. We undergo an enlargement of vision, the realization that what happens in the natural world—the vagaries of chance and law that result in the good of some individuals and species at the expense of others—is part of the complex process that has resulted in us as well as everything else on our planet. Within this enlarged perspective we can no longer consider evil only in terms of what benefits or hurts me or my species.[11] Curiously, we seldom question the random effects of chance that result in good to ourselves. Few of us, for instance, ask, "Why has this good thing happened to me?" though we frequently find the world malevolent if we suffer some diminishment or reversal of fortune. Yet, we cannot have one without the other.[12] My life, your life, all life, is a chance happening; so also are birth defects, cancer cells, and AIDS. This brutal truth is so difficult for us to accept that we instinctively narrow our horizon to ourselves and narrow God to a deity only concerned with my good, or at most, the good of the human species. But a cosmological, ecological perspective demands the enlargement of vision: I am not and we are not the only products of evolution nor the only creatures whose good is a matter of divine concern. In a world as large, as complex, and with as many individuals and species as our planet has, the good of some will inevitably occur at the expense of others.[13] An egocentric or anthropocentric horizon is simply not realistic in light of the common creation story, and it is also contrary to the Christian paradigm of solidarity with the oppressed. A focus on the self and its well-being is not persuasive in either of these pictures of reality; neither a cosmocentric nor a theocentric perspective allows for such limited vision.

Natural evil and sin join at this one point for both are concerned with a limited horizon, the inability to identify with others outside of the self, the refusal to acknowledge that one is not the center of things. Natural evil is narrowly interpreted as bad things happening to *me* and sin is the desire to have everything for *oneself*.[14] And yet, when one's child dies or a brother contracts AIDS, grief, anger, and even rage are appropriate responses, far more appropriate than a measured acceptance of the throw of the dice. There would be something almost obscene in reminding a person in such circumstances that they need a wider vision of things, that neither evolution nor God has any special concern for that child or brother.

What we have been suggesting is that both things are true: we do need a wider vision, painful and difficult as that is to achieve; and God does care about and side with the outcast and

needy, while working in accord with the inexorable caprices of natural selection—God cannot set aside the laws of nature to benefit a
chosen few. Life, diversity, complexity, novelty—and even our
free will—all rest on the randomness of natural selection as well as
the diminishment, waste, and death of its processes. And yet,
while accepting the inevitability of this pattern, we still grieve for
and suffer with—as God does also in the cosmic Christ—those
who are diminished and wasted.

Let us look at both sides of this issue of natural evil more concretely, the side of suffering with the victims of evil and an enlarged vision of evil. To say that God suffers with those who suffer
from the vagaries of random chance—the partner of a young
woman killed in a freak accident, the parents of a child born with
serious birth defects—means one thing in a deistic or monarchical
model of God and the world and something quite different within
the model of the world as God's body. In neither model is God the
cause of these human tragedies, but in the deistic and monarchical
models, God is not involved in the consequences, either, for God is
external to and distant from the world. But this is not the case in
the organic model: God is involved—in fact, is not only involved
but feels the pain of all who suffer within the body.[15] If the world is
God's body, then nothing happens to the world that does not also
happen to God. If we live and move and have our being in God,
then God, though asymmetrically, lives in us as well. A panentheistic model does not reduce God to the world, but God is in
the young woman killed in the accident and in the baby with birth
defects as well as in those who suffer the loss or diminishment of
their loved ones. God is not the cause of these events and cannot
be if we take seriously the contemporary scientific picture of reality, but God is with us in the consequences. The God who is the
breath of our breath is closer to us than we are to ourselves; this
God is in and with us no matter what happens. And this of course
includes death: we do not have to leave God when we die, nor do
we join God in heaven. In the organic model we are with God
whether we live or die, for whether our bodies are alive or return to
the other form of embodiment from which they came, they are
within the body of God. God is not somewhere else so that we
must depart this world to join the source from which we came, but

with us in the earth, the soil, that receives us at our death, or as a version of the Lord's Prayer addresses God, "Loving God, in whom is heaven."[16] The loving God is with us and so, then, is heaven.

This is the pastoral side of the issue of natural evil, and it is very important. Any theodicy that does not attend to it seriously and thoughtfully is usually aesthetic or intellectualistic in outlook. It cares more about justifying God from the perspective of the big picture, the panoramic aeons of time and space within which human, personal concerns are minor blemishes in an otherwise pleasing and ordered creation, than it does about the anguished cry of a bereaved parent or partner.

The other side of the issue of natural evil is that it is not the principal kind of evil that endangers our planet. In the enlarged perspective of both evolution and solidarity with the oppressed, natural evil dims in importance in comparison with human sin. To be sure, terrible things happen to people accidentally and randomly, and species become extinct from natural causes over time, but of equal if not more importance is what *we do* to others of our own species, to other species, and to the planet itself. *The issue facing us is not natural evil but sin,* not the inability to accept the larger picture but the refusal to remove ourselves from the center of it. Children die accidentally and from birth defects and brothers (and sisters) contract AIDS, but many more children die from malnutrition and medical neglect and those at most risk to get AIDS are the poor, the oppressed, the neglected of our society. In other words, we should not use natural evil as a smokescreen to hide the real ecological problem: human selfishness and greed. This view of sin, needless to say, is gender, race, and class specific: it applies most appropriately to first-world people with power. Moreover, as we have already suggested, biological and cultural evolution—or natural evil and sin—are now inextricably joined with us. The distinction between them is blurred, for natural evils seldom occur in our time without human complicity. And it is the latter for which we are responsible and that lie within our power to change. It is not the Mount St. Helens eruptions or Hurricane Andrews that are threatening the planet and its creatures but the depletion of the ozone layer and the desertification of Africa. It is elitist and self-indulgent to dwell on natural evil as if it were, as the insurance writers put it, "an act of God," perpetrated by natural (or supernatural) forces outside our control, when systemic evils of massive proportions, which daily destroy huge numbers of human bodies as well as other bodies, lie within our power—the power of the privileged—to alleviate.

We have suggested two Christian responses of solidarity with the oppressed: liberation and suffering. The first, in light of the Christic paradigm, is to fight with all our intelligence, power, and imagination for the inclusion of all, especially those presently excluded in our particular time and place. That is what emerges from the ministry of Jesus and his followers throughout the centuries. From this first response we derive our models of God (and ourselves) as mother, father, judge, lover, liberator, healer, friend—all the active, interpersonal models of solidarity with the oppressed. It is, I believe, the most important response from a Christian perspective.

The second response is the one that follows from the inevitable absurdity of radical solidarity with the oppressed, both from human conventional standards and from evolutionary biology, from, in other words, sin and natural evil. To suffer with those who suffer is not, then, the primary Christian response, but it is an inescapable secondary one.[17] The first is the active, the second the passive phase of Christian identification with the world. The first is epitomized in Jesus' ministry and life practices; the second, in his death on a cross—the inevitable result, given conventional standards, of siding with the outcast and the vulnerable. In some interpretations the suffering of God is the first and primary divine activity; here, it is secondary. It is, nonetheless, an essential response, for it undercuts any naivete or idealism about results, which is implied if the first response stands alone. Given human sin, the possibility for solidarity with the vulnerable to triumph or even make a significant difference is highly questionable, as anyone knows who has worked on any justice or ecological issue. Add to human sin the vagaries of natural evil, and one must accept the inevitability of intense and massive suffering.[18]

The Scope of the Body:
The Cosmic Christ

The suffering of creation—undoubtedly the greater reality for most creatures, human as well as nonhuman—is addressed by the scope of the body or the cosmic Christ. *Whatever* happens, says our model, happens to God also and not just to us.[19] The body of God, shaped by the Christic paradigm, is also the cosmic Christ—the loving, compassionate God on the side of those who suffer, especially the vulnerable and excluded. All are included, not only in their liberation and healing, but also in their defeat and despair. Even as the life-giving breath extends to all bodies in the universe, so also does the liberating, healing, *and* suffering love of God. The resurrected Christ is the cosmic Christ, the Christ freed from the body of Jesus of Nazareth, to be present in and to all bodies.[20] The New Testament appearance stories attest to the continuing empowerment of the Christic paradigm in the world: the liberating, inclusive love of God for all is alive in and through the entire cosmos. We are not alone as we attempt to practice the ministry of inclusion, for the power of God is incarnate throughout the world, erupting now and then where the vulnerable are liberated and healed, as well as where they are not. The quiescent effect on human effort of the motif of sacrificial suffering in the central atonement theory of Christianity has made some repudiate any notion of divine suffering, focusing entirely on the active, liberating phase of God's relation to the world.[21] But there is a great difference between a sacrificial substitutionary atonement in which the Son suffers for the sins of the world and the model of the God as the body within which our bodies live and who suffers with us, feeling our pain and despair. When we have, as disciples of Jesus' paradigmatic ministry, actively fought for the inclusion of excluded bodies, but nonetheless are defeated, we are not alone, even here. And the excluded and the outcast bodies for which we fought belong in and are comforted by the cosmic Christ, the body of God in the Christic paradigm.

The Direction of Creation and the Place of Salvation

The immediate and concrete sense of the cosmic Christ—God with us in liberation and in defeat—is the first level of the scope or range of God's body. But there are two additional dimensions implied in the metaphor that need focused and detailed attention. One is the relationship between creation and salvation in which salvation is the *direction* of creation and creation is the *place* of salvation. The metaphor of the cosmic Christ suggests that the cosmos is moving *toward* salvation and that this salvation is taking place *in* creation. The other dimension is that God's presence in the form or shape of Jesus' paradigmatic ministry is available not just in the years 1–30 C.E. and not just in the church as his mystical body, but everywhere, in the cosmic body of the Christ. Both of these dimensions of the metaphor of the cosmic Christ are concerned with *place* and *space*, with where God's body is present in its Christic shape.[22] Christian theology has not traditionally been concerned with or interested in spatial matters, as we have already noted, priding itself on being a historical religion, often deriding such traditions as Goddess, Native, and "primitive" for focusing on place, on sacred spaces, on the natural world. But it is precisely place and space, as the common creation story reminds us, that must now enter our consciousness. An ecological sensibility demands that we broaden the circle of salvation to include the natural world, and the practical issues that face us will, increasingly, be ones of space, not time. On a finite, limited planet, arable land with water will become not only the symbol of privilege but, increasingly, the basis of survival. Geography, not history, is the ecological issue. Those in the Christian tradition who have become accustomed to thinking of reality in a temporal model—the beginning in creation; the middle in the incarnation, ministry, and death of Jesus Christ; and the end at the eschaton when God shall bring about the fulfillment of all things—need to modify their thinking in a spatial direction. We need to ask where is this salvation occurring here and now, and what is the scope of this salvation?

In regard to the first dimension of the cosmic Christ, what does it mean to say that salvation is the *direction* of creation and creation is the *place* of salvation? To say that salvation is the direction of creation is a deceptively simple statement on a complex, weighty matter. It is a statement of faith in the face of massive evidence to the contrary, evidence that we have suggested when we spoke of the absurdity of such a claim in light of both conventional standards and natural selection. Some natural theologies, theologies that begin with creation, try to make the claim that evolutionary history contains a teleological direction, an optimistic arrow, but our claim is quite different. It is a retrospective, not a prospective claim; it begins with salvation, with experiences of liberation and healing that one wagers are from God, and reads back into creation the hope that the whole creation is included within the divine liberating, healing powers. It is a statement of faith, not of fact; it takes as its standpoint a concrete place where salvation has been experienced—in the case of Christians, the paradigmatic ministry of Jesus and similar ministries of his disciples in different, particular places—and projects the shape of these ministries onto the whole. What is critical, then, in this point of view about the common creation story is not that this story tells us anything about God or salvation but, rather, that it gives us a new, contemporary picture with which to remythologize Christian faith. The entire fifteen-billion-year history of the universe and the billions of galaxies are, from a Christian perspective, from this concrete, partial, particular setting, seen to be the cosmic Christ, the body of God in the Christic paradigm. Thus, the direction or hope of creation, all of it, is nothing less than what I understand that paradigm to be for myself and for other human beings: the liberating, healing, inclusive love of God.

To say that creation is the place of salvation puts the emphasis on the here-and-now aspect of spatiality. While the direction motif takes the long view, speaking of the difficult issue of an evolutionary history that appears to have no purpose, the place motif underscores the concrete, nitty-gritty, daily, here-and-now aspect of salvation. In contrast to all theologies that claim or even imply that salvation is an otherworldly affair, the place motif insists that salvation occurs *in* creation, in the body of God. The cosmic Christ is the physical, available, and needy outcast in creation, in the space where we live. In Christian thought creation is often seen as merely the backdrop of salvation, of lesser importance than redemption, the latter being God's main activity. We see this perspective in such comments as "creation is the prologue to history" or "creation provides the background and setting for the vocation of God's people,"[23] and in Calvin's claim that nature is the stage for salvation history. In this way of viewing the relation between creation and redemption, creation plays no critical role: it is only the stage on which the action takes place, the background for the real action. But in our model of the body of God as shaped by the Christic paradigm, creation is of central importance, for creation—meaning our everyday world of people and cities, farms and mountains, birds and oceans, sun and sky—is the place where it all happens and to whom it happens. Creation as the place of salvation means that the health and well-being of all creatures and parts of creation is what salvation is all about—it is God's place and our place, the one and only place. Creation is not one thing and salvation something else; rather, they are related as scope and shape, as space and form, as place and pattern. Salvation is for all of creation. The liberating, healing, inclusive ministry of Christ takes place *in* and *for* creation.

These two related motifs of the direction of creation and the place of salvation both underscore expanding God's liberating, healing, inclusive love to all of the natural world. This expansion does not eclipse the importance of needy, vulnerable human beings, but it suggests that the cosmic Christ, the body of Christ, is not limited to the church or even to human beings but, as coextensive with God's body, is *also* the direction of the natural world and the place where salvation occurs.

Nature and the Cosmic Christ

These comments lead us into the second dimension of the metaphor of the cosmic Christ, which also concerns spatiality. The world in our model is the sacrament of God, the visible, physical, bodily presence of God. The cosmic Christ metaphor suggests that Jesus' paradigmatic ministry is not limited to the years 1–30 C.E. nor to the church, as in the model of the church as the mystical body of Christ, but is available to us throughout nature. It is available everywhere, it is unlimited—with one qualification: it is mediated *through* bodies. Our model is unlimited at one end and restrictive at the other: the entire cosmos is the habitat of God, but we know this only through the mediation of the physical world. The world as sacrament is an old and deep one in the Christian tradition, both Eastern and Western. The sacramental tradition assumes that God is present not only in the hearing of the Word, in the preaching and reading of Scripture, and not only in the two (or seven) sacraments of the church, but also in each and every being in creation. While Christian sacramentalism derives from the incarnation ("the Word became flesh"), the sense of the extraordinary character of the ordinary or the sacredness of the mundane is scarcely a Christian insight. In fact, it is more prevalent and perhaps more deeply felt and preserved in some other religious traditions, including, for instance, Goddess, Native, and Buddhist ones.[24] Moreover, Christian sacramentalism has usually been utilitarian in intent, that is, using the things of the world as symbols of religious states. They are often not appreciated in their own integrity as having intrinsic value but rather as stepping stones on one's pilgrimage to God. This perspective is evident in a famous passage from Augustine's *Confessions*, in which all the delights of the senses are transmuted into symbols of divine ecstasy: "But what is it I love when I love You? Not the beauty of any bodily thing . . . Yet in a sense I do love light and melody and fragrance and food and embrace when I love my God—the light and the voice and the fragrance and the food and embrace in the soul . . . ."[25] This tradition is rich and powerful, epitomized in a sensibility that sees God in everything and everything full of the glory of God: the things of this earth are valuable principally as vehicles for communication with the divine. A different sensibility is evident in this Navajo chant:

> May it be delightful my house;
> From my head may it be delightful;
> To my feet may it be delightful;
> Where I lie may it be delightful;
> All above me may it be delightful;
> All around me may it be delightful.[26]

The delight here is in and not through the ordinary; the ordinary is not chiefly a symbol of the divine delight. The difference between these sensibilities is epitomized in two lines, one from Hildegard of Bingen, a medieval German mystic ("Holy persons draw to themselves all that is earthly") and one from Abraham Heschel, a contemporary Jewish theologian ("Just to be is a blessing, Just to live is holy").[27] The first perspective transmutes all things earthly into their holy potential, while the second finds ordinary existence itself to be holy.

Nevertheless, in spite of its limitations, traditional sacramentalism is an important perspective, for it is the major way Christianity has preserved and developed an appreciation for nature. It has encouraged Christians to look upon the world as valuable — indeed, as holy — and has served as a counterforce to two other perspectives on nature within Christian history, one that divorces it totally from God through secularizing it and one that dominates and exploits it. Traditional sacramentalism has, in its own way, supported the principal thesis of this essay: the model of the world (universe) as God's body means that the presence of God is not limited to particular times or places but is coextensive with reality, with all that is. It has been one of the few traditions within Christianity that has encouraged both a spatial and a historical perspective; that is, Christian sacramentalism has included nature as a concern of God and a way to God rather than limiting divine activity to human history. For these and other reasons Christian sacramentalism should be encouraged. It is a distinctive contribution of Christianity. From its incarnational base, it claims that in analogy with the body of Jesus the Christ all bodies can serve as ways to God, all can be open to and give news of the divine presence. But it does not claim, at least primarily, that bodies have intrinsic value. The great theologians and poets of the Christian sacramental tradition, including Paul, John, Irenaeus, Augustine, the medieval mystics (such as Julian of Norwich, Meister Eckhart, Hildegard of Bingen), Gerard Manley Hopkins, and Pierre Teilhard de Chardin, love the things of this world principally *as expressions of* divine beauty, sustenance, truth, and glory.[28] It is not a sensibility that in a homey phrase wants "to hold on hard to the huckleberries."[29] The value of huckleberries as huckleberries is not a major concern of Christian sacramentalism.

Again, we need to remind ourselves that for the purposes of the planetary agenda, no one tradition needs to claim universality or the whole truth. What is more helpful is to specify the *kind* of insights that are distinctive of different traditions. The Christian tradition does not underscore the intrinsic value of all things earthly but does express richly and deeply the symbolic importance of each and every body on the earth: each in its own way expresses divine reality and is valuable for this reason. Unfortunately, traditional sacramentalism is not a central concern for many Christians; in fact, some Protestant churches scarcely attend to it. Yet it can be a way that Christians, at least, might begin to change their exploitative, utilitarian attitudes toward nature—as well as toward other humans whose bodies are also expressions of God. As Hopkins puts it, "Christ plays in ten thousand places, lovely in limbs, lovely in eyes not his."[30] If use is to be made of our earth and its people and other creatures, it can only be a use, says Christian sacramentalism, for God's glory, not for our profit.

Nevertheless, we suggest two qualifications of traditional sacramentalism. The first is implicit in the direction of this entire essay: the need to replace the utilitarian attitude toward other beings that accompanies anthropocentricism with a perspective that values them intrinsically. If we are not the center of things, then other beings do not exist for our benefit—even for our spiritual growth as ways to God. They exist within the vast, intricate web of life in the cosmos, of which they and we are all interdependent parts, and each and every part has both utilitarian and intrinsic value. Within our model of the world as God's body, all of us, human beings included, exist as parts of the whole. Some parts are not merely means for the purposes of other parts, for all parts are valued by God and hence should be valued by us. We do have a distinctive role in this body, but it is not as the ones who use the rest as a ladder to God; rather, it is as the ones who have emerged as the caretakers of the rest.

The second qualification of traditional sacramentalism picks up on this note of care and might be called "negative sacramentalism." It focuses on bodies not as expressions of divinity, but as signs of human sin and destruction. It is a perspective on the earth and its many bodies that sees them not as telling of the glories of

God but of human destruction. The bodies of the earth, human and nonhuman, that are vulnerable and needy cry out for compassion and care. These bodies appear to us, in the closing years of the twentieth century, not primarily as expressions of divine loveliness, but as evidence of human neglect and oppression. The focus is not on their use to help us in our religious pilgrimage but on our misuse of them, our refusal to acknowledge these bodies as valuable in and for themselves and to God. One of the motifs of our analysis of the model of the world as God's body from the perspective of the common creation story is that all bodies are united in webs of interrelatedness and interconnectedness. This motif has been radicalized by the Christic paradigm that reaches out to include especially the vulnerable, outcast, needy bodies. Hence, I would suggest that a form of Christian sacramentalism for an ecological era should focus not on the use of all earthly bodies but on our care of them, in the ways that the Christic paradigm suggests. We are suggesting that the Christic shape to God's body be applied to the full scope of that body, especially to the new poor, the natural world. Nature, its flora and fauna, therefore would not simply be addenda to human salvation, avenues providing deeper communion between God and human beings; rather, the Christic salvific paradigm would also be applied to the earth and its many creatures. This is what a cosmological or ecological context for theological reflection demands: the whole cosmos is God's concern, not just its human inhabitants and not merely as our habitat.

In what ways, then, should the Christic paradigm be applied to the natural world? In the same ways as applied to other outcasts: the deconstructive phase (liberation from oppressive hierarchies as seen in the parables), the reconstructive (physical sustainability as suggested by the healing stories), and the prospective (inclusion of all as manifest in the eating practices). These primary, active dimensions of the Christic paradigm—the shape of the cosmic Christ given to God's body—are balanced by a secondary, passive phase, the suffering of God with the despairing and defeated. What does each of these themes suggest to us as we reflect on the deteriorating, needy body of our planet earth?

Just as, in the overturning of oppressive, dualistic hierarchies, poor people are liberated from their enslavement by the rich, people of color are liberated from discrimination by whites, so also the earth and its many nonhuman creatures are liberated from oppression and destruction by human beings. The dualistic hierarchy of people over nature is an old and profound one, certainly as ancient as the patriarchal era that stretches back some five thousand years.[31] Until the sixteenth-century scientific revolution, however, and the subsequent marriage of science with technology, human beings were not sufficiently powerful to wreak massive destruction on nature. But we now are. The first phase, then, of extending the Christic paradigm beyond human beings is the recognition, which involves a confession of sin, of our oppressive misuse of the major part of God's creation in regard to our planet, that is, everything and every creature that is *not* human. The destructive phase is a breaking down of our "natural" biases against nature; our prejudices that it is, at best, only useful for our needs; our rationalizations in regard to activities that profit us but destroy it. The hierarchy of humans over nature has been, at least in the West, so total and so destructive for the last several hundred years that many people would deny that nature merits a status similar to other oppressed "minorities." Nature is, of course, the *majority* in terms of both numbers and importance (it can do very well without us, but not vice versa). Bracketing that issue for the moment, however, many would still claim that it does not, like poor or oppressed people, deserve attention as intrinsically valuable. Nature is valuable insofar as and only insofar as it serves human purposes. Thus, in a telling phrase, many speak of wilderness as "undeveloped" land, that is, of course, undeveloped for human profit, though it is excellently developed for the animals, trees, and plants that presently inhabit it.

The liberation of nature from our oppressive practices, the recognition that the land and its creatures have rights and are intrinsically valuable, is by no means easy to practice, since immediately and inevitably, especially on a finite planet with limited resources and increasing numbers of needy human beings, conflicts of interest will occur. These conflicts are real, painful, and important, but the point that our model underscores is that the resolution of them from a Christian perspective cannot ignore the value and rights of 99 percent of creation on our planet. The model of the world as God's body denies this attitude, and the model of the cosmic Christ intensifies that denial. Whether we like it or not, these models say that all parts of the planet are parts of God's body and are included in the Christic liberation from dualistic hierarchies. It is for us to figure out what this must, can, mean in particular situations where conflicts arise. The preferential option for the poor is uncomfortable wherever it is applied; it will be no less so when applied to the new poor, nature.

The second phase of the Christic paradigm, the healing phase, is especially appropriate to the nonhuman dimensions of creation. It is increasingly evident that the metaphors of sickness, degeneration, and dysfunction are significant when discussing the state of our planet. The pollution of air and water, the greenhouse effect, the depletion of the ozone layer, the desertification of arable land, the destruction of rainforests are all signs of the poor health of the earth. One of the great values of the organic model is that it not only focuses on bodies and includes the natural world (unlike many models in the Christian tradition), but it also implies that salvation includes, as the bottom line, the health of bodies. While the model helps us to focus on basic justice issues for human beings—the need for food, clean air and water, adequate housing, education and medical benefits—it also insists that we focus on the basics for other creatures and dimensions of our planet. The organic model focuses on the basics of existence: the healthy functioning of all inhabitants and systems of the planet. Jesus' healing stories are extremely valuable in a time of ecological deterioration and destruction such as we are experiencing. They refuse any early and easy spiritualizing of salvation; they force us, as Christians, to face the deep sickness of the many bodies that make up the body of God. These embarrassing stories are part of the mud of our tradition, the blood-and-guts part of the gospel that insists that whatever more or else Christian faith might be and mean, it includes as a primary focus physical well-being. And nature, in our time, is woefully ill.

Most of us, most of the time, refuse to acknowledge the degree of that sickness. It is inconvenient to do so, since curing the planet's illnesses will force human inhabitants to make sacrifices. Hence, denial sets in, a denial not unlike the denial many people

practice in relation to serious, perhaps terminal, illness when it
strikes their own bodies. But denial of the planet's profoundly deteriorating condition is neither wise nor Christian: it is not wise because, as we increasingly know, we cannot survive on a sick
planet, and it is not Christian because, if we extend the Christic
healing ministry to all of creation, then we must work for the
health of its many creatures and the planet itself.

This brings us to the third and final phase of the Christic paradigm as extended to the whole body of God: the inclusive fulfillment epitomized in Jesus' eating practices. As with the healing
stories, the stories of Jesus feeding the multitudes and inviting the
excluded to his table are embarrassments, perhaps scandals, in
their mundanity and inclusivity. Neither conventional standards
nor natural selection operates on the themes of sharing and inclusion; these stories are countercultural and counterbiological, but
they are hints and clues of a new stage of evolution, the stage of
our solidarity with other life-forms, especially with the needy and
outcast forms. The time has come, it appears, when our competition with various other species for survival will not result in a
richer, more complex and diverse community of life-forms. The
human population is already so dominant that it is likely to wipe
out many other forms and probably seriously harm its own, if pre-
dictions of our exponential growth prove true and the profligate
life-style of many of us continues. The good life rests in part, then,
on human decisions concerning sharing and inclusion, with food
as an appropriate and powerful symbol of both bare existence as
well as the abundant life. In the Christian tradition food has always
served these dual functions, though the emphasis has often been
on the latter meaning, especially in the eucharist as a foretaste of
the eschatalogical banquet. But in our time, the value of food is
precisely its literal meaning: sustainability for bodies, especially the
many bodies on our planet that Christians as well as others in our
society think of as superfluous. In a telling reversal of the need of
all bodies for food, many people assume that other creatures not
only do not *deserve* food but are themselves *only* food—food for
us.[32]

The paradigmatic Christic shape of the body of the world,
then, suggests some hints and clues for Christians as we, in an eco-

logical age, extend that shape to be coextensive with the world, su-
perimposing, as it were, the cosmic Christ on the body of God. We
look at the world, our planet and all its creatures, through the
shape of Christ. As we do so, we acknowledge the distinctive features of that form, especially liberation from our destructive oppression, the healing of its deteriorating bodies, and the sharing of
basic needs with all the planet's inhabitants, that the Christian tradition can contribute to the planetary agenda.

But we are not left alone to face this momentous, indeed, hor-
rendous, task. Ecological despair would quickly overwhelm us if
we believed that to be the case. The cosmic Christ as the shape of
God's body also tells us that God suffers with us in our suffering,
that divine love is not only with us in our active work against the
destruction of our planet but also in our passive suffering when we
and the health of our planet are defeated. An attitude of sober realism, in view of the massiveness of ecological and human oppression that faces us in our time, is the appropriate—perhaps the only
possible—attitude. We and our planet may, in fact, be defeated, or,
at least life in community, life worth living, may no longer be possible. The situation we face is similar in many respects to that por-
trayed in Albert Camus's powerful allegorical novel, *The Plague*, in
which a mysterious and devastating plague overwhelmed and destroyed most of the inhabitants of a contemporary Algerian town.
It was a symbol of the modern malaise, but for our purposes "the
plague" can serve as a literal description of deepening planetary
sickness. The response of one of the book's chief activists fighting
the plague is a soberly realistic one: "All I maintain is that on this
earth there are pestilences and there are victims, and it's up to us,
so far as possible, not to join forces with the pestilences."[33] When
the work of healing fails in spite of all efforts to make it work, one
must, Christians must, not "join forces with the pestilences." The
cross in the Christic paradigm does not, in our model, promise victory over the pestilences, but it does assure us that God is with the
victims in their suffering. That is the last word, however, not the
first.

Actually, the cross is not the last word. The enigmatic appearance stories of the risen Christ, the Christ who appeared in bodily
form to his disciples, is the witness to an ancient, indelible strain

within the Christian community. It is the belief and the hope that diminishment and death are not the last word, but in some inexplicable manner, the way to new life that, moreover, is physical. This is an important point for an embodiment theology. The death and resurrection of Jesus Christ are paradigmatic of a mode of change and growth that only occurs on the other side of the narrow door of the tomb. Often that pattern has been absolutized as occurring completely and only in Jesus of Nazareth: his death and resurrection are the answer to all the world's woes. In his death all creation dies; in his resurrection all arise to new life. The absolutism, optimism, and universalism of this way of interpreting the ancient and recurring relationship between death and new life—a relationship honored in most religious traditions as well as in evolutionary biology—are problematic in a postmodern, ecological, and highly diverse cultural and religious era. What is possible and appropriate, however, is to embrace these strains in Christian thought as a deep pattern within existence to which we cling and in which we hope—often as the hope against hope. We must believe in the basic trustworthiness at the heart of existence; that life, not death, is the last word; that against all evidence to the contrary (and most evidence is to the contrary), all our efforts on behalf of the well-being of our planet and especially of its most vulnerable creatures, including human ones, will not be defeated. It is the belief that the source and power of the universe is on the side of life and its fulfillment. The "risen Christ" is the Christian way of speaking of this faith and hope: Christ is the firstborn of the new creation, to be followed by all the rest of creation, including the last and the least.

Face, Body, and Spirit: Some Reflections on the Trinity

We have viewed the relationship between God and the world in light of the model of God as the spirit of the body, the universe, and that body as shaped by the Christic paradigm. What does this suggest in terms of trinitarianism, and is a trinitarian view of God even necessary or important in our model? To answer the latter question first, I would say yes, it is important. The proper function of trinitarianism in the Christian tradition is, I believe, to preserve for an agential theism both radical immanence and radical transcendence. That this is not the purpose of many trinitarian formulations is obvious from even a cursory acquaintance with the tradition, but it is the importance of trinitarianism in our model. Our model is not, as we recall, only agential (God as a transcendent superperson external to creation) nor only organic (God as the immanent power within natural processes) but agential *and* organic: God as the spirit of the body, the life or breath within the entire universe. Moreover, the Christic shape of this body has defined and particularized it further, in ways that have radicalized God's immanence. Divine immanence is empowerment toward the liberation, well-being, and fulfillment of all the bodies within God's body. The spirit that moves in creation giving breath to all bodies becomes also the spirit of Christ that wills the salvation of all bodies. The spirit and the body are both immanental terms, both metaphors pointing to the activity of God in relation to the world. It is this immanence, especially as expanded to include all of nature, that we have stressed in our model, not only because it has been neglected in Christianity, but also because it is what is needed in our time.

But both of these terms, *spirit* and *body*, are, as we have emphasized, backside, not face, terms. One of the distinctive features of both the Jewish and Christian traditions is the insistence that God is not available in or to our categories, any or all of them. This is, I believe, the crucial insight that the notion of the transcendence of God in these traditions points to, rather than that God is an external, all-powerful superperson. *That* description is also a model and only a model. God lies, lives, or whatever beyond, beneath, over and under, that and all other attempts at expression. The transcendence of God is in its primary and most important sense the invisible face of God, that aspect or dimension that we never see, never know. It is what God is when God is not "being God"; it is the mystery, the absoluteness, that relativizes all our notions and models of God; it is the godness of God; it is the silence that surrounds all our paltry and pathetic attempts to speak of God; it is the big no to all our little yeses. This radical transcendence is a reason—and a very good reason—for retaining the trinitarian formula in an agential-organic model of God and the world, for it presses us to acknowledge that both aspects of the model, the spirit and the body, are but our small yeses. It allows us fearlessly and thoroughly to investigate this model for all its life-giving and Christic potential while at the same time realizing that it, like all models, does not describe the face of God. The transcendence of God frees us to model God in terms of what is most significant to us (for instance, the life-giving power in our bodies) and to do so not with the fingertips but with both hands. We can do this because we know that God is not captured in nor exhausted by our models. We have given reasons for adopting one or another model (we have, for instance, suggested four primary criteria), but correspondence with divine reality is not and cannot be one of these reasons. That is, I believe, what the transcendence of God, understood as the unavailable face of God, tells us.

Hence, as a revisioning of traditional trinitarian thinking, I would suggest that rather than "the Father, Son, and Holy Spirit," which does not preserve either the radical transcendence or radical immanence of God, we consider the following: the mystery of God (the invisible face or first person), the physicality of God (the visible body or second person), and the mediation of the invisible and the visible (the spirit or third person). One of the unfortunate effects of using the metaphor of father for the first person is that, in its homey associations of human paternal relations (or even in its less homey patriarchal associations), it does not signify radical transcendence. In saying yes to one metaphor, that of father, it does not implicitly say no to all models, which is what invisible face is meant to imply in our model. Moreover, the close association of the metaphors of father and son also undermines divine transcendence, since biological or generational identification is implied. Finally, the traditional language, as many have pointed out, is exclusive in gender, valorizing only the male parental-filial relationship.

Our suggestion of the invisible face, the visible body, and the mediating spirit is obviously also limited and inadequate. God transcends all our models, but in so doing allows us to imagine the backside in all sorts of ways. Among the most powerful for embodied spiritual creatures such as we are is as embodied spirit. Perhaps, but it is at most just another little yes. One inadequacy of our model is a vagueness as to what "mediating" means in relation to spirit: does it imply that spirit is partly a face term, that spirit mediates the invisible to the visible? In a sense it does, at least if we look at ourselves who, as inspirited bodies, are the model for the model. Who we are is known not through our bodies alone (as a corpse illustrates) but through our enlivened, inspirited bodies. So at the least we can say, in terms of this model, that what we know of God is mediated in the body through the spirit. And it is in this sense that we have spoken of two meanings of God's spirit as mediated through the body: the spirit that empowers all life and the Holy Spirit that, for Christians, gives a direction to the teeming life of creation. We know God—we have some intimation of the invisible face of God—through divine incarnation in nature and in the paradigmatic Jesus of Nazareth, in the universe as God's body and in the cosmic Christ.

In conclusion, let us briefly recall how each of these forms of the incarnation radicalizes divine immanence and transcendence. We suggested earlier that when we contemplate the wonders of evolutionary history in both its smallest and its greatest dimensions, through a microscope or a telescope, what we grasp is a concrete experience of awesomeness that comes as close as may be humanly possible to experiencing immanental transcendence or transcendent immanence. Suddenly to see some aspect of creation naked, as it were, in its elemental beauty, its thereness and suchness, stripped of all conventional categories and names and uses, is an experience of transcendence and immanence inextricably joined. This possibility is before us in each and every piece and part of creation: it is the wonder at the world that young children have and that poets and artists retain. It is to experience the ordinary *as* extraordinary. This is experiencing the world as God's body, the ordinariness of all bodies contained within and empowered by the divine.

Our model has also suggested another way that divine transcendence and immanence join: in the body of Christ, the cosmic Christ. As Dorothee Soelle comments on the parable of the Good

Samaritan: "God is, at it were, lying in the streets, if only we could learn to see."[34] The radicalization of transcendence in the Christic paradigm is the incognito appearance of Christ wherever we see human compassion for the outcast and the vulnerable. Radical love for the "unworthy"—the foreigner lying injured on the road (or a destroyed rainforest, the few remaining individuals in a species, or a hungry child)—is also an image that melds divine transcendence and immanence. God is present when and where the oppressed are liberated, the sick are healed, the outcast are invited in. Just as every flower or insect is the body of God if we can learn to see it as such, so also every creaturely body in need is Christ's body, if we can see it as such. There is nothing novel about this suggestion; in fact, it is biblical to the core, for as we read in Matthew, "just as you did it to one of the least of these who are members of my family, you did it to me" (25:40). Our only addition is to suggest that the least of the family members must include, in our time, the other creatures of the earth and even the planet itself.

i thank You God for most this amazing
day:for the leaping greenly spirits of trees
and a blue true dream of sky;and for everything
which is natural which is infinite which is yes

(i who have died am alive again today,
and this is the sun's birthday;this is the birth
day of life and of love and wings:and of the gay
great happening illimitably earth)

how should tasting touching hearing seeing
breathing any—lifted from the no
of all nothing—human merely being
doubt unimaginable You?

(now the ears of my ears awake and
now the eyes of my eyes are opened)
                                    —e.e. cummings

7 / ESCHATOLOGY

A New Shape for Humanity

A new shape for humanity, a new way of being in the world, began to emerge from our reflections on our place in the scheme of things as pictured by the common creation story. We were decentered as the point and goal of evolutionary history and recentered, in the words of biologist Stephen Jay Gould, as "the stewards of life's continuity on earth."[1] We arrived at these conclusions by looking at ourselves from the pedestrian, mundane, earth-up perspective, by seeing ourselves as part of the profound, intricate kind of unity that characterizes the contemporary organic model of reality, as well as the special sort of difference that distinguishes us from other beings on our planet. The new shape for humanity is not only, however, a product of who we are in the common creation story; for Christians it is also who we are as members of God's body qualified by the liberating, healing, and inclusive love of Christ. This identification presses us beyond stewardship of life on earth to solidarity with all earth's creatures, especially the vulnerable. The Christic shape for humanity is built upon our evolutionary distinction, but it is also a radical intensification of it.

Thus, we have been *decentered* as the point and goal of creation and *recentered* as God's partners in helping creation to grow and prosper in our tiny part of God's body. A new place and vocation have been given to us. It is one that is informed by both contemporary science and by Christian faith, for it is grounded in the mundane and the physical but shaped by a new calling that the common creation story and evolutionary science could never have envisioned — the calling to solidarity with all other creatures of the earth, especially the vulnerable and needy ones.

In this final chapter we will try to say concretely what this new shape for humanity might mean in helping to form a different, better world. First, specifically, what is the new, better world? What kind of eschatological vision, a vision of hope for a different and better future, drives us and invites us? A second issue concerns guidelines for the tough decisions we face as we attempt to make this vision concrete. What does the view from the body mean as it pertains to solidarity not only with human outcasts but also with the natural world, the new poor of our time? A third question involves the church within this new shape for humanity. Is it the community of the saved? the body of Christ? or is it, as we will suggest, a sign and witness to the new vision? The church is a place where people are trying to be formed in and by that shape. We conclude with a few autobiographical afterthoughts.

Eschatology:
The Hope for a New Creation

Eschatology can mean many things. Often in the Christian tradition it has been concerned with death and the afterlife, with "last things" such as judgment, hell and heaven, the second coming. But it can also mean the breaking in of new possibilities, of hope for a new creation.[2] It can mean living from a vision for a different present based upon a new future. The future serves as both a goad and a goal, a goad with which to criticize the reigning paradigm and a goal to encourage us to bring into being a new one. We do not have a utopia, an ideal community to which we can point where the new vision is being realized, where things are the way they ought to be; but we can have an "atopia," an imagined world both prophetic and alluring from which we can judge what is wrong with the paradigm that has created the present crisis on our planet. It also presents a vision luring us to another possible shape for ourselves and our world. Criticism of what is and attraction to what might be — these are the notes of a contemporary eschatology needed in our time. But what, specifically, is that critique and lure? The lure or vision comes first, for it gives us a perspective from which to judge our present situation. From our model of the universe as God's body, a model informed by the common creation story and qualified by the Christic paradigm, several features of a new and better world have emerged. These notes of a new creation are not Christian *or* scientific, but a mix of both, a vision of a world in which one could live as a whole being, physical and spiritual, body and soul. Here are some of these notes.

1. *The new vision underscores the unity of each with all and the distinction of each from all: both interdependence and independence.* Central to the new paradigm is the beyond-all-imagining profound, intricate nature of the interrelationship and interdependence of each and every living and nonliving aspect of creation. From breath to breath we depend upon one another. Nothing is more central to the common creation story than the ancient and present character of mutual dependence of all life-forms on one another and on the life-supporting systems of our planet. Yet, at the same time, we are all different from one another, and our distinctions are many, sometimes awesome (black holes, whales, sequoia trees), sometimes strange (the creatures of the Burgess Shale, quarks, blind fish), sometimes profuse (grains of sand on a beach, drops of water in the ocean). Our new paradigm calls attention to unimaginable unity and unimaginable diversity, radicalizing and appreciating both. That dual radicalization and celebration must penetrate our sensibilities and be a key factor in all our decisions, both personal and public.

2. *In this new vision we must learn to live appropriately within the scheme of things.* If the common creation story has taught us one lesson it is that we are not the center of the universe and not even the center of our tiny planet. It has given us a functional cosmology, a way of seeing where we fit in this planet to which we belong. In the vision of a different, better world, this double reality *that* we belong and *where* we belong will be central. We can, in this

paradigm, no longer live a lie in relation to other human beings, other species, and the planet itself. Ecological sin—wanting to have everything for oneself and one's kind—is not only a sin against God (as it was as well in the old paradigm) but it is also, in the new paradigm, contrary to reality. This absolutely critical acknowledgment and practice, which will allow space and place to others and thus help life on earth to continue, is also curiously satisfying, indeed comforting. It is not only that we must share the space and live in proper relations with others, but by doing so, we realize that we belong here. We are welcomed home.

3. *Salvation, the good life, in the new paradigm means first of all the basic, physical needs of the earth's creatures.* The organic model has caused us to see the world through the eyes of the body. This model has made powerfully real to us what we have often forgotten and sometimes despised: we *are* bodies, as is everything else in creation. Moreover, seeing the world as God's body has deepened our sensibilities to the importance of the physical so that we now know that whatever else good, whole, fulfilled life might include, it starts with the basics needed for physical life—food, clean air and water, shelter, space, and so on. If our model has become an interpretive lens through which we see the world, we can never again think of salvation in spiritual, otherworldly, atemporal, or nonspatial ways. Moreover, if God is embodied, then bodies become special and whatever degrades, oppresses, or destroys bodies affronts God. "Sins against the body," actions that deprive, abuse, mutilate, rape, or murder bodies become heinous from the perspective of the model. The view from the body gives us a new way of seeing salvation and sin: as honoring and fulfilling or degrading and destroying the body.

4. *The good life in the new paradigm also involves solidarity with the oppressed.* The Christic shape given to the body of God has a bias for the excluded in its notes of liberation, healing, and inclusion. The Christic vocation involves more than the stewardship of life or even solidarity with other members of our own species (although these are crucial notes of the new paradigm), for it is a special call to the outcast of creation, whoever or whatever that might be at a particular time. Nature is, in our time, the new poor—oppressed, victimized, deteriorating, excluded—and deserves our solidarity in

its vulnerability. We human beings, especially some of us, have *made* nature poor, and we are being called to redress our excesses. Siding with the outcast is neither a popular nor necessarily a successful position. It will not solve all the complex environmental ills that beset the natural world, but it reminds us of one central conviction: God loves the entire creation. The new creation is for all of creation, with special attention to those beings or aspects of it that are suffering or excluded. A cosmological or ecological theology claims that the good news is not only for individual human beings and not even only for oppressed groups of human beings, but for the entire creation.

5. *In the vision of the new creation, we human beings have a special vocation.* We are the stewards of life's continuity on earth and partners with God in solidarity with the oppressed. It is an awesome vocation, a far higher status than being a little lower than the angels, subjects of a divine king, or even the goal of evolutionary history. We now realize that our knowledge of the common creation story and where we fit into it means that we are responsible for taking evolution to its next step, one in which we will consciously bond with other human beings and other life-forms in ways that will create a sustainable, wholesome existence for the rich variety of beings on our planet. The vision of this new creation takes many forms, from international conferences trying to join economic development with environmental integrity to science fiction utopias embodying aspects of the new paradigm.[3] To be stewards of life on our planet and, even more, to side with the oppressed life-forms on earth, is a sublime, formidable, and baffling vocation for mere human beings. It is not one we probably would have chosen, but it has been thrust upon us as the self-conscious ones on earth and as Christians. Faced with this vocation, however, we ought to remember two things. First, each of us has only to sew one small square in the quilt, do well one necessary task for the planetary agenda. Second, we are not the creators or redeemers of creation, only the partners of the creator and savior. God, in the Christic paradigm, is on the side of the oppressed to liberate, heal, and include them. That is God's main activity—and ours—in relation to creation. God, our embodied God, also suffers with all suffering bodies. And beyond even suffering we live with

the hope against hope that defeat and death are not the last word, but that even the least body in the universe, the most insignificant, most vulnerable, most outcast one will participate in the resurrection of the body.

These notes of the new paradigm, the new creation—radical unity and diversity, appropriate living within the scheme of things, the centrality of basic needs, solidarity with the oppressed, a new vocation for human beings—sketch a different portrait for living on our planet than the dualistic, hierarchical, consumer-oriented, individualistic, anthropocentric, modern paradigm. More than anything else the portrait decenters and recenters human beings: we are both less important and more important in the eschatalogical vision of a new future. We are responsible decision makers, among other things, which brings us to the subject of ethics.

Ethics:
A New Lens for Seeing

As we begin these reflections we need to recall that the principal task of an ecological theology, at least the one attempted in these pages, is not to decide the complex, specific issues facing us. Its main task is to change consciousness, to develop a new sensibility about who we are in the scheme of things so that when we deal with concrete issues we can do so differently than in the past. The focus of this essay is on *thinking differently* so that we might behave differently. The focus is a limited one that does not pretend to solve the intricate, complex dilemmas and issues that we face in every dimension of our personal, communal, and political lives. It will not, for instance, tell us what to do about the consumer-addicted life-style of the first world or the destruction of rainforests; it will not formulate the specific economic, political, and social policies and laws needed to address these issues. But it does insist that we look at these and all other issues from the context of a different paradigm than the one that brought about these crises. It suggests a new vision, a new shape for humanity and for our world, a vision that changes the way we see everything and, hence, the way we decide any specific issue and concern.

This essay has been about ethics, that is, correct human conduct, from the very beginning. The constructs within which we live, such as the organic or machine models, imply a mode of conduct. Conduct is not an addendum or applied from a theory because each model contains within itself a way of being in the world. All the preceding chapters have been focused on unfolding the ecological, theological, and christological implications of the organic model for human behavior, that is, how we consider and comport ourselves in the world and in relation to other beings. Hence, in considering ethics at the close of this essay we mean a particular aspect of our conduct: the relationship of an ecological theology of embodiment to concrete, nitty-gritty decisions on all sorts of difficult issues in our personal and private lives. And there are a vast number of these, needless to say; in fact, there is scarcely any issue facing us in the political, economic, medical, technological, military, educational, or family arenas that lies outside the range of an ecological theology of embodiment. Difficult issues concerning the well-being of bodies, especially the most vulnerable ones, confront us wherever we look: prenatal and nutritional care of the young, experimental genetics, rape and sexual abuse, endangered species, AIDS, the homeless, clear-cut logging practices, affirmative action laws, taxation policies, pollution control and water rights, abortion and contraception availability, immigration laws, health insurance and care, educational costs and opportunities, and on and on. The range of ecotheological issues is endless, and the view from the body, especially the needy body, changes how we see *every* issue. To make things more complex, the rights of some needy bodies are often in competition with the rights of other needy bodies, as in the case of the livelihood of loggers versus the lives of nearly extinct animals or the allocation of scarce funds to meals for disadvantaged school children or for the housebound elderly.

Our new paradigm does help us, however, to ask some novel questions and see some new connections. For instance, we become aware of the deep as well as subtle relationships among issues that in the modern individualistic, anthropocentric paradigm are not connected, such as those involving economic priorities and environmental health. The unwillingness of the American government at the 1992 UN Conference on Environment and Development to support policies on biodiversity and carbon dioxide emissions is a case in point. President Bush claimed that such policies would have adverse effects on American business. From the perspective of the embodiment model that stresses the basic needs of all life-forms, as well as the long-term health of our planet, that claim is parochial and shortsighted. Or the current battle over the right to abortion in the United States, when seen in light of our new paradigm, becomes an issue not of the sacredness of every human embryo, as it is in the individualistic, anthropocentric point of view, but of two other broader and deeper bodily concerns: the right of each child born to be wanted and to have the essentials for a healthy, satisfying life as well as the right of women to control their own bodies. The new paradigm widens the perspective on abortion from a narrow, absolutist one of human embryonic rights to the well-being of those born in addition to the well-being of those who must care for those born.

The view from the body will not tell us precisely what to do about biodiversity, global warming, or abortion, but this paradigm does offer to these issues, as well as others, a way of reflecting upon them within a framework larger than individualistic anthropocentrism. It suggests that the many issues facing us be considered in light of these notes: the need of other life-forms (not just human ones) for the basic essentials; the admonition for humans to live appropriately, allowing space for other species; our vocation to help life continue on our planet and especially to side with the oppressed, which in our time must include the new poor, nature. A shift in paradigm from the modern construct to the organic one involves decentering our species individually and collectively in terms of both numbers and life-style and recentering us as the species responsible for helping the rich, varied, interdependent community of individuals of many species to continue.

Our model, as is true of all models, helps us to see issues through its own lens. It highlights a few insights and blocks out others; it does not give us the whole picture. The major issues before us are difficult, painful, and complex; the point is certainly not to claim our new vision has all the answers and pit it against other positions. Many factors, areas of expertise, personal stories, and values enter into responsible decision making at both the private and public level. Different models suggest different assumptions and sensibilities and provide different perspectives on the issues, whatever they are. Our model—the world as God's body, rooted in the common creation story and qualified by the Christic paradigm—helps us to think differently in a number of important ways about ourselves and where we fit in the world. To think differently in these ways is but one contribution to the planetary agenda, but it is, we have insisted, an essential and neglected different kind of thinking.

Ecclesia:
A Sign of the New Creation

The church is called the body of Christ. The embodiment model has been central to ecclesiology; it has been one of the ways that organic thinking has flourished in Christianity. The model has encouraged a sense of unity of Christians with one another in and across denominational lines as well as with Christ, the head of the body. It has also supported a sense of uniqueness and privilege within the Christian community: we are the body of the savior of the world. While it might seem appropriate that an embodiment theology would culminate in the church as the body of Christ, deeper reflection causes us to pause. The model of the church as the body of Christ is anthropocentric in relation to other species and the natural world for this body is composed only of human beings. The model is also exclusive in relation to people of other religious traditions, for it appropriates divine embodiment for Christians alone. While the model has some advantages, especially when used in conjunction with other very different models, such as the church as a pilgrim people, as a liberating community, or as a fellowship of friends, it should not be seen as the consummation of the model of the world as God's body.[4] Throughout this essay we have been concerned to underscore embodiment as the basis of our common life, linking us in deep, permanent, and intricate ways not only with all other human beings but also with all other life-forms and, most especially, with God, the source of all embodied life. Embodiment is not exclusively a Christian nor a human phenomenon: all creatures are not only embodied but divinely embodied, for we all live and move and have our being within the divine body.

What, then, of the church? Our model suggests, in its recentering of those human beings who stand within the Christic paradigm, a modest though radical metaphor for the church: it is a sign of the new creation. The church is a sign of the inbreaking of the new vision with its several characteristics or notes. Where human beings, decentered as the goal of creation and recentered as those who side with the oppressed, create communities embodying concern for the basic needs of the life-forms on earth, aware of their profound interdependence as well as individuality, *here* is the church from the perspective of the organic model. Where the new vision of the liberating, healing, inclusive love of the embodied God in the Christic paradigm occurs, *there* is the church. The church as institution is called to live out the new creation *in its body*, and, in this sense, the embodiment model is central to its nature and vocation. The institutional church as manifest in concrete, local churches can become a critical social body helping to bring about the new reality. Needless to say, this does not necessarily occur in the institutions we call churches, nor does it occur only in these institutions. It may occur there but it does occur elsewhere.

To say that the church is a sign rather than the symbol of the inbreaking new creation makes a modest statement about the church. It relativizes the church and describes it in terms of its function, not its being. The church is an activity attempting to manifest the new paradigm. The model acknowledges that aspects of this paradigm emerge in other communities as well and that these various communities can work together in their common endeavor. From the perspective of our model the church is one voice in the conversation of the planetary agenda. The well-being of our planet and its life-forms is a common responsibility of all human beings. The world as we have come to know it through the common creation story cannot be saved by Christianity or any other religion, but Christians have some special contributions to make to the planetary agenda. As the incarnational religion *par excellence*, Christianity can offer its basic belief in divine enfleshment, its theology of embodiment in which God, human beings, and everything else in the cosmos are knit together. Christianity can also offer to the planetary agenda its vision of the liberation, healing, and inclusion of the oppressed, and in our day that must include vulnerable nature. Radical embodiment and radical inclusion of the outcast—these are not the only signs of the new creation, but they are essential ones.

Some Afterthoughts

At the end of the day and at the end of a book, especially a book on planetary responsibility, one can easily lose heart. In one of my favorite "Far Side" cartoons two tiny insects are perched on top of a mushroom against a starlit sky and one of them remarks, "Just look at those stars tonight . . . makes you feel sort of small and insignificant."[5] Indeed. The common creation story dwarfs us all; the entire human species from its beginnings a few million years ago until now is but a second in the time frame of the universe. The life of each one of us is too brief even to be counted. We are indeed small and insignificant.

Even in one tiny corner of the universe, our infinitesimal planet, where our species has achieved a dubious dominance, we feel uncertain, discouraged, and often overwhelmed. Even here in this small place with our impressive intelligence, energy, and imagination we often feel worse than small and insignificant—we feel selfish and corrupt or at least indifferent and weary. Planetary responsibility is too much for us; it will involve too much thoughtfulness, too much energy, too many sacrifices. Besides, is not all this talk of stewardship of life's continuity and siding with the oppressed just quixotic jousting with windmills? The decay of our planet is probably inevitable, so we might as well just accept it. What real chance do we have of turning things around?

All of this is probably true. Those who fought the plague in Albert Camus's novel by that name did not expect to exterminate the plague or even to escape it themselves. They only decided to live differently while they did live, to live as if life mattered while they had it, to live with integrity in light of the brutal reality that defined their world. One has to get up in the morning and look in the mirror. It may come to nothing more than that.

But one *does* have to get up in the morning and keep going. How to do that? Throughout the centuries Christians have typically done so by being deeply rooted, personally and daily rooted, in God. Social justice and spirituality are not opposite tracks; rather, staying the course on any justice issue appears possible only by being grounded in a power and love beyond oneself. African-American and Latin American liberation theologies, as well as feminist and womanist ones, insist on the interface of spirituality and the fight for justice. They are continuing the tradition of John Woolman, the eighteenth-century Quaker abolitionist, Sojourner Truth, former slave and champion of women's rights, and Dorothy Day, the Roman Catholic socialist and founder of urban hospitality houses for the destitute—all of whom were profoundly and unabashedly religious. Casting one's despair as well as one's hope for transformation on the source of all breath and new life has been a daily discipline and necessity for most Christians who have tried in small or large ways to make the world a better place.

The ecological crisis is no exception. It may appear to have a greater measure of despair and a lesser one of hope for transformation than some other issues, but in type it is no different. A spiritual grounding is certainly not the only thing needed, for a Christian concerned with the well-being of our planet ought to attend to the issue as a citizen, a worker, a consumer, a householder, a church member, and in whatever other circles one exists. But a spiritual base is an often forgotten *sine qua non*, especially for action-oriented Protestants who are wary of spirituality as too inner-directed or individualistic. There is even more resistance from Protestants to a "nature" spirituality, a spirituality that finds renewal and hope coming from what the eye sees and not just what the ear hears.

As a Protestant and erstwhile Barthian, I was myself for many years such a resister. Only "the Word" that reached my ears conveyed the presence of God, never the sights before my eyes. In these closing pages, I would like to share a little of my own spiritual journey, not because it is in any way exceptional but simply because a particular case can sometimes be helpful.

My first inclination toward nature spirituality occurred while hiking in the White Mountains of New England when I was fourteen years old. I was filled with oceanic feelings of oneness with nature and God as I lay on mountaintops watching billowy clouds form over distant hills. I recall reciting silently to myself, "I lift up my eyes unto the hills from whence cometh my help." Help came from the hills, from the divine through nature. Later, at divinity school, I was taught that the correct translation made a clear division between the hills and the divine: "From where will my help come? My help comes from the Lord . . . ." I quickly learned to listen for the Word of God, which meant averting my eyes from those beckoning hills. Almost thirty years passed before I would dare to look at nature again as a divine habitation, but by now oceanic feelings of oneness had been replaced by wonder at the particular, interest in detail, delight in difference. Annie Dillard's description of a goldfish named Ellery sums it up (the attention to detail in this passage is the basis for the sense of wonder it calls forth in me):

> This Ellery cost me twenty-five cents. He is a deep red-orange, darker than most goldfish. He steers short distances mainly with his slender red lateral fins; they seem to provide impetus for going backward, up, or down. It took me a few days to discover his ventral fins; they are completely transparent and all but invisible—dream fins. He also has a short anal fin, and a tail that is deeply notched and perfectly transparent at the two tapered tips. He can extend his mouth, so it looks like a length of pipe; he can shift the angle of his eyes in his head so he can look before and behind himself, instead of simply out to his side. His belly, what there is of it, is white ventrally, and a patch of this white extends up his sides—the variegated Ellery. When he opens his gill slits he shows a thin crescent of silver where the flap overlapped—as though all his brightness were sunburn.
>
> For this creature, as I said, I paid twenty-five cents. I had never bought an animal before. It was very simple; I went to a store in Roanoke called "Wet Pets"; I handed the man a quarter, and he handed me a knotted plastic bag bouncing with water in which a green plant floated and the goldfish swam. This fish,

two bits' worth, has a coiled gut, a spine radiating fine bones, and a brain. Just before I sprinkle his food flakes into his bowl, I rap three times on the bowl's edge; now he is conditioned, and swims to the surface when I rap. And, he has a heart.[6]

Every time I read this passage I am unnerved by the juxtaposition of twenty-five cents with the elaborateness, cleverness, and sheer glory of this tiny bit of matter named Ellery. Over the years I have learned that the closer attention I pay to whatever piece of the world is before me — the more I know about it, the more open I am to its presence, the closer I look at it or listen to it or touch it or smell it — the more amazed I am by it. It is not that I "see God in it" in any direct or general way; rather, it is the specialness, the difference, the intricacy of each creature, event, or aspect of nature that calls forth wonder. And that wonder helps sustain me; it helps me stay the course.

For instance, while writing this book, I have been hiking in the temperate rainforests along the coast of British Columbia. I have learned a thing or two in these forests about life and death, about the way they intertwine and depend on each other. I've learned this by paying close attention to huge, ancient red cedars and Douglas firs lying on the forest floor. These so-called dead trees are, in fact, far from dead, for they will live several hundred more years as "nurse" trees to countless forms of life, including sapling trees. The new life will use them as a base for their own early, tenuous grasp at existence, for the nurse trees are warmer and have more nutrients than the earth. The fallen trees will eventually decompose into the forest floor to become yet another form of matter to support yet more life. It is not at all clear what is dead and what is alive in these forests, or, more accurately, death and life here are not absolute categories as they are for most of us most of the time. This realization of the intimacy and mutual dependency between life and death is not an "idea" for me, but has become a felt reality as I hike these woods, seeing ragged stumps of cut trees and the bodies of fallen trees serving as the source of new life. In order for this realization to sink in, I've had to pay attention to the detail: to the way the roots of a new sapling grip the trunk of a rotting tree or the way different kinds of mosses covering the logs grow in layers on top of each other. Insight has come through the particular, through paying attention. I knew for years that from death comes new life: I knew it as a platitude and as a Christian mystery, but paying attention to the actual way an old, dying tree nurses new saplings made it a reality for me, a reality that has greatly calmed my terrors of extinction when I was seven. It has also given me heart and hope.

Perhaps this is the way that we see the presence of God in the world and are nurtured and renewed by it—not through feelings of oceanic oneness with nature but by paying attention, listening to, learning about the specialness, the difference, the detail of the "wonderful life" of which we are a part. The body of God is not *a* body, but all the different, peculiar, particular bodies about us. One does not need mountains or rainforests—any body will do, if we are willing to pay attention to it as Meister Eckhart eloquently says: "If I spent enough time with the tiniest creature—even a caterpillar—I would never have to prepare a sermon. So full of God is every creature."[7] Yes, indeed. But only if one spends "enough time" with each creature. "Each creature," of course, includes human ones: the point is that whether we pay attention to the others in nature or to our own kind we do so with love, that is, as Iris Murdoch says, with the "extremely difficult realisation that something other than oneself is real."[8] We do not use nature or other people as a means to an end—our union with God—but see each and every creature, every body, as intrinsically valuable in itself, in its specialness, its distinctiveness, its difference from ourselves. This acknowledgment of difference and intrinsic worth is not only the basis of an ecological ethic as we have seen, but it is also the source of a nature spirituality. The earth becomes the place where we put down our roots and renew ourselves to stay the course, not because all creatures are transparent images of God but because each in its own peculiar, idiosyncratic, special difference is a wonder to behold. The model of the world as God's body encourages us to dare to love bodies and find them valuable and wonderful—just that and nothing more. The "God part" will take care of itself if we can love and value the bodies. That is what an incarnational theology assures us: it is all right to have a nature spirituality. In fact, we should have one.

An incarnational theology assures us as well that we are not alone in loving the bodies of our planet. I close with two brief readings that have helped me. The first is by the medieval mystic Julian of Norwich and could be seen as a meditation on that lovely spiritual, "He's got the whole world in his hands."

> . . . a little thing, the size of a hazelnut, in the palm of my hand, and it was as round as a ball. I looked at it with my mind's eye and I thought, 'What can this be?' And the answer came, 'It is all that is made.' I marvelled that it could last, for I thought it might have crumbled to nothing, it was so small. And the answer came to my mind, 'It lasts and ever shall because God loves it.' And all things have being through the love of God. In this little thing I see three truths. The first is that God made it. The second is that God loves it. The third is that God looks after it. What is God indeed that is maker and lover and keeper. I cannot find words to tell."[9]

This is the hope against hope that our efforts on behalf of our planet are not ours alone but that the source and power of life in the universe is working in and through us for the well-being of all creation, including our tiny bit of it.

Another perspective is that of the contemporary novelist Alice Walker, another lover of the planet.

> Helped are those who love the Earth, their mother, and who willingly suffer that she may not die; in their grief over her pain they will weep rivers of blood, and in their joy in her lively response to love, they will converse with trees . . .
>
> Helped are those who find the courage to do at least one small thing each day to help the existence of another—plant, animal, river, human being. They shall be joined by a multitude of the timid.
>
> Helped are those who lose their fear of death; theirs is the power to envision the future in a blade of grass.
>
> Helped are those who love and actively support the diversity of life; they shall be secure in their differentness.
>
> Helped are those who *know*.[10]

We *do* know, and we ask for help.

Notes

Chapter 1: The Ecological Crisis

1. Jonathan Schell makes this point with chilling eloquence in his book, *The Fate of the Earth* (New York: Avon Books, 1982).

2. While the nuclear threat may be clear and stark, we are now coming to realize in the present post-Cold War era that the elimination of nuclear weapons (not to mention nuclear waste) is a highly complex and difficult matter. Nuclear terrorism, proliferation, and rearmament are all possibilities. We appear, however, to have entered a less immediate and more elusive stage of nuclear danger. See Sharon Welch's fine analysis of living with the continuing nuclear threat: *A Feminist Ethic of Risk* (Minneapolis: Fortress Press, 1990).

3. The phrase is from Bill McKibben's book, *The End of Nature* (New York: Random House, 1989).

4. For an interesting, ambitious example of this mentality by a highly responsible journal, see the fall 1989 issue of *Scientific American*, entitled "Managing the Planet" (note the title!).

5. Herman E. Daly and John B. Cobb, Jr., *For the Common Good: Redirecting the Economy Toward Community, the Environment, and a Sustainable Future* (Boston: Beacon Press, 1989), 400.

6. Thomas Berry develops this point when he insists that we need to widen our "identification horizon" —that is, what we identify with—from the self and its immediate concerns and tribal others to include all others (*The Dream of the Earth* [San Francisco: Sierra Club Books, 1988]). He poignantly sums up our present narrow horizon when he remarks, "a sense of the planet never entered our minds" (44).

7. One recognition of this reality was the "Earth Summit," the UN Conference on Environment and Development held in Rio de Janeiro in June 1992. While its results are debatable, its mission, numbers, and breadth testify to the growing realization that environmental health, economic viability, and human well-being are inextricable issues. Maurice

Strong, the secretary general of the summit, stated its goal as laying "the foundation for a global partnership between developing and more industrialized countries, to ensure the future of the planet." Upwards of 30,000 people from governmental and non-governmental agencies, including 170 heads of state, attended the conference. If it did nothing else, it made clear that the agenda in question involves "everything that is."

8. The complexity and difficulty of this task should not be underestimated, especially for persons in middle-management positions who have little control over the conduct of their work. It is curious but true that householders and chief executives are both better able to change their positions toward planetary responsibility than are the majority of workers who fall in the middle. Thus, the burden of change must come from the top and the bottom, from the leaders of industry (with the insistence of appropriate legislation) and from the grass roots (with the prompting of education for environmental responsibility).

9. An excellent resource on the political and economic dimensions of the ecological crisis can be found in Lester R. Brown et al., *State of the World 1992: A Worldwatch Institute Report on Progress Toward a Sustainable Society* (New York: W. W. Norton and Co., 1993). This report is produced annually and is available in paperback for a small price (if you cannot find it at your bookstore, write to Worldwatch, 1776 Massachusetts Avenue, N.W., Washington, D.C. 20036 or call 202–452–1999). Another very helpful in-depth analysis of economic and political issues and strategies is Al Gore, *Earth in the Balance: Ecology and the Human Spirit* (New York: Houghton Mifflin Co., 1992).

10. See my article, "The Theologian as Advocate," *Theological Education* (Spring 1989): 79–97, in which I discuss the model's strengths and limitations.

11. See my book *Metaphorical Theology: Models of God in Religious Language* (Philadelphia: Fortress Press, 1982) for the deconstructive phase of this task and *Models of God: Theology for an Ecological, Nuclear Age* (Philadelphia: Fortress Press, 1987) for the constructive phase.

12. This correlation is well documented in a number of works; a few of the ones I have found most interesting and persuasive are as follows: Susan Griffin, *Made From This Earth: An Anthology of Writings* (New York: Harper and Row, 1982); Gerda Lerner, *The Creation of Patriarchy* (Oxford: Oxford University Press, 1986); Carolyn Merchant, *The Death of Nature: Women, Ecology and the Scientific Revolution* (New York: Harper and Row, 1980); Martha Weigle, *Creation and Procreation: Feminist Reflections on Mythologies of Cosmogony and Parturition* (Philadelphia: University of Pennsylvania Press, 1989).

13. These terms, especially *matter*, *body*, and *nature*, demand definitions or at least some indication of how they will be used in this essay. The most basic one is *matter*: the term refers to that of which everything is

made, with the differences we see in the world about us consisting of different arrangements of atoms. "Everything you touch or feel, all the objects of our world with their extraordinary range of appearances and properties, consist of different arrangements of atoms" (Robert M. Hazen and James Trefil, *Science Matters: Achieving Scientific Literacy* [New York: Doubleday Anchor Books, 1991], 95). The following list of things are all "matter": an elephant, the Empire State Building, sand, your left ear, the Pacific Ocean, air, tofu, Jupiter, beer, this book. These things differ from one another depending on how their atoms and molecules (clumps of atoms) are organized. The three main styles of organization or "states of matter" are gases, liquids, and solids (*Science Matters*, 94–95). Gases, liquids, and solids can change phase, a critical feature in understanding the interconnectedness of reality in contemporary science. "If an ice cube falls to the floor it melts . . . If you boil water on the stove, you produce a cloud of steam. If you let your paintbrush dry without cleaning it, the brush becomes hard and useless. These are examples of processes in which matter changes phase—from solid to liquid in the first case, from liquid to gas in the second, and from liquid to solid in the third" (*Science Matters*, 99). *Body* in this understanding of matter is, then, a solid state of matter and refers primarily to "the physical or material frame or structure of man [sic] or of any animal: the whole material organism viewed as an organic entity" (*Oxford English Dictionary*, 2d ed., 1989). While the most precise meaning of *body* is, then, a living organism, the term can be used analogously for any solid: "a separate portion of matter, large or small, a material thing; something that has physical existence and extension in space" (*OED*). Finally, *nature* is the sum total of all matter in all its states—the various solids, gases, and liquids that comprise the universe—as well as the laws that regulate its processes ("The creative and regulative physical power which is conceived of as operating in the material world and as the immediate cause of all its phenomena" [*OED*]). More commonly, we refer to "nature" as opposed to "culture," in a way similar to the equally dualistic and hierarchical pairing of matter versus spirit or body versus soul. Contemporary science, however, does not recognize these distinctions, insisting that nature (the sum total of all matter) consists of infinite arrangements of atoms, giving us a picture of reality characterized by continuity, interrelationship, and transformation among states of matter. A theology that attempts to be compatible with this picture should seek ways to affirm these characteristics when it speaks of culture, soul, spirit—and of God.

14. See especially Merchant, *The Death of Nature*; Mary Daly, *Gyn/Ecology: The Metaphysics of Radical Feminism* (Boston: Beacon Press, 1979); Margaret R. Miles, *Carnal Knowing: Female Nakedness and Religious Meaning in the Christian West* (Boston: Beacon Press, 1989).

15. This division is complex and by no means absolute, but it does appear in early examples of the current women's movement (see the distinction between "reformers" and "radicals" in the introduction to *Womanspirit Rising: A Feminist Reader in Religion*, ed. Carol P. Christ and Judith Plaskow [San Francisco: Harper and Row, 1979]), as well as in current work, such as ecofeminism and French feminist deconstructionism, both of which, in different ways and for different reasons, tend to favor embodiment as the way to women's liberation. Goddess traditions, of course, are heavily in favor of women's identification with both embodiment and nature.

16. See, for example, Toril Moi, *Sexual/Textual Politics: Feminist Literary Theory* (New York: Routledge, 1985); Luce Irigaray, *This Sex Which Is Not One*, trans. Catherine Porter (Ithaca, N.Y.: Cornell University Press, 1985); Chris Weeden, *Feminist Practice and Poststructuralist Theory* (Oxford: Basil Blackwell, 1987). See also the fine historical study of this struggle within Christianity in Peter Brown's *The Body and Society: Men, Women, and Sexual Resurrection in Early Christianity* (New York: Columbia University Press, 1988).

17. The full quotation from which this phrase comes is as follows: "Ecology is the study of the organisms in their home: it is the study of the structure and function of the organisms and groups of organisms found in nature and their interactions with one another and with their environment" (G. Tyler Miller, Jr., *Living in the Environment*, 3d ed. [Belmont, Calif.: Wadsworth, 1982], 44).

18. The debate ranges from the extreme organic perspective of deep ecology (see Bill Devall and George Sessions, *Deep Ecology: Living as if Nature Mattered* [Salt Lake City, Ut.: Peregrine Smith Books, 1985]) and the Gaia hypothesis (see James Lovelock, *The Ages of Gaia: A Biography of Our Living Earth* [New York: W. W. Norton and Co., 1988]) to the reductionism of molecular biology, which understands all living organisms in terms of physics and chemistry—in other words, as "nothing but" atoms and molecules. For a description and critique of this latter position, see Arthur Peacocke, *God and the New Biology* (London: J. M. Dent and Sons, 1986). An intermediary position, one that I find agreeable, is voiced by Merchant, *The Death of Nature*, 99–100. "Along with current challenges to mechanistic technology, holistic presuppositions about nature are being revived in ecology's premise that everything is connected to everything else and in its emphasis on the primacy of interactive processes in nature. All parts are dependent on one another and mutually affect each other and the whole. Each portion of an ecological community, each niche, exists in dynamic relationship with the surrounding ecosystem. The organism occupying any particular niche affects and is affected by the entire web of living and nonliving environmental components. Ecology, as a philosophy of nature, has roots in organicism—the idea that the cosmos is an organic entity, growing

and developing from within, in an integrated unity of structure and function."

19. The use of organic and mechanical models is complex in science (especially in fields other than ecology) and only loosely related to the worldviews that rely on them. That is, contemporary science uses both models, finds neither adequate and other models necessary, while also claiming that some phenomena appear to fit no model. On the issue of the mechanical versus the organic model, Robert John Russell asks whether Newtonian mechanics or Darwinian evolution should be considered as mechanical or organic, since "cases can be made for both interpretations in each case, e.g., in Newtonian gravity, presumably a mechanical theory yielding a 'clockwork universe,' all bodies are interconnected; in Darwinian evolution, presumably an organic theory yielding an ecological view of nature, the gene is the 'mechanism' of variation and is unaffected by the environment of the phenotype" (from private correspondence). Our use of the body and machine or organic and mechanical models is at the level of worldviews, not scientific theory and practice—at the level of what Carolyn Merchant calls "the death of nature," the substitution of a view that sees nature as inert, static, atomistic, externally objective ("out there") instead of alive, growing and changing, multilevelled, holistic, and including human beings (*The Death of Nature*, chap. 8). To the extent that mechanism and organism or the machine and the body express some of these characteristics, they serve as models of the two views of reality.

20. For one treatment of holism versus atomism, see Paul Davies, *The Cosmic Blueprint: New Discoveries in Nature's Creative Ability to Order the Universe* (New York: Simon and Schuster, 1988).

21. As Merchant points out, mechanistic thinking, beginning in the 1950s, replaced the organic model in ecology, resulting in a managerial perspective concerning the future use of resources. "The concept of the ecosystem . . . is based on the mathematical modeling of nature. Data are abstracted from the organic context in the form of information bits and then manipulated according to a set of differential equations, allowing the prediction of ecological change and the rational management of the ecosystem and its resources as a whole" (*The Death of Nature*, 103).

22. The term *postmodern* is used in various ways in contemporary thought, but here it will refer to twentieth-century (postmodern) versus Newtonian (modern) science. The following helpful table by Ian Barbour, differentiating the twentieth-century scientific paradigm from the medieval and Newtonian, outlines the postmodern view of nature operative in this essay (*Religion in an Age of Science*, vol. 1 [New York: Harper and Row, 1990], 219).

Medieval	*Newtonian*	*Twentieth Century*
1. Fixed order	Change as rearrangement	Evolutionary, historical, emergent

Medieval	*Newtonian*	*Twentieth Century*
2. Teleological	Deterministic	Law and change, structure and openness
3. Substantive	Atomistic	Relational, ecological, interdependent
4. Hierarchical, anthropocentric	Reductionistic	Systems and wholes, organismic
5. Dualistic (spirit/matter)	Dualistic (mind/body)	Multilevelled
6. Kingdom	Machine	Community

23. In this essay we will confine our focus on *spirit* to indicate the life, animating principle, or meaning of bodies. In this sense, spirit and body are not separable, for an organism, a body, is indistinguishable from the vital principle (literally, the breath) that gives it existence. A body that no longer has spirit or breath becomes a corpse, a *dead* body.

24. For a discussion of this point see *Models of God*, "God as Lover," chap. 5.

25. The connections between our bodies, the body of the earth, and the body of the universe—in other words, various forms of matter—are suggestively captured in this quotation: "My body was originally formed from an ovum and sperm in my mother's body, and this ovum and sperm were formed of matter which came into the bloodstream of my father and mother from the world outside. I am formed of the matter of the universe and am linked through it to the remotest stars in time and space. My body has passed through all the stages of evolution through which matter was first formed into atoms and molecules, when the living cell appeared. I have passed through every stage from protoplasm to fish and animal . . . If I could know myself, I would know matter and life . . . since all are contained within me" (Bede Griffiths, *Return to the Centre* [Springfield, Ill.: Templegate, 1976]).

26. The term *God* is used here and in the other early sections of the book in customary ways in Western religious and cultural thought influenced by the Hebrew and Christian traditions. Thus *God* is, in this monotheistic, ethical worldview, the One object of supreme adoration, who as creator and redeemer of the universe is both its source and its hope as well as the standard of human behavior. This view of God will undergo modification in the course of seeing it through the lens of the body model, but some central continuities will remain, especially its agential monotheistic ethicism.

27. For a fuller discussion of the nature of metaphors and models, see *Metaphorical Theology*, chaps. 2, 3, 4, and *Models of God*, chap. 2.

28. *Immanence* and *transcendence* are complex terms with troubled histories in both Judaism and Christianity. Popularly, these traditions have prided themselves on having transcendent views of God in contrast to the immanent views of "pagan" religions. Here *transcendent* is an honorific term referring to a distant, external, all-powerful, superbeing who is "above and independent of the universe" (OED), while *immanent* is a disreputable designation for the notion of the divine as indwelling (or reduced to) reality. This caricature is not, of course, fair to the ways in which both Judaism and Christianity have imaginatively and at times profoundly expressed God's immanence (most notably in the Wisdom and Logos traditions), but it does suggest a deep and abiding problem of coherence between the two dimensions of divine reality. A central project of this essay will be to redefine divine transcendence and immanence in ways that radicalize each and relate them in credible — as well as religiously significant — ways (see chap. 5, "A Meditation on Exodus 33:23b" and chap. 6, "Face, Body, and Spirit").

29. For wide-ranging analyses of the body from a variety of feminist hermeneutical perspectives, see Alison M. Jaggar and Susan R. Bordo, eds., *Gender/Body/Knowledge: Feminist Reconstructions of Being and Knowing* (New Brunswick, N.J.: Rutgers University Press, 1989) and Susan Rubin Suleiman, ed., *The Female Body in Western Culture: Contemporary Perspectives* (Cambridge: Harvard University Press, 1985). For a recent ecofeminist point of view, see Charlene Spretnak, "Embracing the Body," in *States of Grace: The Recovery of Meaning in the Postmodern Age* (San Francisco: Harpers, 1991), 114–55.

30. One recent and interesting analysis of the way that the success of the women's movement in allowing women to enter nontraditional fields has backlashed is found in Naomi Wolf's thesis that as women have become more powerful, they are being pressured also to become more beautiful: "In the 1980's it was evident that as women became more important, beauty too became more important. The closer women come to power, the more physical self-consciousness is asked of them. 'Beauty' becomes the condition for a woman to take the next step. You are now too rich. Hence, you cannot be too thin" (*The Beauty Myth* [London: Chatto and Windus, 1990], 16). Wolf gives as evidence of this subtle form of control over women's bodies the increase in eating disorders and cosmetic surgery, not to mention the explicit brutal forms of control through rape and sexual abuse. She poses a very serious issue when she asks: "Are women the pliable sex, innately adapted to being shaped, cut, and subjected to physical invasion? Does the female body deserve the same notion of integrity as the male body?" (227).

31. The realization that much of what we take as reality is a construction (interpretation or understanding) by dominant groups for their own benefit is one of the key insights of contemporary hermeneutics, and es-

pecially of the hermeneutics of various liberation movements. This essay will be concerned with suggesting different constructions of both "body" and "nature" than are conventional in our society. The next chapter will critique the classic construction of body and suggest a new construction derived from the common creation story. Other chapters will criticize the subject-object, "us-them" construction of nature in which all other life-forms are viewed dualistically and hierarchically as both beneath human beings and as created for our use. In its place we will suggest a construction in which we learn to assume our proper place *within* nature as *part of* nature.

 32. The term *common creation story* is widely used to refer to the one creation story that all human beings, all other life-forms — and, indeed, everything that is — have in common. It is the story associated with the big bang theory of the beginning of the universe billions of years ago and its subsequent development. The adjective "common" distinguishes this creation story from the cosmogonies and cosmologies of the various religions that, while also providing narratives of the origin and theory of the universe, are accepted only by their adherents. The distinctive characteristic of the common creation story is its inclusiveness, but an inclusiveness marked, in its present stage, by the most radical diversity and individuality imaginable.

Chapter 2: The Organic Model

 1. Ian Barbour, *Religion in an Age of Science*, vol. 1 (New York: Harper and Row, 1990), 147.

 2. Two persuasive, interesting interpretations of the demise of the organic model are found in Carolyn Merchant, *The Death of Nature: Women, Ecology and the Scientific Revolution* (New York: Harper and Row, 1980); and Stephen Toulmin, *The Return to Cosmology: Postmodern Science and the Theology of Nature* (Berkeley: University of California Press, 1982).

 3. For an analysis of deep ecology, see chap. 4, "Us versus It: Living a Lie in Relation to Nature."

 4. Basic scientific literacy is both necessary and difficult to attain. This essay maintains, however, that the needed knowledge is not specialized expertise on quantum physics or differing theories among contemporary evolutionists, but the broadly accepted picture that respected scientists and philosophers of science have of reality. That knowledge is available in a number of recently published works. One very readable one is by Robert M. Hazen and James Trefil, *Science Matters: Achieving Scientific Literacy* (New York: Anchor Books, 1991); see also James Trefil, *1001 Things Everyone Should Know About Science* (New York: Doubleday, 1992).

5. Some are presently voicing this concern. Wolfhart Pannenberg, bemoaning Barth's decision 'in principle' that a theological doctrine of creation should not concern itself with scientific descriptions of the world, concludes: "If theologians want to conceive of God as the creator of the real world, they cannot possibly bypass the scientific description of that world" ("The Doctrine of Creation and Modern Science," in *Cosmos as Creation: Theology and Science in Consonance*, ed. Ted Peters [Nashville: Abingdon Press, 1989], 156–57). Physicist and theologian Arthur Peacocke states: "Any affirmation about God's relation to the world, any doctrine of creation if it is not to be vacuous and sterile, must be about the relation of God to the creation, and this creation is the world that the natural sciences describe. Theology really has no other choice unless it wants to retreat to a ghetto where people just talk to themselves and not to the rest of the world" ("Theology and Science Today," in *Cosmos as Creation*, 30). Physicist Hanbury Brown writes: "When religious beliefs lose touch with reality they are likely to turn *inwards* and present a picture of the world which is no more than a mirror of ourselves, and such a picture . . . is potentially dangerous. If our system of religious beliefs is to form a coherent worldview, as it did in the Medieval Model, it must look *outwards* to what contemporary science is telling us about the world around us" (*The Wisdom of Science: Its Relevance to Culture and Religion* [Cambridge: Cambridge University Press, 1986], 172).

6. The trajectory moving both God and human beings out of nature and into the inner self is a complex one, to say the least. A few critical names, however, are certainly Friedrich Schleiermacher, who based theology in self-consciousness, Karl Barth, who vigorously repudiated Schleiermacher's move, and the line of existentialists from Søren Kierkegaard to Rudolf Bultmann (and Paul Tillich, to a lesser extent), who sealed the mid-twentieth century victory over Barth. None of the players in this contest, however, saw nature as significant: Schleiermacher stated that creation was at most an implication of one's personal sense of dependence; Barth saw creation as enclosed within election and totally defined by it; and Bultmann claimed that God's action was entirely limited to the inner person, with science left to deal with the natural world.

7. For a sampling of the work of theologians influenced by this perspective, see the following: Barbour, *Religion in an Age of Science*; Thomas Berry, *The Dream of the Earth* (San Francisco: Sierra Club Books, 1988); Charles Birch and John Cobb, Jr., *The Liberation of Life: From the Cell to the Community* (Cambridge: Cambridge University Press, 1981); Brown, *The Wisdom of Science*; David Ray Griffin, *God and Religion in the Postmodern World* (Albany, N. Y.: SUNY Press, 1989); Jay McDaniel, *Of God and Pelicans: A Theology of Reverence for Life* (Louisville, Ky.: Westminster/John Knox Press, 1989); Jürgen Moltmann, *God in Creation: A New Theology of Creation and the Spirit of God* (San Francisco: Harper and Row, 1985); A. R.

Peacocke, *Creation and the World of Science* (Oxford: Clarendon Press, 1979); John Polkinghorne, *Science and Creation* (London: SPCK, 1987); Holmes Rolston III, *Science and Religion: A Critical Survey* (New York: Random House, 1987); Toulmin, *The Return to Cosmology*.

8. While the common models of "body" and "machine" as ways of viewing reality assume a distinction if not a dualism between them, the distinction is, as Donna Haraway puts it, a "leaky" one at least in terms of the frontiers of current science. "Late twentieth-century machines have made thoroughly ambiguous the difference between natural and artificial, mind and body, self-developing and externally designed, and many other distinctions that used to apply to organisms and machines. . . . Our best machines are made of sunshine; they are all light and clean because they are nothing but signals, electromagnetic waves, a section of a spectrum. . . . " (*Simians, Cyborgs, and Women: The Reinvention of Nature* [New York: Routledge, 1991], 152–53). She envisions the new being as a "cyborg," one who is not afraid of "joint kinship with animals and machines . . . ." (154). One need only think of severely handicapped persons (such as the renowned physicist Stephen Hawking), whose "bodies" are a complex of highly sophisticated machines as well as what remains of their human tissue, as extreme examples of how machines are daily and common extensions of all our bodies in innumerable ways—the computer being one of the most prevalent. While I acknowledge that the distinction between the body and the machine is a leaky one, as *worldviews* the organic and the machine models suggest significantly different sensibilities.

9. A discussion of holism versus atomism appears in chap. 3, "A Reading of Postmodern Science: Organism or Mechanism."

10. Some recent publications include the following, all from Harper and Row: Joseph Campbell and Charles Musès, eds., *In All Her Names: Four Explorations of the Feminine in Divinity* (1991); Carol P. Christ and Judith Plaskow, eds., *Weaving the Visions: New Patterns in Feminist Spirituality* (1989); Riane Eisler, *The Chalice and the Blade: Our History, Our Future* (1988); Marija Gimbutas, *The Civilization of the Goddess: The World of Old Europe* (1991); Caitlin Matthews, *Sophia: Goddess of Wisdom: The Divine Feminine from Black Goddess to World Soul* (1991); Alix Pirani, ed., *The Absent Mother: Restoring the Goddess to Judaism and Christianity* (1991); Monica Sjöö and Barbara Mor, *The Great Cosmic Mother: Rediscovering the Religion of the Earth* (1987); Charlene Spretnak, *States of Grace: The Recovery of Meaning in the Postmodern Age* (1991).

11. Starhawk, "Feminism, Earth-based Spirituality, and Eco-Feminism," in *Healing the Wounds: The Promise of Ecofeminism*, ed. Judith Plant (Santa Cruz, Calif.: New Society Publishers, 1989).

12. Paula Gunn Allen, "The Woman I Love Is a Planet; the Planet I Love Is a Tree," in *Reweaving the World: The Emergence of Ecofeminism*, ed.

Irene Diamond and Gloria Orenstein (San Francisco: Sierra Club Books, 1990), 52.

13. Spretnak, *States of Grace*, 113.

14. John Seed, "Anthropocentricism," Appendix E in Bill Devall and George Sessions, *Deep Ecology: Living as if Nature Mattered* (Salt Lake City: Peregrine Smith Books, 1985), 243.

15. For different views of the history of the organic model prior to the seventeenth century (as well as reasons for its demise), see James A. Carpenter, *Nature and Grace: Toward an Integral Perspective* (New York: Crossroad, 1988); Amos Funkenstein, *Theology and the Scientific Imagination from the Middle Ages to the Seventeenth Century* (Princeton: Princeton University Press, 1986); Paulos Gregorios, *The Human Presence: An Orthodox View of Nature* (Geneva: World Council of Churches, 1978); Grace Jantzen, *God's Body, God's World* (Philadelphia: Westminster Press, 1984); Merchant, *The Death of Nature*; Eugene TeSelle, "Divine Action: The Doctrinal Tradition," in *Divine Action: Studies Inspired by the Philosophical Theology of Austin Farrer*, ed. Brian Hebblethwaite and Edward Henderson (Edinburgh: T. & T. Clark, 1990), 71–91; Toulmin, *The Return to Cosmology*.

16. Moltmann, *God in Creation*, 299.

17. TeSelle, "Divine Action," 82.

18. See Elisabeth Schüssler Fiorenza's study of this point in her book, *In Memory of Her: A Feminist Theological Reconstruction of Christian Origins* (New York: Crossroad, 1983).

19. TeSelle, "Divine Action," 83.

20. Jantzen, *God's Body, God's World*, 27f.

21. One commentator writes of Augustine's view: "His pronounced tendency to demean nature when considering it in the light of grace arrested the development in Western theology of a positive understanding of nature, and does so yet to the extent that can scarcely be exaggerated" (Carpenter, *Nature and Grace*, 8). On Thomas, Grace Jantzen comments: "Because matter is utterly inert, essentially lifeless, and is passive to all change . . . it is the very antithesis to God who is the living God . . . Thus for Aquinas and many like him, incorporeality was indispensable to any concept of God; it is indeed the central fact about him on which everything else depends. To question it is tantamount to questioning whether God—a living God—exists at all" (*God's Body, God's World*, 29). For a somewhat different (though also ambiguous) assessment of nature in the Eastern tradition, see Hugh Montefiore, ed., *Man and Nature* (London: Collins, 1975).

22. Merchant, *The Death of Nature*, 1.

23. Merchant, *The Death of Nature*, 3.

24. Merchant, *The Death of Nature*, 168.

25. Merchant, *The Death of Nature*, 193.

26. Merchant, *The Death of Nature*, 214.

27. Merchant, *The Death of Nature*, 214.

28. For an analysis of this point, see Ernan McMullin's discussion of physico-theology in "Introduction: Evolution and Creation," *Evolution and Creation*, ed. Ernan McMullin (Notre Dame: University of Notre Dame Press, 1985); "Natural Science and Belief in a Creator: Historical Notes," *Physics, Philosophy and Theology: A Common Quest for Understanding*, ed. Robert John Russell et al. (Vatican City State: Vatican Observatory, 1988), 49–79.

29. Margaret Miles makes this point succinctly when she writes, "In Christianity the body scorned, the naked body, is a female body." She also elaborates the point: "The special affiliation of the female body with the grotesque is founded on the assumption that the male body is the perfectly formed, complete and therefore normative body. By contrast, all women's bodies incorporate parts (like breasts, uterus, and vagina) and processes (like menstruation and pregnancy) that appear grotesque to the authors and artists who represented women" (*Carnal Knowing: Female Nakedness and Religious Meaning in the Christian West* [Boston: Beacon Press, 1989], 185, 155). The dualism in the model is sharply defined by Rosemary Radford Ruether's words, "Women, as representatives of sexual reproduction and motherhood, are the bearers of death, from which the male spirit must flee to 'light and life' " (*Sexism and God-Talk: Toward a Feminist Theology* [Boston: Beacon Press, 1983], 80).

30. "The nuclear world [i.e., the world of exploitation of all sorts, as seen in world hunger and ecological deterioration] is at least partly the product of a tradition in which human bodies have not been sufficiently valued in spite of doctrines of creation, Incarnation, and resurrection of the body that would seem to affirm human body-selves" (Miles, *Carnal Knowing*, 13).

31. This "cultural hegemony," which specifies the characteristics of the ideal, normative human being, has been attributed to the philosopher Antonio Gramsci. A thought-provoking exercise involves judging how much deviance society allows from this ideal. For instance, a car or soup advertisement might include a black woman or an elderly person, but have you seen any physically challenged, elderly Hispanics in mainline advertisements? The issue, for our concerns, is how *different* can people be from the societal or conventional norm and still be considered "representatively human"?

32. Merchant mentions three variations of the organic theory resulting in different forms of governance: the medieval view based on the human body, which is basically conservative; a village-community organicism with more democratic tendencies; and a revolutionary form, as found in utopian societies. The most powerful form was the first, and it lay behind both civil and ecclesiastical governments: "On this model, monarchy was the form of political organization most natural to the cosmic and

divine order. Monarchy derived its authority by divine right from God and distributed authority to the various social estates through civil law. The medieval sovereign represented God in the temporal realm; the church his will in the spiritual realm" (*The Death of Nature*, 72).

33. Merchant notes that ecology in the early part of the twentieth century was built on the organic model, but turned in a "mathematically reductionist direction" with "the emergence of fascist tyranny based on a centralized organismic model glorifying the father as absolute dictator" (*The Death of Nature*, 76); see also John de Graaf, "The Wandervogel," *Co/ Evolution Quarterly* (Fall 1977): 14–21. James Gustafson, in his discussion of the contractual versus the organic models for understanding social relations, notes that in the latter, "The individual is seen primarily as the outcome of the processes of life as a whole, and his or her 'autonomy' is underestimated" (*Ethics from a Theocentric Perspective*, vol. 1, *Theology and Ethics* [Chicago: University of Chicago, 1981], 292). These comments, of course, are based on the analogy with which the classical model works: the human body.

34. The extensive Goddess literature elaborates this point; in addition, see Martha Weigle, *Creation and Procreation: Feminist Reflections on Mythologies of Cosmogony and Parturition* (Philadelphia: University of Pennsylvania Press, 1989).

35. As quoted by Annie Dillard, *Pilgrim at Tinker Creek: A Mystical Excursion into the Natural World* (New York: Bantam Books, 1974), 96.

36. Mary Hesse, "Cosmology as Myth," *Cosmology and Theology*, ed. David Tracy and Nicholas Lash (New York: Seabury Press, 1983), 50. She goes on to say: "In our account of the interaction of cognitive systems of different kinds . . . we need a quite different theory of truth which will be characterized by *consensus* and *coherence* rather than correspondence, by *holism* of meanings rather than atomism, by *metaphor* and *symbol* rather than literalism and univocity, by intrinsic judgments of *value* as well as of fact" (54).

37. See chap. 3, "A Reading of Postmodern Science: Organism or Mechanism."

38. The modesty of some astrophysicists is evident in this statement by two of them: "If we believe that all our descriptions and laws of Nature must at some level be approximations to the true reality, then we will never find the unique and completely accurate description of reality because ultimately our equations cannot describe it" (John D. Barrow and Joseph Silk, *The Left Hand of Creation: The Origin and Evolution of the Expanding Universe* [New York: Basic Books, 1983], 210).

39. For a clear, readable review of current problems associated with the standard big bang theory, see Alan Lightman, *Ancient Light: Our Changing View of the Universe* (Cambridge: Harvard University Press, 1991). His conclusion is that, "given all the difficulties mentioned, most cosmol-

ogists feel that *no* current models are satisfactory. The underlying big bang model could itself be in jeopardy" (85). On the other hand, two other astrophysicists writing in the March 1992 issue of *Scientific American* claim that "the big bang theory, the conceptual foundation of modern cosmology, has grown increasingly certain in recent years" and that the impressive achievements verifying it "have persuaded most physicists and astronomers that, to a first approximation at least, the big bang theory is probably correct" (David N. Spergel and Neil G. Turok, "Textures and Cosmic Structure," 52). Only a month later, in April 1992, important corroboration of the big bang theory by a NASA team claimed to solve one of its riddles—how our present lumpy universe evolved from what until now was believed to be an early smooth one. The team found evidence of ripples in the early universe, thus lending solid, though still not conclusive, evidence for the big bang. Regardless of who turns out to be correct, theologians would be well advised to avoid siding too closely with either position. What is critical are the broad parameters of this story that give a substantially different view of reality than found, for instance, in the medieval or the Newtonian view.

40. David Tracy and Nicholas Lash define the term in the following way: " 'Cosmology' may mean many things. The term can refer to theological accounts of the world as God's creation; or to philosophical reflection on the categories of space and time; or to observational and theoretical study of the structure and evolution of the physical universe; or, finally to 'world views': unified imaginative perceptions of how the world seems and where we stand in it" (*Cosmology and Theology*, vii).

41. Over the past decade or so, a large number of books have appeared written for the educated layperson giving various aspects of this story. Here are a few of them: Robert K. Adair, *The Great Design: Particles, Fields, and Creation* (New York and Oxford: Oxford University Press, 1987); Barrow and Silk, *The Left Hand of Creation*; Marcia Bartusiak, *Thursday's Universe: A Report from the Frontier on the Origin, Nature and Destiny of the Universe* (Redmond, Wash.: Tempus, 1986); Paul Davies, *The Cosmic Blueprint: New Discoveries in Nature's Creative Ability to Order the Universe* (New York: Simon and Schuster, 1988); Freeman Dyson, *Infinite in All Directions* (New York: Simon and Schuster, 1988); George B. Field and Eric J. Chaisson, *The Invisible Universe: Probing the Frontiers of Astrophysics* (Boston: Birkhauser, 1985); Edward Harrison, *Cosmology: The Science of the Universe* (Cambridge: Cambridge University Press, 1981); Stephen Hawking, *A Brief History of Time: From the Big Bang to Black Holes* (New York: Bantam Books, 1988); Carl Sagan, *Cosmos* (New York: Random House, 1980); James S. Trefil, *The Moment of Creation: Big Bang Physics from Before the First Millisecond to the Present Universe* (New York: Charles Scribner, 1983); Steven Weinberg, *The First Three Minutes* (New York: Basic Books, 1977).

42. Trefil elaborates on this point: "The most important and dramatic evidence for the Big Bang picture of the beginning of the universe comes from the discovery of universal microwave radiation. This radiation is of the type that would be associated with a body at a temperature of 30 [degrees] above absolute zero—just the temperature that the expanding radiation gas resulting from the Big Bang should have reached by this time. In a sense, the microwave experiments are hearing the reverberations of the explosion with which the universe began" (*The Moment of Creation*, 20). Just *what* happened, however, is a matter of considerable speculation: for a recent sampling, see the October 1990 issue of *Scientific American*. A noted astrophysicist, Eric Chaisson, gives a summary view: "By most accounts, the Universe began with an explosion of something hot and dense—hotter than the tens of millions of degrees Celsius in the cores of most stars, denser than the trillions of grams per cubic centimeter in the nucleus of any atom. Precisely what that 'something' was, we cannot currently say with much certainty. Perhaps nothing more than a bolt of energy. Or perhaps nothing at all, if some of the latest physics harbors any measure of truth" ("Credo: Our Cosmic Heritage," *Zygon* 23 [December 1990]: 472).

43. There is considerable debate on the possibility of this enterprise. Hawking, for instance, believes that it *is* possible (and he might be the one to do it!), while others are far less optimistic.

44. I am especially indebted to Hawking, *A Brief History of Time* and Trefil, *The Moment of Creation* for the following overview.

45. Hawking, *A Brief History of Time*, 120–21.

46. There is probably no issue that has received more attention from theologians in the current—as well as ancient—conversation between religion and science than the issue of purpose or meaning in the natural order. For a fuller analysis of the issue, see chap. 3, "Natural Theology," as well as chap. 5, "A Meditation on Exodus 33:23b" and "Major Models of God and the World."

47. John Polkinghorne writes: "A random event (an aggregation of atoms, a genetic mutation) produces a new possibility which is then given a perpetuating stability by the regularity of the laws of nature. Without contingent chance, new things would not happen. Without lawful necessity to preserve them in an environment whose reliability permits competitive selection, they would vanish away as soon as they were made" (*The Way the World Is* [Grand Rapids: William B. Eerdmans, 1983], 11).

48. John Polkinghorne, *One World: The Interaction of Science and Theology* (London: SPCK, 1986), 56.

49. For a discussion of this point, see Adair, *The Great Design*, 9.

50. For a discussion of holism versus atomism, see Davies, *The Cosmic Blueprint*; the same matter is dealt with in terms of unifiers and di-

versifiers by Dyson, *Infinite in All Directions*; Arthur Peacocke analyzes the issue in light of present-day sociobiology in his book, *God and the New Biology* (London: J. M. Dent and Sons, 1986).

51. *Wonderful Life: The Burgess Shale and the Nature of History* (New York: W. W. Norton and Co., 1989), 14.

52. See chap. 3, "Natural Theology."

53. Barbour, *Religion in an Age of Science*, 124.

54. For a different view of this matter, one which attempts, with extreme subtlety, to introduce such a principle, see Rolston, *Science and Religion*.

55. Philosopher and ethicist Mary Midgley points out that contractual ethics is limited to rational human beings, but our duties, in this view, leave out many human beings (babies, the mentally handicapped, the senile), not to mention a great number of other contexts. "People have duties *as* farmers, parents, consumers, forest-dwellers, colonists, species-members, ship-wrecked mariners, tourists, potential ancestors and actual descendants" (*Evolution as a Religion: Strange Hopes and Stranger Fears* [London: Methuen and Co., 1985], 160).

56. Margaret Miles, *Carnal Knowing*, 28.

57. Process thought and American pragmatism come to mind. The centrality of embodiment and especially of the analogy of God as related to the world as the mind (or self) is to the body can be seen in writings by Charles Hartshorne, David Ray Griffin, John B. Cobb, Jr., and others. For ways that embodiment functions in American pragmatism, see Nancy Frankenberry, *Religion and Radical Empiricism* (Albany, N. Y.: SUNY, 1987); William Dean, *American Religious Empiricism* (Albany, N. Y.: SUNY, 1986); and Dean, *History Making History: The New Historicism in American Religious Thought* (Albany, N. Y.: SUNY, 1988).

58. Iris Murdoch, *The Sovereignty of the Good* (London: Routledge and Kegan Paul, 1970), 84.

59. Murdoch, *The Sovereignty of the Good*, 85.

60. Iris Murdoch, "The Sublime and the Good," *Chicago Review* 13 (Autumn 1959): 51.

61. As quoted by A. S. Byatt, *Iris Murdoch*, ed. Ian Scott-Kilvert (London: Longman Group, 1976), 23–24.

62. One of the grandest sacramental poets in the Christian tradition, Gerard Manley Hopkins, was also one with the keenest eye for the differences in which and with which each thing celebrated its Creator. He called it "inscape," that special, unique, radical, and inimitable individuality of each and every scrap of creation that became its special "news" that it rang out of God.

63. Jonathan Edwards, *The Nature of True Virtue* (Ann Arbor, Mich.: University of Michigan Press, 1960), 3.

64. Three very different theologies that incorporate aspects of what I have termed *attention epistemology* are the following: Edward Farley, *Good and Evil: Interpreting a Human Condition* (Minneapolis: Fortress Press, 1990); Gustafson, *Ethics from a Theocentric Perspective*; Catherine Keller, *From a Broken Web: Separatism, Sexism and Self* (Boston: Beacon Press, 1986).

65. For a treatment of McClintock's work, see Evelyn Fox Keller, *Reflections on Gender and Science* (New Haven: Yale University Press, 1985), chap. 7. For another analysis of attention epistemology, see Karen J. Warren, "The Power and Promise of Ecological Feminism," *Environmental Ethics* 12 (Summer 1990): 125–46.

66. Keller, *Reflections on Gender and Science*, 163–64.

67. Marilyn Frye, "In and Out of Harm's Way: Arrogance and Love," *The Politics of Reality* (New York: The Crossing Press, 1983), 66–72.

68. For a general treatment of the relationship of knowledge and embodiment, one that insists that concepts have a bodily basis, as seen, for instance, in our tendency to structure the world in cycles (hours, days, weeks, years) and from cycles in our bodies (heartbeat, breathing, digestion, menstruation, waking and sleeping, circulation), see Mark Johnson, *The Body in the Mind: the Bodily Basis of Meaning, Imagination, and Reason* (Chicago: University of Chicago Press, 1987). Feminists would claim, however, that such a treatment deals with the body in a universalist, essentialist way, since no gender, class, racial, or other context of embodiment is considered in the analysis.

69. This criticism has been levelled against some of the French feminist deconstructionists as well as against Mary Daly. For one such treatment, see Chris Weeden, *Feminist Practice and Poststructuralist Theory* (Oxford: Basil Blackwell, 1987).

70. For a discussion of this phenomenon, see Barbar Hilkert Andolsen, *"Daughters of Jefferson, Daughters of Bootblacks": Racism and American Feminism* (Macon, Ga.: Mercer University Press, 1986).

71. Elizabeth V. Spelman, *Inessential Woman: Problems of Exclusion in Feminist Thought* (Boston: Beacon Press, 1988), 129–30.

72. Spelman, *Inessential Woman*, 126f.

73. Spelman, *Inessential Woman*, 128.

74. One interesting example here is recent work in chaos theory, especially the importance of initial conditions in nonlinear systems that result in massive and unpredictable changes down the line. James Gleick mentions that we see this phenomenon in everyday life: a woman leaves the house thirty seconds late, a flowerpot misses her head, and she is run over by a truck. "In science as in life, it is well known that a chain of events can have a point of crisis that could magnify small changes. But chaos meant that such points were everywhere. They were pervasive. In systems like the weather, sensitive dependence on initial conditions was an inescapable consequence of the way small scales intertwined with large"

(*Chaos: Making a New Science* [New York: Penguin Books, 1987], 23). Chaos writers insist that linear models are too simplistic for understanding nature, which is complex, nonlinear, surprising, and random—yet with what as Gleick describes as "richly ordered patterns, sometimes stable and sometimes unstable, sometimes finite and sometimes infinite, but always with the fascination of living things" (43).

75. The full definition reads as follows: "That area of human understanding that deals with the interrelatedness between living things and the non-living environment is *ecology*; it is more specifically defined as that branch of science that deals with the structure and function of nature. Since the term 'ecology' is derived from the Greek *oikos* (meaning house or home), ecology may also be simply defined as a study of the household of organisms with everything that affects them there" (Paul E. Lutz, "Interrelatedness: Ecological Pattern of the Creation," *Cry of the Environment: Rebuilding the Christian Creation Story*, ed. Philip N. Joranson and Ken Butigan [Santa Fe, N. M.: Bear and Co: 1984], 253).

76. James Lovelock, who has popularized the controversial notion of the earth (Gaia) as a living organism that is self-regulating, has also given us another, perhaps more important and certainly less controversial notion: we need to develop a perspective for the health of the earth. We need, he claims, general physicians who are concerned not for the well-being of this or that species (including our own), but for the health of the entire planet. And it was precisely the sight, for the first time, of earth from space that prompted his insight of a "planetary perspective," "the top-down physiological view of life as a whole" (*The Ages of Gaia: A Biography of Our Living Earth* [New York: W. W. Norton and Co., 1988], 29).

77. "We can do our best to build up a conception of 'the overall scheme of things' which draws as heavily as it can on the results of scientific study, informed by a genuine piety in all its attitudes toward creatures of other kinds: a piety that goes beyond the consideration of their usefulness to Humanity as instruments for the fulfillment of human ends. That is an alternative within which human beings can both *feel*, and also *be*, at home. For to be at home in the world of nature does not just mean finding out how to utilize nature economically and efficiently—home is not a hotel!" (Toulmin, *The Return to Cosmology*, 272).

78. The Second Law is considerably more complex than our description of it; see, for instance, the fascinating qualifications of its workings in the analysis of Ilya Prigogine on self-organizing systems far from equilibrium in which disorder or randomness at one level leads to order or dynamic patterns at a higher level (I. Prigogine and I. Stengers, *Order Out of Chaos* [New York: Bantam Books, 1984]. Our more mundane use of the law is well expressed in the following remarks by Hazen and Trefil. " 'Entropy' is the scientist's measure of a system's randomness or disorder. The

. . . Second Law says that in any closed system entropy either increases or (at best) remains the same over time. Disorder never decreases. Having said this, however, we have to admit that some systems can become more ordered—but at the expense of making things more disordered someplace else. You can vacuum your room, but you also have to pay the electric bill. When you make an ice cube in your refrigerator the water becomes more ordered as it freezes. The refrigerator, however, is not an isolated system—it is connected to the power plant that generates its electricity. The Second Law says that an increase in the orderliness of the water's atoms must be balanced by an increase in disorder in the atmosphere around the generating plant, an increase that is sure to result from waste heat.

"Living systems are the most highly ordered form of matter we know. Staggering numbers of atoms must fit together in a precisely dictated way to make even the simplest cell. Creationists sometimes argue that evolution theories violate the Second Law because they assume that life appeared spontaneously. Nothing so ordered, they argue, could arise from disorder, because of the Second Law. Just as was the case with the ice cube, however, you have to consider the energy and randomness of the *entire system in which life arose*. That system includes not just the earth, but the earth's energy source—the sun—as well. The relative increase in order seen in living systems on the surface of our planet is more than balanced by the disorder created by the nuclear furnace that supplies the sun with energy; and the total entropy of the earth-sun system increases all the time. The Second Law tells us that in nature, as in life, you have to pay for what you get" (*Science Matters*, 32–33).

79. Erwin Schroedinger, as quoted by Ian G. Barbour, *Issues in Science and Religion* (Englewood Cliffs, N. J.: Prentice-Hall, 1966), 319.

80. I am indebted for the following analysis to Lutz, "Interrelatedness."

81. Wendell Berry, ecologist and poet, expresses this cyclical process eloquently: "In an energy economy appropriate to the use of biological energy, all bodies, plant and animal and human, are joined in a kind of energy community . . . They are indissolubly linked in complex patterns of energy exchange. They die into each other's life, and live into each other's death. They do not consume in the sense of using up. They do not produce waste. What they take in they change, but they change it always into a form necessary for its use by a living body of another kind. And this exchange goes on and on, round and round, the Wheel of Life rising out of the soil, descending into it, through the bodies of creatures" (*The Unsettling of America: Culture and Agriculture* [San Francisco: Sierra Club Books, 1977], 86).

Chapter 3: A Theology of Nature

1. In chap. 1 of his book, *Theology of Nature* (Philadelphia: Westminster Press, 1980), George S. Hendry describes these three contexts—the psychological, political, and cosmological—from historical and theological perspectives.

2. This perspective is evident in the history of the Hebrew people, in which the writings dealing with the liberation of the people were recorded prior to those concerned with creation (see, for instance, Bernard W. Anderson, "Creation in the Bible," in *Cries of the Environment: Rebuilding the Christian Creation Story,* ed. Philip N. Joranson and Ken Butigan [Santa Fe, N. M.: Bear and Co., 1984]). An illustration of the priority of liberation to creation in early Christian writings is seen in the importance of the notion of "second Adam" in relation to the "first Adam."

3. A theology of nature is also different from a doctrine of creation, as John Cobb suggests when he writes that the latter is one doctrine whereas the former is a whole theology from the perspective of what we are learning about nature from contemporary science. "We are not trying only to spell out what traditional theology implies about nature. Instead, we want to see the whole of theology influenced and reconceived in light of what we are learning about nature. This makes 'the theology of nature' something different from 'the doctrine of creation' " ("The Role of Theology of Nature in the Church," *Liberating Life: Contemporary Approaches to Ecological Theology,* ed. Charles Birch et al. [Maryknoll, N. Y.: Orbis Books, 1990], 263).

4. For a more complete analysis of this point, see my article, "An Earthly Theological Agenda," *Christian Century* (January 2–9, 1991): 12–15.

5. While "creation spirituality" is a loose rubric and could include such diverse writers as Alice Walker, James Lovelock (of the Gaia thesis), Susan Griffin, and Starhawk, our use of it is fairly narrow, focused on those influenced by the Christian tradition who opt for a creation in contrast to the traditional redemption priority. A few key works include the following: Thomas Berry, *The Dream of the Earth* (San Francisco: Sierra Club Books, 1988); Thomas Berry with Thomas Clarke, *Befriending the Earth: A Theology of Reconciliation Between Humans and the Earth* (Mystic, Conn.: Twenty-Third Publications, 1991); Michael Dowd, *EarthSpirit: A Handbook for Nurturing an Ecological Christianity* (Mystic, Conn.: Twenty-Third Publications, 1991); Matthew Fox, *The Coming of the Cosmic Christ: The Healing of Mother Earth and the Birth of a Global Renaissance* (San Francisco: Harper and Row, 1989); Fox, *Creation Spirituality: Liberating Gifts for the Peoples of the Earth* (San Francisco: Harpers, 1990) plus several other books; Anne Lonergan and Caroline Richards, eds., *Thomas Berry and the New Cosmology* (Mystic, Conn.: Twenty-Third Publications, 1987); Brian Swimme, *The Uni-*

verse Is a Green Dragon: A Cosmic Creation Story (Santa Fe, N. M.: Bear and Co., 1984).

6. For the past two hundred years at least, and perhaps as far back as Luther's retreat to the self as the locus of contact between God and the world, the natural world has been considered irrelevant to theology. Only history, and only human history, has been seen as the place where God touches our reality. Since the Reformation, redemption of human beings has been the focus of divine activity, with creation similarly focused on human existence. Thus, Luther could say, "I believe that God created *me*," or Calvin could see nature as the stage of salvation history, or Schleiermacher could deal with creation as merely an extension of the feeling of absolute dependence. This tradition continued into our century with Karl Barth's insistence that the reality of creation is known in the person of Jesus Christ (creation is enclosed within redemption) and in Rudolf Bultmann's claim that belief in creation means confessing oneself to be a creature.

7. Berry, *Dream of the Earth*, 121.

8. Brian Swimme writes about this story as follows: "For suddenly, the human species has a common cosmic story. Islamic people, Hopi people, Christian people, Marxist people, and Hindu people can all agree in a basic sense on the birth of the Sun, on the development of the Earth, the species of life, and human cultures. For the first time in human existence, we have a cosmic story that is not tied to one cultural tradition, or to a political ideology, but instead gathers every human group into its meanings" ("The Cosmic Creation Story," in *The Reenchantment of Science: Postmodern Proposals*, ed. David Ray Griffin [Albany, N. Y.: SUNY, 1988], 52). The dangers of universalism and eliding differences are evident in this quotation; nonetheless, there is value in the perspective as one kind of unity that, according to the picture of reality current in our time, does bind all human beings together.

9. Berry, *Dream of the Earth*, 37.

10. Berry, *Dream of the Earth*, 5.

11. Berry, *Dream of the Earth*, 197.

12. Berry, *Dream of the Earth*, 11.

13. Berry, *Dream of the Earth*, 2.

14. Berry, *Dream of the Earth*, 120. Compare the following statement by Matthew Fox: "Creation is the source, the matrix, and the goal of all things—the beginning and the end, the alpha and the omega. Creation is our common parent, when 'our' stands for all things. Creation is the mother of all things and the father of all beings, the birther and the begetter. It is all-holy; it is awe-filled, from the tiniest onion seed to the towering redwood tree. It is all-powerful; it resurrects" (*Creation Spirituality*, 10). There is much in Fox's statement with which I agree—at least

metaphorically—but it is difficult to sort out theologically and epistemo-
logically the kind of statement he is making.

15. See his book *Creation Spirituality*.

16. Fox, *Creation Spirituality*, 40–41.

17. Fox, *Creation Spirituality*, 29.

18. One of my favorite examples of this genre is Ursula K. LeGuin, *Always Coming Home* (New York: Bantam Books, 1986).

19. Berry, *Dream of the Earth*, 9–10.

20. Alan Richardson and John Bowden, *The Westminster Dictionary of Christian Theology* (Philadelphia: Westminster Press, 1983).

21. Examples of the strong version—divine purpose or teleology—can be found in the notion of "downward causation" as understood (somewhat differently) by Paul Davies, *The Cosmic Blueprint: New Discoveries in Nature's Creative Ability to Order the Universe* (New York: Simon and Schuster, 1988) and Holmes Rolston III, *Science and Religion: A Critical Survey* (New York: Random House, 1987). The latter writes: "There are selective principles at work, as well as stabilities and regularities, which order the story and perpetuate a swelling wave over the transient particles. This portrays in some respects a loose teleology, a soft concept of creation . . . We have in the life adventure an interaction phenomenon, where a prolife principle is overseeing the affairs of matter" (132). The weak version evident in the notion of "consonance" or "congruence" is widespread among theologians involved in the science-religion conversation and means, simply, that theology ought to be done in the context of the contemporary worldview (see, for instance, Arthur Peacocke's several volumes that are based on this assumption).

22. A host of books and essays are available for laypersons to read on this conversation. The following list is merely suggestive of some that have influenced me: Ian G. Barbour, *Myths, Models and Paradigms: A Comparative Study in Science and Religion* (New York: Harper and Row, 1974); Barbour, *Religion in an Age of Science*, vol.1 (New York: Harper and Row, 1990); Charles Birch and John Cobb, Jr., *The Liberation of Life: From the Cell to the Community* (Cambridge: Cambridge University Press, 1981); Hanbury Brown, *The Wisdom of Science: Its Relevance to Culture and Religion* (Cambridge: Cambridge University Press, 1986); Willem B. Drees, *Beyond the Big Bang: Quantum Cosmologies and God* (LaSalle, Ill.: Open Court, 1990); David Ray Griffin, *God and Religion in the Postmodern World* (Albany, N. Y.: SUNY Press, 1989); David Ray Griffin, ed., *The Reenchantment of Science: Postmodern Proposals* (New York: SUNY Press, 1988); James M. Gustafson, *Ethics from a Theocentric Perspective* (Chicago: University of Chicago Press, 1981); John E. Haught, *The Cosmic Adventure: Science, Religion and the Quest for Purpose* (New York: Paulist Press, 1984); Conrad Hyers, *The Meaning of Creation: Genesis and Modern Science* (Atlanta: John Knox Press, 1984); Gordon D. Kaufman, *In Face of Mystery: A Constructive Theology* (Cam-

bridge: Harvard University Press, 1993); Jay McDaniel, *Of God and Pelicans: A Theology of Reverence for Life* (Louisville, Ky.: Westminster/John Knox Press, 1989); Ernan McMullin, ed., *Evolution and Creation* (Notre Dame: University of Notre Dame Press, 1985); John M. Mangum, ed., *The New Faith-Science Debate: Probing Cosmology, Technology, and Theology* (Minneapolis: Fortress Press, 1989); Jürgen Moltmann, *God in Creation: A New Theology of Creation and the Spirit of God* (San Francisco: Harper and Row, 1985); Arthur R. Peacocke, *Creation and the World of Science* (Oxford: Clarendon Press, 1979); Peacocke, *Theology for a Scientific Age: Being and Becoming — Natural and Divine* (Oxford: Basil Blackwell, 1990); Arthur R. Peacocke, ed., *The Sciences and Theology in the Twentieth Century* (Notre Dame: University of Notre Dame Press, 1981); Ted Peters, ed., *Cosmos as Creation: Theology and Science in Consonance* (Nashville: Abingdon Press, 1989); John Polkinghorne, *Science and Creation* (London: SPCK, 1988); Polkinghorne, *One World: The Interaction of Science and Theology* (London: SPCK, 1986); Robert John Russell et al., eds., *Physics, Philosophy and Theology: A Common Quest for Understanding* (Rome and Notre Dame: Vatican Observatory and University of Notre Dame Press, 1988); David Schindler, ed., *Beyond Mechanism: The Universe in Recent Physics and Catholic Thought* (New York: University Press of America, 1986); Stephen Toulmin, *The Return to Cosmology: Postmodern Science and the Theology of Nature* (Berkeley: University of California Press, 1982); David Tracy and Nicholas Lash, eds., *Cosmology and Theology* (Edinburgh and New York: T. & T. Clark and Seabury Press, 1983).

23. See Hanbury Brown's illuminating point that the reason many Christian doctrines are considered obsolete is that they are based on a very different picture of the world than the current one. "It was a picture based largely on the physics and sociology of Aristotle (4th century B.C.) which was later elaborated into the Medieval Model . . . In that picture Heaven was completely separated from the Earth . . . things in Heaven were not only made of a different substance from those on Earth but they obeyed different physical laws. Man [sic] and the Earth were central to the whole scheme of things; Heaven was above [man's] head and Hell was beneath his feet. Every detail of what Man did and thought was closely watched over by God and His angels" (*The Wisdom of Science*, 167). As Brown notes, only in such a cosmology would divine intervention make sense, but sadly, many people still believe in this picture, and it forms the background for the supernaturalist interpretation of many doctrines, including incarnation, redemption, and resurrection.

24. See chaps. 3 and 4 of my book, *Metaphorical Theology: Models of God in Religious Language* (Philadelphia: Fortress Press, 1982), for a discussion of how metaphors and models operate in science and theology.

25. For instance, Arthur Peacocke claims that both science and theology are intellectual in character, with science being a search for intelligi-

bility while theology is a search for meaning. Theology is "the reflective and intellectual analysis of the experience of God" in Christian form (*Theology for a Scientific Age*, 6).

26. Philip Hefner asks this question in the following way: "What is at issue is whether or not we will treat with consistency and continuity the cosmic-physical processes and the biological-cultural developments . . . How can we paint a picture of the meaningfulness of human developments when the canvas of interpretation is the unfolding of cosmic processes over an enormous 18-billion-year span" ("The Evolution of Created Co-Creator," in *Cosmos as Creation*, 218).

27. See his book *In Face of Mystery*, chap. 19.

28. As Ernan McMullin notes: "Making God a 'God of the gaps' is a risky business. Gap-closing is the *business of science*. To rest belief in God on the presence of gaps in the explanatory chain is to put religion *against* science, ultimately" ("Introduction: Evolution and Creation," in *Evolution and Creation*, 35). The statement of Pope Pius XII in regard to the news from the scientific world of the big bang is a classic example of physico-theology: "[Science] has confirmed the contingency of the universe . . . when the cosmos came forth from the hands of the Creator. Hence, creation took place in time. Therefore, there is a Creator. Therefore, God exists! Although it is neither explicit, nor complete, this is the reply we were awaiting from science, and which the present human generation is awaiting from it" (Address to the Pontifical Academy of Sciences, 22 November 1951, as quoted in Stanley L. Jaki, *Cosmos and Creator* [Edinburgh: Scottish Academic Press, 1980], 19). In addition to McMullin's critique, see Drees, *Beyond the Big Bang* for another treatment of the issue.

29. See especially Pierre Teilhard de Chardin, *The Phenomenon of Man* (New York: Harper and Row, 1968).

30. See John Barrow and Frank Tipler, *The Anthropic Cosmological Principle* (Oxford and New York: Oxford University Press, 1986).

31. Stephen Jay Gould, *The Flamingo's Smile: Reflections in Natural History* (New York: W. W. Norton and Co., 1985), 397.

32. The recent spectacular corroboration of the big bang theory by a NASA team has been seized upon by some theologians and scientists as further evidence of this God of natural theology. Scientists aid and abet theologians with remarks such as that of NASA team leader George Smoot: "If you're religious, it's like looking at God" (*The Globe and Mail*, 24 April 1991). Danah Zohar, trained in physics and theology at the Minnesota Institute of Technology and Harvard, chimes in with: "It's like seeing the first ripple of God's thoughts in Creation" (*The Globe and Mail*, 2 May 1991). Some are more skeptical: John Polkinghorne, physicist and theologian at Queen's College, Cambridge, is doubtful whether the latest discovery will change the positions of believers or unbelievers (*The Globe and Mail*, 2 May 1991). Still others advise theological restraint, such as zoolo-

gist Richard Dawkins, who pleads: "Please, don't call it the fingerprint of God. Religious people will seize on it like ferrets" (*The Globe and Mail,* 2 May 1991). Indeed, some will, but the gains from this version of natural theology are as slim as from all others. Moreover, as Rudolf Bultmann rightly pointed out early in the century, no amount of scientific evidence can relieve us of the need to trust, or, more colloquially, science does not provide us with an end-run around faith.

33. Universal subjectivity or panpsychism presents profound problems if taken literally, for example, the "subjectivity" of an atom. However, if the analogical or metaphorical character of the proposal remains central—that the base of the notion of self is the human self and that other applications of it are more or less appropriate—this view of cosmic significance is attractive, especially its support for intrinsic value.

34. Kaufman, *In Face of Mystery*, chap. 20.

35. Ernan McMullin puts compatibility or coherence in a broad context in his discussion of consonance between science and theology. The theologian "should aim at some sort of coherence of world-view, a coherence to which science and theology, and indeed many other sorts of human construction like history, politics, and literature, must contribute" ("How Should Cosmology Relate to Theology" in *The Sciences and Theology in the Twentieth Century,* 52). What is at stake here is the possibility of holistic thinking in the broadest context; compatibility between science and theology is only one aspect of such thinking.

36. Process theology has taken this issue with utmost seriousness and has advanced some novel and provocative proposals. For two interesting ones, see David Ray Griffin, *God, Power, and Evil: A Process Theodicy* (Philadelphia: Westminster Press, 1976) and McDaniel, *Of God and Pelicans,* especially chap. 1.

37. For a discussion between Gordon Kaufman and myself on this issue, see "A Discussion of Sallie McFague's *Models of God*" by Mary Joe Weaver, Gordon Kaufman, Rosemary Radford Ruether, David Tracy, and James G. Hart with a response from McFague in *Religion and Intellectual Life* 5 (Spring 1988): 9–44. The dilemma is summed up by philosopher of science Mary Hesse concerning the only kind of God that science appears to tolerate: "Even if 'God' is allowed to emerge from the design-like arguments of the anthropic principle, this god will be simply defined to do what is required: a Deist God who is allowed to choose the right constants at the creation. Nothing follows that is like the God of Abraham, Isaac, and Jacob and our Lord Jesus Christ, nor of any other traditional religion" ("Physics, Philosophy, and Myth" in *Physics, Philosophy and Theology,* 198).

38. A refinement on Thomas Kuhn's notion of paradigm shifts by Imre Lakatos is helpful here: Lakatos distinguishes between "hard core" commitments and "auxiliary hypotheses," the former being preserved by making adjustments in the latter ("Falsification and the Methodology of

Scientific Research Programmes," in *Criticism and Growth of Knowledge*, ed.
I. Lakatos and A. Musgrave [Cambridge: Cambridge University Press,
1970]; see also *Philosophical Papers*, vol. 1, ed. John Worall and Gregory
Currie [Cambridge: Cambridge University Press, 1978]). My project of investigating other and presumably better personal models of God can be
put in this context of preserving the hard-core commitment to personal
metaphors by making adjustments at the level of particular historical ones
in the tradition.

39. I am reminded here of a statement by H. Richard Niebuhr that
has haunted and fascinated me for many years. He wrote that belief was
"becoming suspicious of one's own deep suspicion of the Determiner of
Destiny" (this is quoted from memory because I am unable to find the reference). This is a minimalist definition of belief, to put it mildly, but I have
always found it refreshingly realistic in its understatement.

40. See, for instance, three books by Gould: *The Flamingo's Smile; The
Mismeasure of Man* (New York: W. W. Norton and Co., 1981); *Wonderful
Life: The Burgess Shale and the Nature of History* (New York: Norton and Co.,
1989).

41. Gould, *Wonderful Life*, 25.

42. Gould, *Wonderful Life*, 14.

43. Gould, *Flamingo's Smile*, 409–10.

44. And this is especially true of ourselves—a highly improbable
creature who almost didn't make it numerous times. Gould comments on
our surprising presence: "*Homo sapiens*, I fear, is a 'thing so small' in a vast
universe, a wildly improbable evolutionary event well within the realm of
contingency. Make of such a conclusion what you will. Some find the
prospect depressing; I have always regarded it as exhilarating and a source
of both freedom and consequent moral responsibility" (*Wonderful Life*,
291).

45. See chap. 6 of this essay; also chap. 2 of *Models of God: Theology for
an Ecological, Nuclear Age* (Philadelphia: Fortress Press, 1987).

46. See chap. 2, *Models of God*; also *Metaphorical Theology: Models of
God in Religious Language* (Philadelphia: Fortress Press, 1982).

47. Carolyn Merchant makes a trenchant point in this regard: "It is
important to recognize the normative import of descriptive statements
about nature. Contemporary philosophers of language have critically re-
assessed the earlier positivist distinction between the 'is' of science and the
'ought' of society, arguing that descriptions and norms are not opposed to
one another by linguistic separation into separate 'is' and 'ought' statements, but are contained within each other. Descriptive statements about
the world can presuppose the normative; they are then ethic-laden" (*The
Death of Nature: Women, Ecology and the Scientific Revolution* [New York:
Harper and Row, 1980], 4).

48. Claude Stewart says of Teilhard's accomplishment: "What we finally find going on in Teilhard is an elaborate process of *resacralization* of the natural order through *remythologization*. His grand conceptual synthesis passes over into, and the results function as, a new creation myth . . . His conceptual synthesis—which, as we have argued, is best viewed on one level as a thought experiment in the area of the theology of nature—functions finally as a new myth" (*Nature in Grace: A Study of the Theology of Nature* [Macon, Ga.: Mercer University Press, 1983], 228).

49. See, for instance, Ian G. Barbour's "Teilhard's Process Metaphysics," in *Process Theology: Basic Writings*, ed. Ewart H. Cousins (New York: Newman Press, 1971).

50. As quoted in *The Oxford Book of Prayer*, ed. George Appleton (Oxford: Oxford University Press, 1988), 57.

51. Pierre Teilhard de Chardin, "Pantheism and Christianity," *Christianity and Evolution* (London: Collins, 1971), 73–74.

52. Moltmann, *God in Creation*, 53.

53. William R. Stoeger, S.J., makes this point when he says that the sciences influence religion by modifying the common cultural field, the symbols and images we use to speak of God: "Contemporary scientific and technological culture, along with other areas of modern life and history provide new images and metaphors, corresponding to some extent to a continually new and fuller description of ourselves and of the reality which surrounds us and nourishes us. There are rich and more powerful images of the mysterious immensity and complexity of physical reality, of the unity, the beauty, the inter-relatedness, the interdependence and the fragility of all things, at both the physical and biological and psychological levels, of the numinous, and the transcendentally immanent" ("What Contemporary Cosmology and Theology Have to Say to One Another," *CTNS Bulletin* 9 [Spring 1989]: 1–15).

54. My position here has some similarities to (and has been informed by) that of Francis Schüssler Fiorenza's notion of a "wide reflective equilibrium," a method that "presupposes a diversity of judgments, principles, and theories, each entailing different kinds of justification that come together to support or to criticize, to reinforce or to revise" (*Foundational Theology: Jesus and the Church* [New York: Crossroad, 1984], 302). "There is not one single element of foundation; rather, the foundation consists in the constant interchange among the diverse sources and principles" (303).

55. I have been aided in these reflections by the work of some American pragmatists, most notably Nancy Frankenberry and William Dean. The pragmatist tradition attempts to reach to the most elemental level of experience, as captured in this comment by William James on our experience of relations: "a feeling of *and*, and a feeling of *if*, and a feeling of *but*, and feeling of *by*, quite as readily as we say a feeling of *blue* or a feeling of *cold*" (as quoted by Frankenberry, *Religion and Radical Empiricism* [Albany,

N. Y.: SUNY Press, 1987], 91). American pragmatism attempts to place human experience, at its most primordial level, in the web of natural (not just historical) life, difficult as this is to reach or to talk about. This assumption not only supports the priority of the body but is also a context for inclusive sympathy with other life-forms. As Frankenberry states, "For Kant, the world emerged from the self; for radical empiricism, the subject emerges from the world" (173). See also William Dean, *History Making History: The New Historicism in American Religious Thought* (Albany, N. Y.: SUNY Press, 1988) and *American Religious Empiricism* (Albany, N. Y.: SUNY Press, 1986).

56. The movement during this century toward identifying the human world as totally linguistic, highlighted in the work of Ludwig Wittgenstein, Martin Heidegger, and now deconstruction, makes our connections with other life-forms more difficult and tenuous. It is the assumption of this essay that that line of demarcation is neither justified in relation to other animals (who do have forms of communication) nor absolute in relation to ourselves (we do experience more than we can express in language—otherwise, why are poets and mystics dissatisfied with their efforts at expressing their experiences?).

57. See chap. 1, "A Meditation on the Body."

58. The view of experience here has been informed by the very helpful (and complex) position of James M. Gustafson, who sees experience as prior to reflection as well as deeply social, and religion as a matter of affections and emotions—a natural piety and affection for God and others that is fulfilled when one loves God rightly and all other things as related to God. This gross summary of Gustafson's position does not begin to suggest its richness and subtlety. See *Ethics from a Theocentric Perspective*.

59. See the classic work on this subject by H. Richard Niebuhr, *The Meaning of Revelation* (New York: Macmillan, 1955).

60. The current, loosely connected movement called narrative theology makes this point vividly. See George A. Lindbeck, *The Nature of Doctrine: Religion and Theology in a Postliberal Age* (Philadelphia: Westminster Press, 1984). My chief criticism of this position is that while it rightly stresses the necessity of *formation* into a religious community, it neglects the other necessity of *reforming* the tradition.

61. An important distinction here is between the "essence" of a religious tradition (a futile task) and an interpretation or construal. The latter is open to revision, to conversation with alternative readings, to acceptance of its own partiality and even error.

62. The writings of Thomas Kuhn on this subject are of course by now classics, but a recent comparison and contrast of methods in science and theology by Ian G. Barbour is also instructive (see part 1, "Religion and the Methods of Science," in *Religion in an Age of Science*).

63. These comments are not meant as historical judgments on the work of Plato and Aristotle but rather refer to broad traditions stemming from and influenced by their work.

64. See works mentioned in n. 55; also Rebecca Chopp, "Feminism's Theological Pragmatics: A Social Naturalism of Women's Experience," *Journal of Religion* 67 (April 1987): 239–56 and Chopp, *The Praxis of Suffering: An Interpretation of Liberation and Political Theologies* (Maryknoll, N. Y.: Orbis Books, 1986).

65. One powerful and eloquent expression of this position is by Gordon Kaufman: "To believe in God, thus, is to commit oneself to a particular way of ordering one's life and action: it is to devote oneself . . . to working toward a fully humane world within the ecological constraints here on planet Earth, while standing in piety and awe before the profound mysteries of existence" (*In Face of Mystery*, 347).

66. Freeman Dyson describes the two groups in the following way: "Unifiers are people whose driving passion is to find general principles which will explain everything. They are happy if they can leave the universe looking a little simpler than they found it. Diversifiers are people whose passion is to explore details. They are in love with the heterogeneity of nature and they . . . are happy if they leave the universe more complicated than they found it" (*Infinite in All Directions* [New York: Harper and Row, 1988], 45).

67. Arthur Peacocke offers an excellent discussion of this issue in *God and the New Biology* (London: J. M. Dent and Sons, 1986).

68. The success of reductionism often blinds one to its limitations. Ian Barbour reminds us of them: "It would be the ultimate in *reductionism* to expect that all events could be predicted from one principle. It would deny the emergence of new kinds of phenomena at higher levels of organization and activity in life, mind, and culture. The price of simplicity and abstractness of an equation in physics is that it ignores the multiplicity and diversity of things in the world, from galaxies, apples, and robins, to human love" ("Creation and Cosmology," in *Cosmos as Creation*, 136).

69. See Barbour, "Scientific Materialism," in *Religion in An Age of Science*, 4–8. Robert John Russell's statement on the issue is a helpful one: "When scientists try to explain everything they can with a given theory, it is called methodological reductionism, and as such it is a legitimate research strategy. When they claim, however, that ultimately every other field of inquiry will be explained by their own field (usually physics!), it becomes epistemological reductionism" ("Agenda for the Twenty-First Century," *The New Faith-Science Debate*, 69, 94).

70. Supposing that one construction of reality *is* reality falls under the "fallacy of misplaced concreteness": "It is 'misplaced concreteness' to take the abstractions of any theory, old or new, as an all-inclusive clue to reality. Neither classical nor modern physics—nor any other specialized

science—can do justice to all aspects of human experience or provide a comprehensive world-view" (Ian G. Barbour, *Issues in Science and Religion* [Englewood Cliffs, N. J.: Prentice-Hall, 1966], 290).

71. The reduction of all the complexity and diversity we see about us to one principle is vividly stated in this remark: "We stand . . . on the verge of the ultimate triumph of the reductionist idea. Within a few years, we may very well realize that if we probe deeply enough, we will find a universe that is the ultimate in simplicity and beauty. All of the apparent complexity we see will be understood in terms of an underlying system in which particles of one type interact with each other through one kind of force" (James S. Trefil, *The Moment of Creation: Big Bang Physics From Before the First Millisecond to the Present Universe* [New York: Charles Scribner, 1983], 220).

72. Stephen Jay Gould calls this third alternative "organizational" or "holistic": "Life acquires its own principles from the hierarchical structure of nature. As levels of complexity mount along the hierarchy of atom, molecule, gene, cell, tissue, organism, and population, new properties arise as results of interactions and interconnections emerging at each new level. A higher level cannot be fully explained by taking it apart into component elements and rendering their properties in the absence of these interactions. Thus, we need new, or 'emergent' principles to encompass life's complexity; these principles are additional to, and consistent with, the physics and chemistry of atoms and molecules" (*Flamingo's Smile*, 379–80).

73. The role of metaphor and models in science has created a substantial literature over the past thirty years. For a review and analysis of some of these materials see chap. 3 of *Metaphorical Theology*. Here are two recent comments by philosophers of science. Mary Hesse: "Clearly the whole imperialist aim of theoretical science to be the royal and single road to knowledge has been a profound mistake . . . Scientific theory is just one of the ways in which human beings have sought to make sense of their world by constructing schemes, models, metaphors and myths. Scientific theory is a particular kind of myth that answers to our practical purposes with regard to nature. It often functions as myths do, as persuasive rhetoric for moral and political purposes" (*New York Times*, October 22, 1989, sec. 4, 24). Hanbury Brown: "We can think of our whole scientific picture of the physical world . . . as a *metaphor* which describes what we observe of a complex, perhaps incomprehensible, reality in terms which we can grasp and use. This picture is limited, not only by our understanding, but also by our tools of observation, so that it is always incomplete, always unfolding and always provisional. It can never claim to be the absolute truth, but at any given time it is the best picture we have" (*The Wisdom of Science*, 140).

74. "Whatever Happened to Immanuel Kant: A Preliminary Study of Selected Cosmologies," in *The Church and Contemporary Cosmology*, ed.

James B. Miller and Kenneth E. McCall (Pittsburgh: Carnegie-Mellon University Press, 1990), 164.

75. The full statement is worth quoting: "I criticize the myth that science itself is an objective enterprise, done properly only when scientists can shuck the constraints of their culture and view the world as it really is . . . Science, since people must do it, is a socially embedded activity. It progresses by hunch, vision, and intuition. Much of its change through time does not record a closer approach to absolute truth, but the alteration of cultural contexts that influence it so strongly" (Gould, *Mismeasure of Man*, 21–22).

76. Two vocal and eloquent spokeswomen for this position are Donna Haraway, "Situated Knowledges: The Science Question in Feminism and the Privilege of Partial Perspective," *Feminist Studies* 14 (Fall 1988): 575–99; Sandra Harding, *The Science Question in Feminism* (Ithaca, N. Y.: Cornell University Press, 1986); Harding, *Whose Science? Whose Knowledge? Thinking from Women's Lives* (Ithaca, N. Y.: Cornell University Press, 1991); Harding, "Taking Responsibility for Our Own Gender, Race, Class: Transforming Science and the Social Studies of Science," in *Rethinking Marxism* (Amherst, Mass.: Association for Economic and Social Analysis, 1989), 8–19. See also Helen E. Longino, *Science as Social Knowledge: Values and Objectivity in Scientific Inquiry* (Princeton: Princeton University Press, 1990) and Lynn H. Nelson, *Who Knows: From Quine to Feminist Empiricism* (Philadelphia: Temple University Press, 1990).

77. Harding, "Taking Responsibility," 15–16.

78. "Only science for the people (in Galileo's phrase), not for the elites, can be justifiably supported in a society committed to democracy. There are plenty of useful projects for such sciences, but they do not include research that provides resources for militarism or ecological disaster, or continues to move resources away from the underprivileged and toward the already overprivileged" (Harding, *Whose Science?* 101–2).

79. See Haraway for her treatment of the difference between these two views ("Situated Knowledges," 590).

80. The position intends to avoid both absolutism and relativism with its view of a stronger objectivity: "The science question in feminism is about objectivity as positioned rationality. Its images are not the products of escape and transcendence of limits (the view from above) but the joining of partial views and halting voices into a collective subject position that promises a vision of the means of ongoing finite embodiment, of living within limits and contradictions—of views from somewhere" (Haraway, "Situated Knowledges," 590). The resultant view of objectivity "privileges contestation, deconstruction, passionate construction, webbed connections, and hope for transformations of systems of knowledge and ways of seeing" (585).

81. Haraway, "Situated Knowledges," 579.

Chapter 4: At Home on the Earth

1. See the treatment of space in chap. 6 of Jürgen Moltmann, *God in Creation: A New Theology of Creation and the Spirit of God* (San Francisco: Harper and Row, 1985). He gives a definition of the ecological concept of space: "Every living thing has its own world in which to live, a world to which it is adapted and which suits it" (147).

2. See Gordon D. Kaufman, *In Face of Mystery: A Constructive Theology* (Cambridge: Harvard University Press, 1993) for a thorough treatment of theological reconstruction in this context.

3. Space can also be seen as a hierarchical category. Whereas time and history may provide egalitarian opportunities for change, space—suggesting high and low, up and down, as well as static equilibrium—can be interpreted in a conservative direction. This is both interesting and true, but shows, I think, the Western bias to see history as progress, improvement, betterment. Many of us in the closing years of the twentieth century are chastened on that score as we consider the devastation of our planet and its creatures. (I am indebted to Catherine Keller of Drew University for this insight.)

4. Brian Swimme, "Science: A Partner in Creating the Vision," in *Thomas Berry and the New Cosmology*, ed. Anne Lonergan and Caroline Richards (Mystic, Conn.: Twenty-Third Publications, 1987), 87.

5. Thomas Berry speaks of our need to reinvent the human as a species among species: "We need a constitution for the North American Continent. We need a United Species, not simply a United Nations" (*The Dream of the Earth* [San Francisco: Sierra Club Books, 1988], 161). While this perspective tends to undercut the diversity that is also a central aspect of the postmodern scientific view of reality, it is nonetheless important and neglected.

6. Mary Midgley, *Beast and Man: The Roots of Human Nature* (Ithaca, N. Y.: Cornell University Press, 1978), 194–95.

7. A qualification is necessary here. It might be more accurate to say that for the last five thousand years, during the period of patriarchy, we have lost our primitive and ecologically correct sense of our place in the scheme of things. As contemporary research into early matriarchal Goddess religions shows, human awareness of belonging to the earth is very old. Other religions, including Native American ones, also attest to the awareness of human embeddedness in nature that seems to come naturally to people who live in close contact with the earth.

8. In addition to Mary Midgley, some philosophers and theologians are currently exploring these themes. Stephen Toulmin speaks of living in the world as a home rather than as a hotel; the former way "means making sense of the relations that human beings and other living things have toward the overall patterns of nature in ways that give us some sense of

their proper relations to one another, to ourselves, and to the whole" (*The Return to Cosmology: Postmodern Science and the Theology of Nature* [Berkeley: University of California Press, 1982], 272). James M. Gustafson, writing as Toulmin also does in the context of postmodern science, says that "we are to conduct life so as to relate to all things in a manner appropriate to their relations to God" (*Ethics from a Theocentric Perspective*, vol. 1, *Theology and Ethics* [Chicago: University of Chicago Press, 1981], 113).

9. The notions here of "where we fit" and "proper place" in the scheme of things are *not* meant to support, in any fashion, cultural stereotypes of subservience and quietism, as when certain ethnic groups or children are told to "know their place" or "keep their place." Rather, the concept of a limited space and a proper place for human beings vis-à-vis other species (as well as other members of our own species) carries the connotation of not taking more than one's share: the implication is of justice for all, not the subservience of some.

10. Gustafson, *Ethics from a Theocentric Perspective*, 96–97.

11. See, for instance, the interpretations by Paul Ricoeur, *The Symbolism of Evil* (New York: Harper and Row, 1967); Phyllis Trible, *God and the Rhetoric of Sexuality* (Philadelphia: Fortress Press, 1978); Anne Primavesi, *From Apocalypse to Genesis: Ecology, Feminism and Christianity* (Minneapolis: Fortress Press, 1991).

12. To say that sin is selfishness does not entail claiming that righteousness is selflessness. Traditional understandings of sin as pride fail, as Valerie Saiving pointed out in her classic essay over thirty years ago, to acknowledge women's problem of a lack of self in our society ("The Human Situation: A Feminine View," *Womanspirit Rising: A Feminist Reader*, ed. Carol P. Christ and Judith Plaskow [San Francisco: Harper and Row, 1979], 25–42). Moreover, as we have stressed repeatedly, in the organic model human beings have a grand, not selfless, role to perform for the good of the whole.

13. The brevity of this section in relation to the following ones on other animals and the natural world is due to the large and impressive literature documenting injustice among human beings. The various liberation theologies from oppressed communities around the world make an important contribution to the case for injustice among our own species. The present section assumes the reader's acquaintance with at least some of this literature.

14. The stubbornness of greed and immediate gratification and thus the thwarting of justice as sharing is evident in this rather chilling question from economist Robert Heilbroner: "Suppose we . . . knew with a high degree of certainty that humankind could not survive a thousand years unless we gave up our wasteful diet of meat, abandoned all pleasure driving, cut back on every use of energy that was not essential to the maintenance of the bare minimum. Would we care enough for posterity to pay

the price of its survival?" (from *An Inquiry into the Human Prospect*, as quoted by John Carmody, *Ecology and Religion: Toward a Christian Theology of Nature* [Ramsey, N. Y.: Paulist Press, 1983], 179). If we would not cut back on our life-style for our grandchildren, it is unlikely we will do so for the distant poor of the two-thirds world, short of a conversion of some substantial sort.

15. "The global balance-sheet is sobering. Since the 1972 United Nations Conference on the Human Environment the gap in living standards between the world's rich and poor has steadily grown. Industrialized countries and some parts of the developing world have prospered, but a billion people live in absolute poverty. Per capita income in the world's 41 poorest countries is well below $300, a sharp contrast to the $14,500 average of developed market-economy countries. Some 70 per cent of the world's income is produced and consumed by 15 per cent of the population. Living standards in Latin America are lower today than in the 1970's. African living standards have slipped to the level of the 1960's" (foreword, *Notes for Speakers*, Earth Summit '92: The United Nations Conference on Environment and Development [New York: United Nations Department of Public Information, 1991]).

16. See "Us versus It: Living a Lie in Relation to Nature" for a fuller discussion.

17. Carl Sagan, *Cosmos* (New York: Random House, 1980), 34.

18. Contemporary views tend toward "putting us in our place," and this is certainly the case with the Gaia theory, which, as its chief spokesman James Lovelock, says "is out of tune with the broader humanist world . . . In Gaia we are just another species, neither the owners nor the stewards of this planet. Our future depends much more upon a right relationship with Gaia than with the never-ending drama of human interest" (*The Ages of Gaia: A Biography of Our Living Earth* [New York: Norton and Co., 1988], 14). James Gustafson quotes an amusing exchange between a scientist and a pastor who protested that a human being could not be a naked ape: "Only a naked ape! You should be grateful if you were an atomic nucleus. You ought to praise the Lord if you were a living cell. A naked ape is something enormously fine that none of us could ever deserve to be!" (*Ethics from a Theological Perspective*, 6).

19. See Tom Regan, *The Case for Animal Rights* (Berkeley, Calif.: University of California Press, 1983); Carol J. Adams, *The Sexual Politics of Meat: A Feminist-Vegetarian Critical Theory* (New York: Continuum, 1991). Tom Regan's comment is thoughtful and hard-hitting: "For I find in that account [Genesis] the unmistakable message that God did not create nonhuman animals for the purpose of vanity products, not for our entertainment, not for sport or recreation, not even for our bodily sustenance. On the contrary, the nonhuman animals currently exploited by these human practices were created to be just what they are—*independently good* expres-

sions of the divine love which, in ways that are likely always to remain to some degree mysterious to us, was expressed in God's creative activity" ("Christianity and Animal Rights: The Challenge and the Promise," *Liberating Life: Contemporary Approaches to Ecological Theology*, ed. Charles Birch et al. [Maryknoll, N. Y.: Orbis Books, 1990], 81).

20. As quoted by Midgley, *Beast and Man*, 219.

21. See Midgley, *Beast and Man*, 206ff.; also Midgley, *Animals and Why They Matter* (Athens, Ga.: University of Georgia Press, 1983).

22. The "roots of human nature" as well as the analysis of this concept are from Midgley, *Beast and Man*. See also Ian Barbour's discussion of sentience and purpose in animals in *Religion in an Age of Science*, vol. 1 (New York: Harper and Row, 1990), 170–72.

23. Midgley, *Beast and Man*, 255–56.

24. Midgley, *Beast and Man*, 206.

25. Midgley, *Beast and Man*, 358.

26. Midgley, *Beast and Man*, 225ff.

27. For an interesting discussion of this phenomenon, see Midgley, *Animals and Why They Matter*, chap. 10. See also the analysis of his own wonder and affection towards otters at play by biologist Lewis Thomas: "We are stamped with stereotyped, unalterable patterns of response, ready to be released. And the behavior released in us, by such confrontations, is, essentially, a surprised affection. It is compulsory behavior and we can avoid it only by straining with the full power of our conscious minds, making up conscious excuses all the way. Left to ourselves, mechanistic and autonomic, we hanker for friends" (*The Medusa and the Snail: More Notes of a Biology Watcher* [New York: Viking Press, 1974], 9).

28. The phrase "second naïvete" is Paul Ricoeur's and refers to the possibility of returning to the most basic roots of our being by a conscious, informed route when the intuitive acceptance found in our own youth and the youth of the human community is no longer possible for us.

29. See Midgley's discussion of "the pathology of egalitarianism" in *Animals and Why They Matter*, 78.

30. One of the most delightful and consciousness-raising short pieces on our relationship with the other animals is "She Unnames Them," by Ursula K. LeGuin, originally published in *The New Yorker*, 21 January 1985. In it Eve "unnames" the animals so that, without language to interfere, human beings might feel closer to them: "They seemed far closer than when their names had stood between myself and them like a clear barrier: so close that my fear of them and their fear of me became one same fear. And the attraction that many of us felt, the desire to smell one another's smells, feel or rub or caress one another's scales or skin or feathers or fur, taste one another's blood or flesh, keep one another warm—that attraction was now all one with the fear, and the hunter could not be told from the hunted, nor the eater from the food."

31. Midgley states the centrality of wonder in human experience with eloquence: "We are receptive, imaginative beings, adapted to celebrate and rejoice in the existence, quite independent of ourselves, of the other beings on this planet. Not only does our natural sympathy reach out easily beyond the barrier of species but we rejoice in the mere existence of plants and lifeless bodies—*not* regarding them just as furniture provided to stimulate our pampered imagination . . . We need the vast world, and it must be a world that does not need us; a world constantly capable of surprising us, a world we did not program, since only such a world is the proper object of wonder" (*Beast and Man*, 361–62).

32. Annie Dillard, *Pilgrim at Tinker Creek: A Mystical Excursion into the Natural World* (New York: Bantam Books, 1974), 81.

33. The classical discussion of free will in relation to the divine will, death, and tragedy are huge subjects in themselves, but they have been made considerably more complex by liberation theologians with the introduction of issues of power, the social construction of reality, and dualistic hierarchicalism, not to mention the loss of the subject and the end of history in the work of deconstruction. Our discussion brackets these matters, focusing only on the issue of self-consciousness.

34. As quoted by Bill Devall and George Sessions, *Deep Ecology: Living as if Nature Mattered* (Salt Lake City: Peregrine Smith Books, 1985), 205.

35. Susan Griffin, *Made from This Earth: An Anthology of Writings* (New York: Harper and Row, 1982), 343.

36. This distinction is from the introduction to *Dharma Gaia: A Harvest of Essays in Buddhism and Ecology*, ed. Allan Hunt Badiner (Berkeley, Calif.: Parallax Press, 1990), xiv. One definition of deep ecology goes like this: "It is the idea that we can make no firm ontological divide in the field of existence: That there is no bifurcation in reality between the human and the nonhuman realms . . . to the extent that we perceive boundaries, we fall short of deep ecological consciousness" (Warwick Fox, "The Intuition of Deep Ecology," *The Ecologist* [Fall 1984]: 66).

37. As quoted by Devall and Sessions, *Deep Ecology*, 85.

38. As one deep ecologist puts it: "The superorganism expresses the idea of holism in a compact and concrete form. It is a reference point for the imagination, summarizing the fundamental truth of ecology: that living things are so deeply interrelated, so profoundly dependent upon each other, that their lives are in effect one" (David Oates, *Earth Rising: Ecological Belief in an Age of Science* [Corvallis, Ore.: Oregon State University Press, 1989], 51).

39. Richard Nelson, *The Island Within* (New York: Random House, 1989), 249.

40. As quoted by Devall and Sessions, *Deep Ecology*, 13.

41. As quoted by Marti Kheel, "Ecofeminism and Deep Ecology: Reflections on Identity and Difference," in *Reweaving the World: The Emergence of Ecofeminism*, ed. Irene Diamond and Gloria Orenstein (San Francisco: Sierra Club Books, 1990), 136.

42. Warwick Fox, *Toward a Transpersonal Ecology: Developing New Foundations for Environmentalism* (Boston: Shambhala Publications, 1990), 239.

43. For an analysis of the ecological self, see Fox, *Toward a Transpersonal Ecology*, chap. 8.

44. As quoted in the introduction to *Nature in Asian Traditions of Thought: Essays in Environmental Philosophy*, ed. J. Baird Callicott and Robert Ames (Albany, N. Y.: SUNY Press, 1989), 62.

45. Aldo Leopold, *A Sand County Almanac and Sketches Here and There* (New York: Oxford University Press, 1949), 110.

46. Deep ecologists sometimes appear insensitive to human suffering, but they do help bring us to the awareness that we are not the only ones who suffer: "It is an intensely disturbing idea that man [sic] should not be the master of all, that other suffering might be just as important. And that individual suffering—animal or human—might be less important than the suffering of species, ecosystems, the planet" (Bill McKibben, *The End of Nature* [New York: Random House, 1989], 182).

47. See the critique of deep ecology's organic model by Jim Cheney, "Ecofeminism and Deep Ecology," *Environmental Ethics* 9 (1987): 115–45.

48. See Marilyn Frye, "In and Out of Harm's Way: Arrogance and Love," in *The Politics of Reality* (Trumansburg, N. Y.: The Crossing Press, 1983), 66–72.

49. Karen J. Warren, "The Power and Promise of Ecological Feminism," *Environmental Ethics* 12 (Summer 1990): 138. See also Marti Kheel, who writes: "Ecofeminist philosophy must be wary of a holistic philosophy that transcends the realm of individual beings. Our deep, holistic awareness of the interconnectedness of all of life must be a *lived* awareness that we experience in relation to *particular* beings *as well as* the larger whole" ("Ecofeminism and Deep Ecology," 136–37).

50. Arne Naess as quoted by Fox, *Toward a Transpersonal Ecology*, 217.

51. Leopold, *A Sand County Almanac*, 203.

52. Leopold, *A Sand County Almanac*, 224–25.

Chapter 5: God and the World

1. For an analysis of the monarchical model, see *Models of God: Theology for an Ecological, Nuclear Age* (Philadelphia: Fortress Press, 1987), chap. 3.

2. See chap. 6, "The Shape of the Body: The Christic Paradigm."

3. Vincent McNabb, ed., *The Decrees of the Vatican Council* (London, 1907) as quoted by Grace Jantzen, *God's World, God's Body* (Philadelphia: Westminster Press, 1984), 102.

4. Process theologians have pressed this point repeatedly. Charles Hartshorne, for instance, describes such a God as "ECK," the supreme Eternal Consciousness, Knowing but not including the world. See his *Philosophers Speak of God* (Chicago: University of Chicago Press, 1953); also see John B. Cobb, Jr., and David R. Griffin, *Process Theology: An Introductory Exposition* (Philadelphia: Westminster Press, 1976), chap. 3.

5. For two treatments of the following models see chap. 8 of Ian G. Barbour, *Myths, Models and Paradigms: A Comparative Study in Science and Religion* (New York: Harper and Row, 1974) and the last chapter of Claude Y. Stewart, Jr., *Nature in Grace: A Study of the Theology of Nature* (Macon, Ga.: Mercer University Press, 1983).

6. See "Christ and Culture in Paradox" in H. Richard Niebuhr's classic study, *Christ and Culture* (New York: Harper and Bros., 1951).

7. Barbour writes as follows of this model: "The *monarchical model* of God as King was developed systematically, both in Jewish thought (God as Lord and King of the Universe), in medieval Christian thought (with its emphasis on divine omnipotence), and in the Reformation (especially Calvin's insistence on God's sovereignty). In the portrayal of God's relation to the world, the dominant western historical model has been that of the absolute monarch ruling over his kingdom" (*Myths, Models and Paradigms,* 156).

8. For a further elaboration of this model, see chap. 3 in *Models of God.*

9. For two treatments, see chap. 6 of Gordon Kaufman, *God the Problem* (Cambridge: Harvard University Press, 1972) and Barbour, *Myths, Models and Paradigms,* 158ff.

10. For a review of this point and literature, see Ian G. Barbour, *Religion in an Age of Science,* vol. 1 (New York: Harper and Row, 1990), 256–58.

11. For analyses of this point in Teilhard's work, see Barbour, *Myths, Models and Paradigms,* 160f.; also Ian G. Barbour, "Teilhard's Process Metaphysics," in *Process Theology: Basic Writings,* ed. Ewart H. Cousins (New York: Newman Press, 1971).

12. Teilhard speaks of this as the "economy of salvation," in which, through stages, the natural order is transformed first by its being taken up by humanity and then by Christ (see, for instance, the discussion in *The Divine Milieu: An Essay on the Interior Life* [New York: Harpers, 1960], 25).

13. A. N. Whitehead, *Process and Reality: An Essay in Cosmology* (New York: Macmillan, 1929), 16f. The classic process theology essay on the model of the world as God's body is by Charles Hartshorne, "The Theo-

logical Analogies and the Cosmic Organism," *Man's Vision of God and the Logic of Theism* (New York: Willett, Clark, and Co., 1941), 171–211. While Hartshorne uses the human body as the base of his organic model, he does so with a fine eye to sociality and diversity by focusing on the complex cellular constitution of the body.

14. See James M. Gustafson, *Ethics from a Theocentric Perspective*, vol. 1, *Theology and Ethics* (Chicago: University of Chicago Press, 1981), 179–89. See also Gordon Kaufman's critique of Gustafson's position ("How Is God to Be Understood in a Theocentric Ethics?" in *James M. Gustafson's Theocentric Ethics: Interpretation and Assessments*, ed. Harlan R. Beckley and Charles M. Swezey [Macon, Ga.: Mercer University Press, 1988]: 13–35), as well as Kaufman's own highly nuanced discussion of nonreified uses of personal metaphors for God (see especially chaps. 22 and 23, *In Face of Mystery: A Constructive Theology* [Cambridge: Harvard University Press, 1993]). Although the positions of Gustafson and Kaufman are substantially different, both are wary of agential personalism and neither suggests new personal metaphors in place of the traditional ones.

15. This present work is meant, in part, to balance the limitations of my use of these metaphors in *Models of God*. However, there is a basic compatability and complementarity between the model of spirit and those of mother, lover, and friend.

16. Even a very brief survey from an encyclopedia makes this point. In the Hebrew Scriptures, the Spirit of God is active in history, prophecy, and many other ways, but especially as the source of life: "As the divine power is evident in a special way in the bringing forth and the maintenance of life, the Spirit of God is considered as the source of life (Gen.1:2, 2:7, 6:3; Ps. 33:6, 104:29f, 146:4; Job 12:10, 27:3, 34:14f; Ezek. 37:7–10)" (article on the Holy Spirit, *Encyclopedia of Theology: The Concise "Sacramentum Mundi,"* ed. Karl Rahner [New York: Seabury Press, 1975], 643). In the New Testament, the redeemed community is constituted by the Holy Spirit. Christ is conceived through the Spirit, equipped with the Spirit at baptism, and driven into the desert by the Spirit: "The Spirit is the moving power behind every activity of Jesus. The opposition of men [sic] to the Spirit is called by Christ the unpardonable sin." Christ promised the Spirit in his absence and it was given at Pentecost: "The pentecostal outpouring of the Spirit is the beginning of the communication of the Spirit which continues through all time." In Paul one finds a wide field of Spirit theology too complex to define. The Spirit is active in everyday life, is the animating principle of the church, and is especially connected with baptism and the life of the baptized as well as the pledge of eschatological fulfillment (*Encyclopedia of Theology*, 643).

17. Steven G. Smith, in his study of the concept of spirit, notes that there are two central traditions: one, connected with Hegel, which posits spirit in history and mind; the other, from Martin Buber, which sees spirit

in nature and especially in relationships. The first tradition focuses on
spirit as mind, the second on spirit as breath or life. See *The Concept of the
Spiritual: An Essay in First Philosophy* (Philadelphia: Temple University
Press, 1988). It is obviously the second tradition that an ecological theology
relies upon, as it allows not only for continuity across all forms of life, but
also for relationship among the diverse forms. Jürgen Moltmann makes a
related point when he notes that definitions of human death either unite
or dissociate us from other forms: if death is defined as "brain death," the
focus is on the head, but if breath is the criterion of life, then life is located
in the whole living body (*God in Creation: A New Theology of Creation and the
Spirit of God* [San Francisco: Harper and Row, 1985], 255).

18. The literature on this analogy for God's action in the world is
large and complex. A classic essay on embodiment within a nondualistic
mind/body framework is P. E. Strawson's "Persons," in *Individuals: An
Essay in Descriptive Metaphysics* (Garden City: Doubleday-Anchor, 1963):
83–113. Theological positions range widely from Grace Jantzen's view of
God's more or less total embodiment as a solution to both divine immanence and transcendence (*God's World, God's Body* [Philadelphia: Westminster Press, 1984]) to John Polkinghorne's rejection of divine embodiment as
resulting in either God's tyranny over the world or capitulation to it (*Science and Providence: God's Interaction with the World* [Boston: New Science
Library, 1989]). The tradition is full of examples of God's tyranny over the
world, due to its refusal to consider any kind of embodiment, but God's
absorption into the world is also a genuine problem if the classic organic
model is operative. Thus, Thomas Tracy says that if we "construe our
world as a single, functionally unified individual," then "to say that
the world is God's body is to say that the processes unfolding in the universe are the processes of God's life, that God does not exist except in
and through these processes" (*God's Action and Embodiment* [Grand Rapids:
Eerdmans, 1984], 112). Our embodiment model attempts to avoid that
collapse, while it also tries to avoid tyranny. Some other recent treatments
of God's action in the world that radicalize both divine immanence and
transcendence are the following: 1) Jay McDaniel's process relational
panentheism, in which the world has some degree of independence, even
as our bodies have some independence from our psyches, a view that
sees both God and the world as agents and patients (*Of God and Pelicans: A
Theology of Reverence for Life* [Louisville, Ky.: Westminster/John Knox,
1989]); 2) Arthur R. Peacocke's unitive mind/brain/body view with top-
down (transcendent) as well as bottom-up (immanent) action: "Just as
our human personal subjectivity (the sense of being an 'I') is a unitive, unifying, centered influence on the conscious, willed activity of our bodies,
and this is what characterizes personal agency, so God is here conceived
as the unifying, unitive source and centred influence of the world's activity" (*Theology for a Scientific Age: Being and Becoming—Natural and Divine*

[Oxford: Basil Blackwell, 1990], 161); 3) Catherine Keller's claim that the "politics of individualism" and a "theology of sheer transcendence" are connected—that a view of the self as separated from others and the world underlies a view of God as "pure structure of reflexive self-hood," curved in upon the divine self and essentially unrelated to the world (*From a Broken Web: Separatism, Sexism and Self* [Boston: Beacon Press, 1986], 37–43); 4) Gordon Kaufman's reconstruction of divine imma-nence and transcendence in terms of biological and cultural historical evolution, a view that, while not using the embodiment model, speaks of God as "the serendipitous cosmic process" in a way that at the same time preserves the mystery and transcendence of God, since God is beyond all our constructions as their "ultimate point of reference" (*In Face of Mystery*, chap. 19). What all of these attempts (including my own) to speak of divine action in the world have in common is the desire to avoid occasional or interventionist divine action while stressing the continuity and thoroughness—but noncontrolling and nondeterministic—character of the action. The sensibility behind this perspective was well ex-pressed in 1889 by Aubrey Moore: "Those who oppose the notion of evolution in defence of a 'continued intervention' of God seem to have failed to notice that *a theory of occasional intervention implies as its correlative a theory of ordinary absence*" (as quoted by Arthur R. Peacocke in *Religion and Public Policy*, ed. Frank T. Birtel [New York: Crossroad, 1987], 32). See also Owen Thomas's helpful anthology of a variety of theological positions on divine action (*God's Activity in the World*, AAR Studies in Religion No. 31 (Atlanta, Ga.: Scholars Press, 1983), and Barbour's critique of various con-temporary positions (*Religion in an Age of Science*, chap. 9, "God and Nature").

19. One of the richest and most moving treatments of the Holy Spirit is Korean theologian Chung Hyun-Kyung's address at the Canberra assembly. Here she invokes the Spirit through the spirits of all the op-pressed, from the murdered "spirit of the Amazon rainforest" to the spir-its of exploited women and indigenous peoples, victims of the Holocaust and of Hiroshima, as well as Hagar, Jephthah's daughter, Malcolm X, Oscar Romero and all other lifeforms, human and non-human, that like "the Liberator, our brother Jesus," have been tortured and killed for greed and through hate. The closing words sum up this stunning hymn to the Spirit that moves through and empowers all life. "Dear sisters and broth-ers, with the energy of the Holy Spirit let us tear apart all walls of division and the culture of death which separate us. And let us participate in the Holy Spirit's political economy of life, fighting for our life on this earth in solidarity with all living beings and building communities for justice, peace, and the integrity of creation. Wild wind of the Holy Spirit blow to us. Let us welcome her, letting ourselves go in her wild rhythm of life. Come Holy Spirit, renew the whole creation. Amen!" ("Welcome the

Spirt; hear her cries: The Holy Spirit, creation, and the Culture of Life"
[*Christianity and Crisis*, 51 (July 15, 1991), 223]).

20. For an introductory overview of the Spirit tradition, especially as
oriented in an ecological direction, see Krister Stendahl, *Energy for Life: Reflections on the Theme "Come, Holy Spirit—Renew the Whole Creation"*
(Geneva: World Council of Churches, 1990). For an extensive, ecologically
oriented theology of the Spirit, see Jürgen Moltmann's *The Spirit of Life: A
Universal Affirmation* (London: SCM Press, 1992).

21. Stendahl supports this usage, as it frees us from the overperson-
alism of the tradition: "The Spirit is the indispensable vehicle to take us
towards an all-inclusive theology" (*Energy for Life*, 5).

22. Alice Walker makes this point in the following excerpt between
Celie and Shug: "It? I ast. Yeah, It. God ain't a he or a she, but a It . . . It
ain't something you can look at apart from anything else, including your-
self. I believe God is everything, say Shug. Everything that is or ever was
or ever will be" (from *The Color Purple*, in *Weaving the Visions: New Patterns
in Feminist Spirituality*, ed. Carol P. Christ and Judith Plaskow [New York:
Harpers, 1989], 103).

23. Raymond Keith Williamson, *Introduction to Hegel's Philosophy of
Religion* (Albany, N. Y.: SUNY Press, 1984), 254.

24. Apart from process theology, two other notable panentheistic
traditions are the Hegelian and the Tillichian. In spite of Hegel's focus on
history to the detriment of nature, he insisted on both intimacy between
God and the world and the mediation of God in the world: God "is not the
world, nor is the world God, but the world is God's appearing, God's activity of self-manifestation, appearing which is completed in man. The
world, and man in it, are real only to the extent that God is in them, and
their true being is in God, which is another way of saying that the finite is
the appearing of the infinite and has its being in the infinite" (quoted in
Williamson, *Hegel's Philosophy of Religon*, 270). One of Tillich's central contributions was his insistence that Spirit is the most adequate term for God
as it unites power (the depths of the divine) with meaning (the Logos) and
together they account for "life" or the spirit: "The statement that God is
Spirit means that life as spirit is the inclusive symbol for the divine life"
(*Systematic Theology*, vol. 1 [Chicago: University of Chicago Press, 1951],
250). One of the values of Tillich's position is that life rather than mind is
the primary designation of the divine spirit; hence, a foundation is laid for
an inclusive theology. A contemporary follower of the Hegelian/Tillichian
panentheistic tradition, Peter Hodgson, moves it yet further in that direction: "When I say 'world,' I mean the whole world—the cosmos as we
know it, the stars and planets, biological life, human consciousness, culture and history. This whole world is the figure, shape, or gestalt of God in
the moment of *difference*; It is 'God's body.' 'God's got the whole world in

his hands' " (*God in History: Shapes of Freedom* [Nashville: Abingdon Press, 1989], 106).

25. "The doctrine of creation . . . is preeminently an affirmation about the sovereignty of God and the absolute dependence of the creatures" (Bernard W. Anderson, "Creation in the Bible," in *Cry of the Environment: Rebuilding the Christian Creation*, ed. Philip N. Joranson and Ken Butigan [Santa Fe, N. M.: Bear and Co., 1984], 28). "In both testaments, the doctrine stresses the transcendence and freedom of God, the complete dependence of the whole creation upon the Creator, the reverence for all forms of life" (19). See also Richard J. Clifford, "Creation in the Hebrew Bible," in *Physics, Philosophy and Theology: A Common Quest for Understanding* (Vatican City State: Vatican Observatory, 1988).

26. The following analysis, especially of the procreative model, is indebted to Martha Weigle, *Creation and Procreation: Feminist Reflections on Mythologies of Cosmogony and Parturition* (Philadelphia: University of Pennsylvania Press, 1989).

27. This way of thinking has found favor in relatively establishment Christian circles. For instance, Arthur Peacocke claims that in the past, divine creation has been dominated by external, masculine images and a more internal one is needed, such as female birth: "Mammalian females . . . create within themselves and the growing embryo resides within the female body and this is a proper corrective to the masculine picture—it is an analogy of God creating the world within herself . . . God creates a world that is, in principle and in origin, other than him/herself but creates it, the world, within him/herself" (*Creation and the World of Science* [Oxford: Clarendon Press, 1979], 142). Grace Jantzen, in her book on the universe as God's body, writes: "God formed it [the world] quite literally 'out of himself'—that is, it is his self-formation—rather than out of nothing" (*God's World, God's Body*, 135). The strangeness of using the male pronoun here seems to have escaped Jantzen.

28. Hugh Montefiore gives a helpful analysis of three models of creation: making, organism, and emanation. In the emanation model, creation is empowered by the life-giving energy of the divine spirit and word (Gen. 1:2, 2:7; Ps. 104:30; Prov. 8:30). The Wisdom tradition picks up on the emanationist strand as does the Neoplatonic, in which all life comes from God and will return to God. See his "Report of a working group on environment in the Church of England," in his edited volume, *Man and Nature* (London: Collins, 1975).

29. The addition of the emanation component is not meant, however, to undercut in any way the foundation that the procreative model gives us in physical reality. Weigle points out that cosmogonies in which male creation predominates (creation by spirit, breath, dream, speech) are more highly valued by anthropologists than those with female procreation (creation by physical or natural means). "The former are too readily re-

garded as male and more highly valued, especially when they can be associated with the monotheism of a supreme (preferably masculine) deity; the latter are often considered female and less valuable for being related to nature and animism" (*Creation and Procreation*, 7). Gerda Lerner notes that because monotheism arose within the context of patriarchy, images of creation were exclusively masculine and severed from procreation; thus, not only was divine creation understood entirely in terms of mental production but so was human creation (*The Creation of Patriarchy* [Oxford: Oxford University Press, 1986], 198). This division has meant a dualism between creation (masculine, mind, "higher things") versus procreation (feminine, body, "lower things"). The problem, however, is not monotheism but patriarchy: the Source of life in the universe can be (and, we are suggesting, ought to be) imaged as procreation rather than production.

30. In different ways, one sees this tendency in Augustine and Hegel, and also in Tillich, whose treatment of the fall is, in significant ways, indistinguishable from creation (see *Systematic Theology*, vol. 2).

31. Conrad Hyers describes the imagery of Genesis 1 as imperialistic and intellectual: "The Priestly account . . . favors the image of the divine king who issues royal commands, organizes territories, and rules over his dominion. In Genesis 1 the imagery is lofty and transcendent, after the manner in which an imperial ruler is elevated a considerable distance above his subjects" (*The Meaning of Creation: Genesis and Modern Science* [Atlanta: John Knox, 1984], 98). The Genesis 2 tradition is more homey and softer, with God as maker (potter and clay), but even here Hyers claims that the biblical tradition steers clear of female birth imagery, seeing creation as "a neuter category" of making—God as artist, architect, sculptor (135).

32. *Webster's New World Dictionary*, 2d ed., 1974.

33. Gerard Manley Hopkins, *Poems and Prose*, ed. W. H. Gardner (London: Penguin, 1953), 27.

34. Weigle, *Creation and Procreation*, 7.

Chapter 6: The Body of God

1. For a treatment of the authority of Scripture, see *Models of God: Theology for an Ecological, Nuclear Age* (Philadelphia: Fortress Press, 1987), 43ff.

2. See *Models of God*, 45ff., for another analysis of this point.

3. My position is close to that of liberation theologian Ingemar Hedstrom: "In light of [the] ravaging of people and land in Central America, we realize that the preferential option for the poor, characteristic of Latin American liberation theologies, must be articulated as a preferential *option for life*. To exercise this option is to defend and promote the fundamental right to life of *all* creatures on earth. The right to life in all its fullness involves partaking of the material base of creation, that is, of the material

goods that permit life" ("Latin America and the Need for a Life-Liberating Theology," in *Liberating Life: Contemporary Approaches to Ecological Theology*, ed. Charles Birch et al. [Maryknoll, N. Y.: Orbis Books, 1990], 120). This position is substantially different from that of deep ecology, which also defends the rights of all life-forms (see chap. 4, "Us versus It: Living a Lie in Relation to Nature."

4. *Liberating Life*, 277.

5. As Jay B. McDaniel writes, "the phrase 'integrity of creation' refers to both kinds of value simultaneously. It is 'the intrinsic and instrumental value of every living organism in its relation to its environment and to God' " ("Revisioning God and the Self: Lessons from Buddhism," *Liberating Life*, 231). See also the discussion of instrumental and intrinsic value in Charles Birch and John Cobb, Jr., *The Liberation of Life: From the Cell to the Community* (Cambridge: Cambridge University Press, 1981), chap. 5.

6. Charles Birch, "Christian Obligation for the Liberation of Nature," *Liberating Life*, 64.

7. This perspective is thoroughly and eloquently argued by James M. Gustafson in *Ethics from a Theocentric Perspective*, vol. 1, *Theology and Ethics* (Chicago: University of Chicago Press, 1981).

8. To speak of natural bodies as the *representative* bodies is analogous to speaking of the representative human being of our time as a third-world woman of color. In both cases, we are pointing to the numbers and vulnerability that epitomize the category. In our time, because of the severe deterioration and destruction facing natural bodies (animals, trees, oceans, and so forth), their bodies rather than ours should stand as the symbol of bodily life. Such bodies are *primarily* body and they are at severe risk.

9. See *Models of God*, 51ff.

10. One of the first to recognize what is now broadly accepted, namely, the importance of cultural evolution as a further stage beyond biological evolution, as well as a counterforce to it, was Pierre Teilhard de Chardin. See especially *The Future of Man*, trans. Norman Denny (New York: Harper and Row, 1964) and *Science and Christ*, trans. René Hague (New York: Harper and Row, 1965). Also, for an analysis of Teilhard's position, see Philip Hefner, *The Promise of Teilhard* (Philadelphia and New York: J. B. Lippincott, Co., 1970). Another and very interesting version of cultural evolution, and one to which my analysis is indebted, is by Gerd Theissen in *Biblical Faith: An Evolutionary Approach* (Philadelphia: Fortress Press, 1985). See also Philip Hefner, "The Evolution of the Created Co-Creator" in *Cosmos as Creation: Science and Theology in Consonance*, ed. Ted Peters (Nashville: Abingdon Press, 1989), 211–33.

11. Gustafson writes of this enlarged perspective: "The arena of goodness, of value, is expanded. Good for whom? For individuals living in a given time and place? For our generation more than for future generations? For man [sic], rather than for the world of plants and animals? If

one's basic theological perception is of a Deity who rules all of creation, and one's basic perception of life in history and nature is one of patterns of interdependence, then the good that God values must be more inclusive than one's normal perception of what is good for me, what is good for my community, and even what is good for the human species" (*Ethics from a Theocentric Perspective*, 96).

12. Arthur Peacocke expresses this point in the following way: "The chance disorganization of the growing human embryo that leads to the birth of a defective human being and the chance loss of control of cellular multiplication that appears as a cancerous tumor are individual and particular results of that same interplay of 'chance' and 'law' that enabled life to exist at all . . . The interplay of 'chance' and 'law' is the necessary condition for the existence of certain good eventualities and the 'natural evil' consequences need not be regarded as either avoidable or as intended in themselves by God. Even God cannot have one without the other" (*Theology for a Scientific Age: Being and Becoming—Natural and Divine* [Oxford: Basil Blackwell, 1990], 126).

13. It is also the case that good and evil are correlates; that is, what gives us the greatest pain—our bodies, for instance—is also the source of great joy, and loving others brings intense joy but their loss the most unbearable pain. David Ray Griffin makes this point in a vivid and somewhat amusing way: "Precisely the same conditions that allow us to enjoy those experiences that we value most highly and would not want to live without are the conditions that lead us to suffer so intensely. Cats enjoy experiences far beyond the reach of lowly amoebae; but amoebae are not susceptible to the variety and intensity of pain that can be undergone by cats. Human beings can enjoy riches of experience far beyond the wildest feline dreams; but cats have no inkling of the depths of suffering undergone by those fellow creatures who share their dwelling and give them milk—few cats commit suicide" (*God, Power, and Evil: A Process Theodicy* [Philadelphia: Westminster Press, 1976], 294).

14. See chap. 4, "Sin: The Refusal to Accept Our Place," for an analysis of sin.

15. Process theologies have stressed this point, claiming that the tradition, which has insisted on the unchangeability and impassivity of God—a non-suffering God—ended up with a doctrine of God contrary to its christology. A suffering, changing, involved God is not only, they claim, the implication of the life of Jesus as paradigmatic of God but also consonant with the postmodern view of reality that does not allow divine control over natural or historical events.

16. From the New Zealand/Maori Anglican liturgy.

17. For a further discussion of this point, see *Models of God*, 148ff.

18. The problem of evil in its many forms, including natural evil and human sin, is heightened in an evolutionary perspective, for it is obvious

that not all species, let alone all individuals in any species, *do* flourish, and this for a variety of reasons. A gospel of inclusive fulfillment for *all* of creation must face what the physical and biological sciences must also face: both the Second Law of Thermodynamics as well as current evolutionary theory underscore what Robert John Russell calls "a world of dissipation, decay and destruction." See "Entropy and Evil," *Zygon* (December 1948): 449–68. The way that many theologians (Moltmann, Peacocke, Barbour, process thinkers, and so on) as well as philosophers of science speak to this issue is through the concept of the suffering God who participates in the pain of the universe as it gropes to survive and produce new forms. Here, Gethsemane, the cross, and the resurrection are important foci for underscoring the depths of God's love. In creating an unimaginably complex matrix of matter eventuating finally in persons able to *choose* to go against God's intentions, God nonetheless grieves for and suffers with this beloved creation, both in the pain its natural course brings to all its creatures and in the evil that its human creatures inflict upon it. I find this discussion rich and important; nonetheless, I would raise a caveat concerning what it tends to underplay—human sin and responsibility. By locating the discussion of evil in the context of the entire cosmic complex, one may overlook the particularly powerful role that human beings increasingly play in inflicting evil on their own species and on other species as well. Divine suffering for the cosmos must not obscure human responsibility for a tiny corner of it—our earth.

19. See John Hick's analysis of major theodicies; he supports the contemporary one in which God suffers with those who suffer (*Evil and the God of Love* [New York: Macmillan, 1966]).

20. For a brief but excellent treatment of the cosmic Christ in the tradition, see Rosemary Radford Ruether, *Gaia and God: An Ecofeminist Theology of Earth Healing* (San Francisco: Harper Collins, 1992), 321ff. For two very different twentieth-century reconstructions of the cosmic Christ, see various works by Pierre Teilhard de Chardin, and Matthew Fox, *The Coming of the Cosmic Christ* (San Francisco: Harper and Row, 1988).

21. This tendency is evident in some forms of liberation theology, especially reform feminism, which is understandably cautious about embracing motifs of divine sacrifice and suffering that might encourage similar passive behavior among the oppressed.

22. One of the few instances of serious attention to the notion of space by a Christian theologian is interesting treatment by Jürgen Moltmann in *God in Creation: A New Theology of Creation and the Spirit of God* (San Francisco: Harper and Row, 1985), chap. 6.

23. Bernhard W. Anderson, "Creation in the Bible," in *Cry of the Environment: Rebuilding the Christian Creation Story*, ed. Philip N. Joranson and Ken Butigan (Santa Fe, N. M.: Bear and Co., 1984), 25.

24. Two collections of poems and prayers illustrate this point: Marilyn Sewell, ed., *Cries of the Spirit: A Celebration of Women's Spirituality* (Boston: Beacon Press, 1991); Elizabeth Roberts and Elias Amidon, eds., *Earth Prayers from Around the World* (San Francisco: Harpers, 1991).

25. *The Confessions of St. Augustine*, Bks. I–X, trans. F. J. Sheed (New York: Sheed and Ward, 1942), 10.6.

26. *Earth Prayers*, 366.

27. *Earth Prayers*, 360, 365.

28. This is a complex issue to which we cannot here do justice. There are at least two directions within this tradition, one from Augustine's Neoplatonism, which tends to absorb the things of the world into God, and the other from Thomas's Aristotelianism, which supports greater substance for empirical reality. One sees the former epitomized in the extreme realism of the doctrine of transubstantiation in which the eucharistic elements are wholly converted into the body and blood of Christ, and the latter in a poet such as Gerard Manley Hopkins with his notion of "inscape," the particular, irreducible, concrete individuality of each and every aspect of creation that is preserved and heightened in its sacramental role as a sign of God's glory. But between these poles are many other positions, with the unifying factor being that in some way or other the things of this world are valuable because of their connection to God.

29. The phrase is from an essay by the literary critic, R. W. B. Lewis, and refers to the "suchness" and "thereness" of ordinary things in the world that stand against all attempts to translate them into or use them for spiritual purposes.

30. Gerard Manley Hopkins, *Poems and Prose*, introd. by W. H. Gardner (London: Penguin Books, 1953), 51.

31. See an analysis by Gerda Lerner, *The Creation of Patriarchy* (New York: Oxford University Press, 1986).

32. On animal rights and vegetarianism, see the following: Carol J. Adams, *The Sexual Politics of Meat: A Feminist-Vegetarian Critical Theory* (New York: Continuum, 1991); Tom Regan, *The Case for Animal Rights* (Berkeley, Calif.: University of California Press, 1983).

33. Albert Camus, *The Plague*, trans. Stuart Gilbert (New York: Alfred A. Knopf, 1954), 229.

34. Dorothee Soelle, *Thinking about God: An Introduction to Theology* (Philadelphia: Trinity Press, International, 1990), 192.

Chapter 7: A New Shape for Humanity

1. Stephen Jay Gould, *The Flamingo's Smile: Reflections in Natural History* (New York: W. W. Norton and Co., 1985), 431.

2. The advent of the coming reign of God in the public ministry of Jesus, his death and resurrection, as well as the outpouring of the Spirit at Pentecost, is the scriptural basis for a substantially different eschatology in the twentieth century than what was widespread in the church for centuries. The dawning of a new creation, the irruption of hope, the critique of the present by the future, are all motifs of the "theology of hope" that is profoundly eschatological and in fact claims that eschatology is the major Christian doctrine (see, for instance, Jürgen Moltmann, *The Theology of Hope* [London: SCM Press, 1967]). Various liberation theologies have been deeply influenced by this eschatological perspective as a way both to criticize present social and political regimes and to envision a different future for the oppressed.

3. Two examples are the Earth Summit '92: The United Nations Conference on Environment and Development (Rio de Janeiro, Brazil, June 1992) and works by Ursula K. LeGuin, especially *Always Coming Home* (New York: Bantam, 1986). Another is Wendell Berry's "small-scale elegance": "Beware the justice of nature. Understand that there can be no successful human economy apart from Nature or in defiance of Nature. Understand that no amount of education can overcome the innate limits of human intelligence and responsibility. We are not smart enough or conscious enough or alert enough to work responsibly on a gigantic scale . . . Learn, therefore, to prefer small-scale elegance and generosity to large-scale greed, crudity, and glamour. Make a home. Help to make a community. Be loyal to what you have made" ("The Futility of Global Thinking," *Harpers Magazine*, September 1989, 22). See another fine example of "small-scale elegance" that includes a critique of both wilderness and deep ecology perspectives: Michael Pollan, *Second Nature: A Gardener's Education* (New York: Laurel, 1991). Ecofeminists such as Carolyn Merchant and Ynestra King insist that any vision of the future must unite economic and environmental issues. "A socialist feminist environmental ethic involves developing sustainable, non-dominating relations with nature and supplying all peoples with a high quality of life" (Merchant, "Ecofeminist and Feminist Theory," *Reweaving the World: The Emergence of Ecofeminism*, ed. Irene Diamond and Gloria Orenstein [San Francisco: Sierra Club Books, 1990], 105). King claims that the vision of the future involves another stage of evolution, not a return to nature: cultural feminism must address "history as well as mystery" ("Healing the Wounds: Feminism, Ecology, and the Nature/Culture Dualism," *Reweaving the World*, 117). This next stage of evolution is "one where we will fuse a new way of being human on this planet with a sense of the sacred, informed by all ways of knowing— intuitive *and* scientific, mystical *and* rational. It is the moment where women recognize ourselves as agents of history—yes, even as unique agents—and knowingly bridge the classic dualisms between spirit and

matter, art and politics, reason and intuition. This is the potentiality of a *rational reenchantment*. This is the project of ecofeminism" (120–21).

4. The document of Vatican II on the church frequently uses the model of a pilgrim people, a refreshing change from the triumphalistic view of the church in documents from Vatican I. For treatments of the church as a liberating community, see Leonardo Boff, *Ecclesiogenesis: The Base Communities Reinvent the Church* (Maryknoll, N. Y.: Orbis Books, 1986) and Rosemary Radford Ruether, *WomanChurch* (San Francisco: Harper and Row, 1985). For a discussion of the church as a fellowship of friends, see chap. 6 of my *Models of God: Theology for an Ecological, Nuclear Age* (Philadelphia: Fortress Press, 1987).

5. Gary Larson, 1980 Chronicle Features, 2-15, Universal Press Syndicate.

6. Annie Dillard, *Pilgrim at Tinker Creek: A Mystical Excursion into the Natural World* (New York: Bantam Books, 1975), 126.

7. *Earth Prayers from Around the World*, ed. Elizabeth Roberts and Elias Amidon (San Francisco, Calif.: Harpers, 1991), 251.

8. Iris Murdoch, *The Sovereignty of the Good* (London: Routledge and Kegan Paul, 1970), 84.

9. The text of Julian of Norwich, modernized from *A Revelation of Love*, ed. Marian Glasscoe (Exeter: University of Exeter Press, 1988), chap. 5.

10. Alice Walker, "The Gospel According to Shug," *The Temple of My Familiar* (New York: Simon and Schuster, 1989), 288–89.

Name Index

Subject Index

266

CPSIA information can be obtained
at www.ICGtesting.com
Printed in the USA
FFOW02n0528171116
29467FF